Critical Essays on
JOHN O'HARA

CRITICAL ESSAYS
ON
AMERICAN LITERATURE

James Nagel, General Editor
University of Georgia, Athens

Critical Essays on
JOHN O'HARA

edited by

PHILIP B. EPPARD

G. K. Hall & Co. / New York
Maxwell Macmillan Canada / Toronto
Maxwell Macmillan International / New York Oxford Singapore Sydney

G. K. Hall & Co.
Macmillan Publishing Co.
866 Third Avenue
New York, New York 10022

Maxwell Macmillan Canada, Inc.
1200 Eglinton Avenue East
Suite 200
Don Mills, Ontario M3C 3N1

Library of Congress Cataloging-in-Publication Data

Critical essays on John O'Hara / edited by Philip B. Eppard.
    p.   cm.—(Critical essays on American literature)
    Includes bibliographical references and index.
    ISBN 0-7838-0026-6
    1. O'Hara, John, 1905–1970—Criticism and interpretation.
I. Eppard, Philip B. II. Series.
PS3529.H29Z63   1994
813'.54—dc20   94-6642
                                                 CIP

---

10   9   8   7   6   5   4   3   2   1

Printed in the United States of America

Contents

◆

General Editor's Note

♦

This series seeks to anthologize the most important criticism on a wide variety of topics and writers in American literature. Our readers will find in various volumes not only a generous selection of reprinted articles and reviews, but original essays, bibliographies, manuscript sections, and other materials brought to public attention for the first time. This volume, *Critical Essays on John O'Hara*, is the most comprehensive collection of essays ever published on one of the most important modern writers in the United States. It contains both a sizable gathering of early reviews and a broad selection of more modern scholarship as well. Among the authors of reprinted articles and reviews are R. P. Blackmur, Dorothy Canfield Fisher, Malcolm Cowley, Mark Schorer, Leslie Fiedler, John Cheever, Shirley Ann Grau, Scott Donaldson, and George Monteiro. In addition to a substantial introduction by Philip B. Eppard, there are also two original essays commissioned specifically for publication in this volume. Charles W. Bassett explores the role of Gibbsville in O'Hara's novel and stories, exploring the unique mix of sexual frankness and social morality in these works. Thomas P. Coakley examines O'Hara's technical skill in handling point of view to create depth of character, a matter of critical neglect in O'Hara studies. We are confident that this book will make a permanent and significant contribution to the study of American literature.

JAMES NAGEL
University of Georgia

Publisher's Note

♦

Producing a volume that contains both newly commissioned and reprinted material presents the publisher with the challenge of balancing the desire to achieve stylistic consistency with the need to preserve the integrity of works first published elsewhere. In the Critical Essays series, essays commissioned especially for a particular volume are edited to be consistent with G. K. Hall's house style; reprinted essays appear in the style in which they were first published, with only typographical errors corrected. Consequently, shifts in style from one essay to another are the result of our efforts to be faithful to each text as it was originally published.

Publisher's Note

Introduction

◆

Philip B. Eppard

John O'Hara engaged in a running battle with the critics throughout his lengthy and prolific career as a professional author. In both his private letters and in his published pronouncements he seems to have relished attacking book reviewers and academic critics. His adversarial stance toward the critics is neatly summarized in a 1964 letter to James Gould Cozzens: "They, the reviewers, are not us. We tend to overlook that fact when we get intelligent, understanding reviews; but they are still not us. They and we are as different as touch football and the genuine article. No training, no tackling, no risk of any kind, and no enduring skill. And, to continue the analogy a little further, no hope of ever getting a varsity letter. But they sure as hell talk big."[1] Clearly O'Hara subscribed to the view that most book reviewers and critics were little more than frustrated novelists or story writers. In his acerbic foreword to *The Cape Cod Lighter*, O'Hara wrote, "In other words, it might be said that there is a pool of unsuccessful writers of fiction who are all too readily available for occasional reviews. With their background it is not surprising that there is so much spiteful condescension in the pieces they write for the Sunday supplements."[2] Such public utterances obviously won him no friends in some critical quarters.

Though he disdained the critics, at the same time O'Hara was deeply concerned with his critical reputation. He cultivated certain reviewers who were favorably disposed toward his work. Beginning with *The Farmers Hotel* in 1951, O'Hara even arranged to publish most of his books on Thursdays because on that day they would be reviewed in the *New York Times* by Charles Poore and not by Orville Prescott, who had been hostile to his work.[3] O'Hara was not hesitant in boasting about his own skills as a writer; for example, he did not shy away from openly lobbying for the Nobel Prize for Literature. This dual response to the critics was only one manifestation of the many contradictions that marked O'Hara's personality.

There are times, of course, when every author feels misunderstood or

1

mistreated by the critics, but O'Hara often had concrete grounds for complaining. As a writer who prided himself on his mastery of detail (among other things), John O'Hara expected the critics to pay as much attention while reading as he did while writing. One can only imagine the scorn he would have heaped on Arthur Mizener, who had earned O'Hara's contempt for his devastating review of *From the Terrace*, for writing a review of *Ourselves to Know* and continually referring to it as *Thyself to Know*.[4] Another instance of careless critical reading concerns the foreword to O'Hara's collection of short stories, *The Horse Knows the Way*. He ended the foreword by proclaiming, "I have work to do and I am afraid not to do it." Some reviewers misread O'Hara and quoted him as saying, "I have work to do and I am not afraid to do it." As Albert Erskine, O'Hara's editor at Random House, noted, it was a case of reviewers reading what they expected O'Hara to say. To them it was just another example of O'Hara's belligerent attitude toward the critics.[5] O'Hara was notoriously thin-skinned, but ultimately even he realized that responding to bad reviews "is a waste of time, even when you have the critic dead to rights."[6]

O'Hara at least had the satisfaction of knowing that the reading public responded enthusiastically to his books. "I get so many hostile reviews that critical reception does not really affect the general reception of my books," he wrote in 1959.[7] The academic critics, however, were not impressed by large sales, and in fact O'Hara's popularity no doubt worked against him in the eyes of the critical establishment. But while O'Hara eagerly cultivated a mass popular audience for his novels and stories, he shunned one avenue leading toward academic respectability by generally refusing to allow his work to be included in the anthologies used in college literature classes. Since the core of the American literature curriculum represents the accepted canon of important writers, O'Hara's refusal paradoxically worked to exclude him from the select group of writers with whom he felt he should be included.[8]

In 1966 Sheldon Grebstein published the first book-length study of John O'Hara as a volume in Twayne's United States Authors Series. His first chapter, "O'Hara and the Critics," is a valuable summary of the critical responses that O'Hara's writings had provoked. Grebstein notes three characteristics of the critical response to O'Hara: the criticism consists largely of reviews in newspapers and magazines; hostile reviews of O'Hara "are remarkable for their vehemence and ferocity"; and serious critical writing about O'Hara by academic scholars is negligible, particularly compared to the vast amount of attention paid to other authors.[9] O'Hara's death in 1970 finally stemmed the flood of words flowing from his typewriter, and apart from a few posthumous publications, there have been no new books to attract the praise or hostility of the reviewers. In the area of academic criticism, the situation is much the same as Grebstein noted nearly 30 years ago. Despite three biographies, a descriptive bibliography, two scholarly conferences, and a short-lived journal devoted to O'Hara, there has not been any heightened level of interest in his work from the academic world. Even the general public's awareness of O'Hara is fading as many of his books gradually drift out of print. In the mid-1960s O'Hara was enough of a fixture in the public consciousness to be on the cover of *Newsweek* and to merit mention in Simon and Garfunkel's song "A Simple Desultory Philippic (Or How I Was Robert MacNamara'd Into Submission)." If O'Hara were merely a popular writer, such a gradual fading from prominence would be understandable. But with few exceptions, even O'Hara's most severe critics have admitted that he was not simply a hack writer. The cause of this critical neglect has been a popular topic of speculation among O'Hara scholars.

Grebstein provides a useful summary of the reasons for O'Hara's being given short shrift by academic critics. It is clear that many of the reasons have their roots in the cultural and literary ethos of the 1930s, the decade of O'Hara's emergence upon the American literary scene. Early on, he was typed in part as a "tough-guy" writer because of the dispassionate point of view pervading his early novels and stories and because of "his candid, even brutally frank treatment of sexuality."[10] He also came of age as a writer in a decade when politics pervaded literature, and yet unlike John Steinbeck, for example, O'Hara had no real political axe to grind in his fiction. His tendency, more pronounced in his later writings, to devote attention to the well-to-do, made him even more out of step with the prevailing literary climate, a fact of which he was well aware. In submitting a piece to Kyle Crichton of *Scribner's Magazine* in 1933, he commented that "it doesn't say anything about how lovely it is to be hungry in Vermont, or how terrible it is to see someone die in Amsterdam Avenue, so I suppose it can be turned down on the ground that the people written about are not worthy of a writer's talent, if any."[11]

Clearly O'Hara's straightforward style has also worked against him with academic critics, who require complexity and nuance in literature in order to facilitate classroom discussions or provide grist for articles for critical journals. An unabashed realist, O'Hara's work seemed old-fashioned at best, or simply irrelevant to most of the trends in modern literature. Finally, O'Hara's shift from New Deal Democracy in the 1930s to Goldwater Republicanism in the 1960s, and his willingness to vent his opinions in print did little to endear him to the generally leftist academy.

While O'Hara's work often attracted lavish praise from some reviewers, a sizable group of critics objected to it on several grounds. Among the objections raised are that his work only reports surface details and lacks an overarching vision; his long novels in particular fail because of the weight of irrelevant social details; his emphasis on the sexual activities of his characters is excessive; the objectivity of his writing is "either a disguise for his mindlessness or the expression of his essential callousness and moral indifference," in Grebstein's summary of the critics.[12]

One encounters a host of critical commonplaces in writing on O'Hara. Critics often contend that his first novel, *Appointment in Samarra*, was his best and that he failed to develop as a novelist after that. They also often claim that his short stories are far better than his novels. Though critics usually agree that he had a wonderful ear for the English language as spoken by twentieth-century Americans, many seem to suggest that somehow this is merely a technical skill, something akin to having a photographic memory. There is certainly some truth to these assertions, but too often they have been tossed out almost automatically without much thought or analysis. Critics and book reviewers tend to repeat themselves and each other. (Irving Howe's reviews of *Assembly* and *Lovey Childs: A Philadelphian's Story*, reprinted in this volume, are good examples of a critic's recycling of material in reviews, albeit with some substantive additions.) John O'Hara exemplifies the case of a writer who is tagged early on in his career with certain characteristics that then tend to be solidified in the eyes of the critics with each succeeding publication.

John O'Hara's literary career can be divided into three phases, which can also be seen as marking three phases in his critical reception. The first phase dates from the early 1930s, with the establishment of his literary reputation as a writer of stories and sketches for the *New Yorker* and with the publication of *Appointment in Samarra* in 1934. Publication of *A Rage to Live* in 1949 inaugurated the second phase, which was marked by the production of most of his long Pennsylvania novels, including *Ten North Frederick, From the Terrace,* and *Ourselves to Know.* A third phase may be dated from 1960, when O'Hara began writing short fiction again after an 11-year hiatus. In the final 10 years of his life he published 140 stories as well as five novels, five plays, and a volume of newspaper columns. The abundance and variety of O'Hara's work in the 1960s made him a fixture on the American literary landscape.

When *Appointment in Samarra* was published in August of 1934, it attracted two broad kinds of responses from the reviewers. There were enthusiastic reviewers like William Soskin, writing for the Hearst newspapers, who proclaimed the arrival of a real writer who unflinchingly presented an accurate slice of American life. Several reviewers described it as a book they couldn't put down. Nevertheless, many critics favorably disposed toward the novel felt compelled to call attention to its frank treatment of sex. Inevitably, a small but influential contingent of reviewers could not get over what they regarded as the book's essential vulgarity. Dorothy Canfield Fisher spoke for these people when she wrote in her short review in the *Book-of-the-Month Club News* that "[i]t will make a good many other people physically sick."[13]

O'Hara's work was panned twice in the *Saturday Review of Literature*, first in a review of *Appointment* by Henry Seidel Canby, who admired O'Hara's writing skills but decried "an insufferable vulgarity, which has crept into so many of our supposedly advanced novels that someone not squeamish, nor unread in earlier literatures must protest against what is cheapening American fiction."[14] Several weeks later, Sinclair Lewis, an author who had clearly influenced O'Hara's early work, managed to incorporate an attack on *Appointment in Samarra* in his review of Canby's volume of memoirs, *The Age of*

Confidence. Lewis concurred with Canby's evaluation of the book, declaring that O'Hara's novel "for all the cleverness of its observation, the deftness of its tempo, the courage of its vocabulary, was inherently nothing but infantilism—the erotic visions of a hobbledehoy behind the barn, even though the barn does figure in the novel as a 'country club.' "[15]

Beyond the author's use of sex, reviews of O'Hara's first novel noted several other aspects of his writing that came to be perennial features of later criticism. O'Hara's skill in recording the patterns of American speech and his use of telling bits of detail are duly noted. A more philosophical issue was raised by R. P. Blackmur, who objected to the apparent pointlessness of Julian English's suicide, or at least to the author's failure to clarify its causes for the reader.[16] In the *New York Times*, John Chamberlain also addressed the question of the motivation for Julian's suicide but held that O'Hara had presented it "true to life," for we can never "untangle absolute reasons for any individual act." He went on to add that "what makes the story . . . convincing is precisely the natural interaction of pure fluctuating chance and latent characteristics to produce tragedy."[17] In a sense, therefore, Blackmur's criticism was one of the first to level the charge that O'Hara's work possesses no cosmic vision. Other critics, such as Chamberlain, have praised O'Hara's skillful rendering of the complexities of life and the ways in which events are shaped by a combination of chance and human character.

O'Hara quickly followed *Appointment in Samarra* with a collection of stories, *The Doctor's Son and Other Stories*, and then with his second novel, *Butterfield 8*. The stories were praised for their skill as character studies, but Fred T. Marsh felt that O'Hara's gifts were too good to be wasted on these bits of realism.[18] *Butterfield 8*, like O'Hara's first novel, received a mixture of praise and condemnation, with some reviewers finding it even more shockingly vulgar. In 1938, with the publication of *Hope of Heaven* (his short Hollywood novel), O'Hara was beginning to disturb some critics like Clifton Fadiman, who concluded "that there has been no growth since the brilliant 'Appointment in Samarra.' "[19]

In April 1938 O'Hara was trying to convince his publisher Samuel Sloan to bring out a second collection of short stories. "I know there are people who like my short stories who cannot abide my novels," he wrote presciently.[20] *Files on Parade*, his second story collection, appeared in 1939. It contained several notable tales praised by the reviewers, including "Price's Always Open," "Lunch Tuesday," "Do You Like It Here?" "Days," and "The Gentleman in the Tan Suit." The volume also contained four "Pal Joey" sketches, which were republished with other Joey stories in 1940. Reviewers often commented on O'Hara's disagreeable characters. Joey was disreputable, but pathetic and almost lovable at the same time. Robert van Gelder wrote that O'Hara presented Joey "with such perfect precision, such absolute accuracy" that he avoided making him just a comic figure. He pronounced the book "a minor masterpiece."[21] With the success of the Rodgers and Hart musical *Pal Joey*, for which O'Hara wrote the libretto, the character of Pal Joey became widely regarded as one of O'Hara's most enduring fictional achievements.

An early and influential critique of O'Hara by Edmund Wilson appeared in the *New Republic* on 11 November 1940.[22] "The cruel side of social snobbery is really Mr. O'Hara's main theme," Wilson declared. He praised O'Hara's faithful rendering of "the social surface," but added, "His grasp of what lies underneath it is, however, not so sure." He complained about the disorganization of his novels and questioned the relevance of some of the characters or scenes O'Hara chose to include. Wilson found O'Hara's novels becoming progressively less successful while his short stories have "distinctly improved." He concluded, "The truth is perhaps that Mr. O'Hara has never really had his bearings since he abandoned the subject of Gibbsville, Pa." Virtually all of Wilson's major criticisms have been echoed through the years by later critics, a tribute, no doubt, to Wilson's critical perception, but also to the power of an influential critic to shape later judgements.

Lionel Trilling's favorable review of O'Hara's third collection of short stories, *Pipe Night*, published in 1945, was one of the most significant reviews of O'Hara's entire career. It was the most serious consideration of O'Hara as a literary artist to come from an academic critic, and its publication on the front page of the *New York Times Book Review* gave it added weight. Trilling placed O'Hara in the tradition of William Dean Howells and Edith Wharton, writers concerned with the American social scene. "More than anyone now writing, O'Hara understands the complex, contradictory, asymmetrical society in which we live."[23] His vision of society was more complex and sophisticated than that of Dreiser or Sinclair Lewis. Trilling even suggested that the novel was the more appropriate venue for O'Hara's subject matter, a suggestion that may have encouraged O'Hara to get to work on a new novel, a book that would mark a change in his literary career.

When *A Rage to Live*, O'Hara's first long Pennsylvania novel, appeared in 1949, it was the first novel he had published since *Hope of Heaven* in 1938. Some critics were undoubtedly genuinely curious as to whether O'Hara's newest work would at last represent a real advance on the solid beginning he had made with *Appointment in Samarra* 15 years earlier. O'Hara anticipated that the book would be controversial, and although the critics were more or less evenly divided in their opinions, the negative reviews made it clear that O'Hara's credit with the critical establishment had run out. In the *Partisan Review*, Irving Howe proclaimed the book "a disaster, John O'Hara's own appointment in Samarra."[24] He argued that O'Hara was not a serious artist but at best only a super reporter who was unequipped to delve into the psychology of his characters. In the *New York Times Book Review*, A. C. Spectorsky objected to the absence of any "wider horizons" in the story of the Tates and Fort Penn.[25] On the other hand, Morton Fineman, writing in the *Philadelphia Inquirer*, called it O'Hara's best work. "There is proof on every page of an advancement to a new and greater level of creativeness and maturity."[26]

Of all the reviews of *A Rage to Live*, Brendan Gill's savage attack in the *New Yorker* had ultimately the greatest impact on O'Hara's career. Gill found *A Rage to Live* "bears little or no resemblance to any of" O'Hara's three earlier novels. He criticized "the recurrent passages of maudlin sexuality" in the book, and charged that "Dr. O'Hara's handy guide to healthy sex practices has been tucked inside the disarming wrapper of the formula family novel" of the type turned out by "writers of the third and fourth magnitude." His conclusion was devastating. "It is hard to understand how one of our best writers could have written this book, and it is because of O'Hara's distinction that his failure here seems in the nature of a catastrophe."[27]

During the preceding two decades O'Hara had been the *New Yorker's* most prolific contributor of stories, and he was understandably hurt by the magazine's publication of such a brutal review. His response was to break his long connection with the *New Yorker*. Since the magazine was the only outlet he felt he had for his short stories, the result was that he stopped writing stories altogether. During the 1950s, therefore, he devoted his energies to the novel. For many critics *A Rage to Live* confirmed their opinion that O'Hara was better when he confined himself to shorter forms. Producing long novels filled with social history was unlikely to enhance O'Hara's critical stature.

Of O'Hara's longer novels, *Ten North Frederick*, which won the National Book Award for 1956, has generally been accorded the warmest reception. Somewhat shorter and more tightly structured than *A Rage to Live*, the story of Joe Chapin seemed to some reviewers a more solid achievement. In the *New York Herald Tribune Book Review* Milton Rugoff wrote:

> Perhaps the most impressive quality of "Ten North Frederick" is the evident maturity of the artist who composed it. One feels that it is based on a profound grasp of its characters and their world, a passion to record them as they are— but with much less of the sexual shock treatment that marked "A Rage to Live"—and a mastery of the novelist's technique for doing so. We are persuaded that these pages tell us all any one could know of Joseph Chapin. We understand him better than he understood himself—better, I dare say, than we understand ourselves. And that is about as significant an experience as fiction can afford us.[28]

Saunders Redding defended O'Hara's art as "the art of the story-teller," marked by "a learned knowledge of his people uncomplicated by philosophy, or social theories or any brooding notions about the meaning of life."[29] Other reviewers, such as Stanley Cooperman in the *Nation*, echoed old complaints that O'Hara provides an abundance of physical details, but never adds a dimension of meaning. The result is "journalistic fiction without the social insight of Dreiser or the lyric sensitivity of Hemingway."[30]

John O'Hara regarded *From the Terrace* as his greatest achievement as a novelist. With its publication, he felt the critics would now consider it the benchmark of his career, rather than judging his later books by the standard of his first novel. For those critics who had balked at the bulk of detail or the sexuality of O'Hara's earlier Pennsylvania chronicles, *From the Terrace* was the last straw. Alfred Kazin, who throughout his long career has had little praise for O'Hara, pronounced the book not the Great American Novel, but "The Great American Bore."[31] For the third time, an O'Hara book was featured on the front page of the *New York Times Book Review*. Only this time the review, by Arthur Mizener, ominously titled "Something Went Seriously Wrong," lamented O'Hara's failure as a novelist.[32] Pointless detail, surface reality, sexual titillation with no real artistic intent—these were some of the charges leveled against O'Hara's magnum opus.

Nevertheless, O'Hara did have his champions. Robert Kirsch in the *Los Angeles Times* hailed the novel and said that O'Hara deserved the Nobel Prize.[33] Charles Poore agreed that it was O'Hara's best, and in response to those who might be daunted by its length, he wrote, "A man needs every bit of the space he can get when he wants to write his own 'Moby Dick,' his own 'War and Peace,' his own requiem, if you will, for a time when the only change we can confidently expect is change itself."[34]

O'Hara presumed that *Ourselves to Know*, his next novel—the story of Robert Millhouser, who murdered his young wife—would surprise or baffle critics because it was such a decided change from *From the Terrace*. The novel's structure was convoluted, with Millhouser's story filtered through the narrator, Gerald Higgins. Most critics welcomed the return to a novel of more manageable proportions. Others noted that the novel's form might cause some readers difficulty, and there were still reviewers bothered by the sexually aggressive, amoral Hedda Millhouser. John Chamberlain noted the Dostoevskian character of the book, but concluded that it "is fundamentally a social, not a psychological novel."[35] William May found that "it is quieter, more reflective, more compassionate in its approach to character than recent works by O'Hara."[36] In a letter written nearly two years after the book's publication, O'Hara described *Ourselves to Know* as "the one where the serious critics missed the boat." He added, "Some day critics now unborn and removed from contemporary influences may argue that it is my best."[37]

In 1960 O'Hara reconciled with the *New Yorker* and once again began writing short fiction. Reviews of *Sermons and Soda-Water*, a set of three novellas, were generally good. Some critics were obviously relieved not to have to deal with another mammoth O'Hara novel. Phoebe Adams in the *Atlantic Monthly* wrote, "As one who has suffered intensely from Mr. O'Hara's works in the long form, I am perfectly willing to applaud any reason at all for his abandonment of it and thank providence that, for whatever motive, he has decided to stay his hand."[38] George Steiner suggested that "the craftsman in O'Hara must know that he has always fared better in the shorter forms."[39] Many reviewers also took note of O'Hara's foreword to the trilogy in which he staked out a role for himself as a recorder of the way life really was in the twentieth century, saying, "I want to get it all down on paper while I can."[40] This frank acknowledgement by O'Hara of his role as a social historian in his fiction, together with the reflective mood of the novellas themselves, provoked positive responses from the critics, many of whom seemed content to let O'Hara stand his ground.

The return to shorter forms in *Sermons and Soda-Water* was followed by a flood of short stories in the 1960s, collected in six volumes beginning with *Assembly* in 1961. His skill in the short story form was widely praised, though often accompanied by derogatory comments on his novels. The retrospective quality of his stories had a powerful appeal even to critics who were not always favorably disposed toward O'Hara. In reviewing *The Cape Cod Lighter*, for example, Benjamin DeMott said, "The book does offer the reader a curious pleasure—that of an evening under lamplight with the photograph album." He said that O'Hara's concern with social detail had in the past "resembled pedantry more than poetry," but that this was not true of the stories in *The Cape Cod Lighter*.[41]

O'Hara's novels in the 1960s were generally less well received than his stories. *The Big Laugh, The Instrument*, and *Lovey Childs: A Philadelphian's Story* received generally poor or mediocre reviews. *The Lockwood Concern*, the last of his long Pennsylvania chronicles, demanded attention, but critical opinions on O'Hara were so solidified by the time of its publication in 1965 that little new was said. John O'Hara died in 1970. Interest in his work had dropped so much that his posthumous novel *The Ewings* and two volumes of uncollected short stories published in 1972 and 1974 attracted relatively little critical attention upon publication.

The earliest scholarly criticism of O'Hara was John Portz's article "John O'Hara Up to Now" published in *College English* in May 1955. Portz was largely critical of O'Hara, arguing that O'Hara's work fails because of "his inability to discover in his books and to reveal to us the true meaning of people and things."[42] He finds O'Hara's view of human nature lopsided in its emphasis on depravity. He considers O'Hara one of the hardboiled school of writers, "caught up in the transitory and ephemeral."[43] Portz's article is an intelligent presentation of most of the criticisms made of O'Hara's work during the first two decades of his career.

The first extended critical discussion of John O'Hara was Edward Russell Carson's 1961 pamphlet *The Fiction of John O'Hara*.[44] Carson's brief study focuses on the Pennsylvania novels and the stories from the first phase of O'Hara's career. Carson provides some insightful readings of the major novels, but concludes that much of what O'Hara has written is written out of a snobbish contempt for his characters.

Sheldon Grebstein's *John O'Hara*, the first book-length study of O'Hara, provides a comprehensive analysis of O'Hara's writings through *The Horse*

Knows the Way (1964). After his initial discussion of the critical response to O'Hara and a biographical chapter covering O'Hara's Pennsylvania years, Grebstein devotes separate chapters to the Pennsylvania fiction, O'Hara's fictional use of New York and Hollywood, and his short stories. Grebstein finds O'Hara's work deficient in part because it lacks a philosophical dimension, and he suggests that O'Hara sacrifices artistic achievement to his preoccupation with social history. He also faults O'Hara's use of language, saying, "There is too rarely *beauty* in it."[45] Nevertheless, Grebstein argues persuasively that O'Hara has been unfairly neglected or maligned by the critics. He praises O'Hara's "penetrating glimpses into the human heart," his depiction of "the power of compulsion over man's behavior" and "the necessity for love and compassion."[46] Grebstein's volume remains a valuable introduction, providing a solid and balanced appraisal of all of O'Hara's major works through the early 1960s.

Charles Child Walcutt's *John O'Hara*, one of the University of Minnesota Pamphlets on American Writers, provides a brief overview of O'Hara's work and brief readings of several of his novels and the stories in *Pipe Night*.[47] Walcutt sees O'Hara's short stories as superior to his novels, and he offers a long list of qualities that limit the achievement of his novels. Walcutt ponders the reasons for O'Hara's immense readability, suggesting, "Perhaps the heart of it is that the characters come alive because the reader is completely involved in the living instant when he sees them responding—often surprisingly—to the problem and the situation through which they exist and grow."[48]

The most recent comprehensive critical survey of O'Hara's life and work is Robert Emmet Long's *John O'Hara*.[49] Long endeavors to show how "O'Hara's own psychological patterns" relate "to the conflicts involved in his fictional conceptions."[50] He discusses O'Hara's vision of society as a menacing force (particularly in relation to sex), the theme of personal isolation that pervades much of his fiction, and his use of symbolism. Long even suggests that "O'Hara's interest is to a large degree aesthetic." "He is capable of very refined observation and great finesse in his handling of characters and their developing situations. His short stories reveal these qualities continually, but they appear in the novels too, and in one special quality he is approached by no one. Although his characters are characteristically two-dimensional, he creates a psychological atmosphere around them at times that is extraordinary. His ability to 'sense' or 'feel' a character within the context of an introspective mood can be seen in even his worst novels."[51] Long concludes that O'Hara is not a major novelist ranking with Hemingway, Fitzgerald, or Faulkner, but that he merits comparison with contemporaries such as Steinbeck, Cozzens, Farrell, and Marquand.

Appointment in Samarra, the story of Julian English's swift descent to suicide, has widely been considered O'Hara's finest novel. Consequently it has received the most sustained critical analysis of any of O'Hara's fiction. The prevailing critical attitude is neatly summed up in the title of Jesse Bier's article, "O'Hara's *Appointment in Samarra*: His First and Only Real Novel."[52] Bier discusses the environmental, circumstantial, and hereditary factors that lead to Julian's suicide. He focuses on the theme of war in the book, particularly O'Hara's use of military imagery to depict Julian's conflict with society. In "Appointment with the Dentist: O'Hara's Naturalistic Novel," Scott Donaldson explores the issue of the inevitability of Julian's suicide. He suggests that it "is not an incomprehensible and foreordained fate," but argues that when society rejects him for his actions, Julian is helpless to do anything but accept society's judgment as both inevitable and final.[53] Charles W. Bassett's essay "Naturalism Revisited: The Case of John O'Hara" focuses on *Appointment in Samarra* as the best example of O'Hara's "naturalistic values and techniques translated into" their most "noteworthy imaginative expression."[54]

O'Hara's other novels have received relatively little attention from the critics. John L. Cobbs examines O'Hara's detailed portrait of the city of Fort Penn in *A Rage to Live*, considering it "the apotheosis of O'Hara's vision of society."[55] Rex Roberts has written an analysis of *Ten North Frederick* in which he proclaims it to be "the Great American Novel." Roberts makes this admittedly bold claim because the book "says more about America than any novel written in the American century between the Industrial and Technological Revolutions. Its subject is the most powerful American myth our culture has created, that any boy can grow up to be President."[56]

Critics have often treated O'Hara as a latter-day naturalist, but they have also considered him in the tradition of the novel of manners as exemplified by Henry James, Edith Wharton, and John P. Marquand. This is certainly a logical approach, given O'Hara's obvious interest in the role of class in American society, and the life of the rich in particular, and his professed vow to accurately record life in America during the first half of the twentieth century. James W. Tuttleton devotes a chapter to O'Hara in his book *The Novel of Manners in America*.[57] Entitled "John O'Hara: Class Hatred and Sexuality," Tuttleton's chapter provides an extended analysis of O'Hara's view of society as manifested in his Pennsylvania novels. He sees O'Hara's vision of society as "an arena of social warfare" where "the cruel realities and illusions of caste" prevent individuals from achieving true love.[58] Tuttleton calls attention to O'Hara's use of the phrase "spurious democracy" to describe the group of boys from different social classes that Julian English played with as a child and suggests that O'Hara uses this as a metaphor for society at large. In *The Sense of Society*, Gordon Milne detects a seriousness of purpose in O'Hara's novels of manners, whose themes go "beyond a superficial account of the cruelty of snobbery to a thoughtful pondering of the futility and tragedy of the waste of life within the social system."[59]

Lee Sigelman builds on Tuttleton's analysis of O'Hara's view of class hatred to show that O'Hara's fiction presents a sophisticated view of society in which "the most important parties to class conflict have a mutual stake in assuring that it does not turn into class warfare."[60] Sigelman also provides a close reading of the political elements in O'Hara's most clearly political works: *The Farmers Hotel*, the posthumously published play *Far from Heaven*, and *Ten North Frederick*.

Given the fact that O'Hara's short stories have been so widely praised, it is surprising that more critical attention has not been directed toward them. Charles W. Bassett's article in the *Dictionary of Literary Biography* volume on *American Short Story Writers* provides a comprehensive overview of O'Hara's short fiction.[61] Nancy Walker has written a lengthy article on O'Hara's use of the novella form, and Edgar McD. Shawen has treated one of O'Hara's short story collections as a whole in "The Unity of John O'Hara's *Waiting for Winter*."[62] Kathryn Riley has used a thematic approach to analyze O'Hara's treatment of suburbia in his short fiction.[63] Brief articles on individual stories include Bassett's on "Alone" and George Monteiro's on *A Family Party*.[64] For an author with over 400 stories to his credit who has been hailed by many as one of the best short story writers of his time, this seems to be a clear case of critical neglect.

If O'Hara has not attracted extended attention from literary critics, he has at least been more fortunate with literary biographers. Within a decade after his death in 1970, John O'Hara was the subject of three biographies. Finis Farr's *O'Hara: A Biography* was the first to appear.[65] Farr was a journalist and biographer who had been a friend of O'Hara's since the 1930s. His book is a well-written overview of O'Hara's life that is particularly good in evoking O'Hara's Pottsville years and in showing how O'Hara used his own experiences in his fiction.

In the academic world, no one has labored harder to promote interest in John O'Hara than Matthew J. Bruccoli. Bruccoli began doing bibliographical work on O'Hara in the 1960s and in 1968 contributed an article on O'Hara to David Madden's influential collection of essays *Tough Guy Writers of the Thirties*.[66] After O'Hara's death Bruccoli became for a few years almost a one-man O'Hara cottage industry. His *The O'Hara Concern: A Biography of John O'Hara* remains the standard source for the facts of O'Hara's personal life and professional career. In Bruccoli's own words it is a "critical biography" that is "intentionally biased by my conviction that John O'Hara was a major writer who was underrated by the critical-academic axis sometimes called the Literary Establishment."[67] Bruccoli does not fail to note the weaknesses of some of O'Hara's books, particularly his late novels *The Instrument* and *Lovey Childs: A Philadelphian's Story*, but concludes by asserting, "He was one of our best novelists, our best novella-ist, and our greatest writer of short stories."[68]

Bruccoli has also provided three other essential tools for students of O'Hara's works. *John O'Hara: A Descriptive Bibliography* provides a full record of O'Hara's publications, the essential facts for studying his career as a professional author.[69] Bruccoli utilized the letters he had assembled in researching *The O'Hara Concern* to produce *Selected Letters of John O'Hara*, a volume which shows O'Hara at his quirkiest and crankiest, but also shows him as a conscious artist deeply committed to the craft of writing. The letters should continue to prove useful to critics interested in O'Hara's techniques, which he would often discuss in letters to friends, reviewers, and his editors. Finally Bruccoli edited *"An Artist Is His Own Fault,"* a volume of O'Hara's unpublished and published speeches, reviews, and statements on writers and writing.[70] At the very least, many of the pieces in this book, particularly the Rider College Lectures, give the lie to those severe critics who charge that O'Hara was little more than a popular writer with no artistic purpose.

The third full-length biography of O'Hara, *The Life of John O'Hara* by Frank MacShane, has as its stated purpose "to renew an interest in O'Hara's work through a look at his life."[71] MacShane weaves critical discussion of O'Hara's work into his biography to a greater extent than either Farr or Bruccoli, thereby giving it an interest that extends beyond the contours of O'Hara's life. For example, MacShane provides a brief discussion of *Hope of Heaven*, O'Hara's third novel, and the ways in which it represents an advance of O'Hara's writing techniques even though the book as a whole was flawed. MacShane also provides an interesting analysis of *The Lockwood Concern*, which he considers the most enduring product of O'Hara's last years as a novelist. Although O'Hara himself had written that the book was "an old-fashioned morality novel,"[72] MacShane suggests that O'Hara's art was too sophisticated for the story to be considered simply a morality tale in which the hubris of George Lockwood ultimately leads to his destruction. Rather O'Hara created his wealthy characters "with rare compassion and understanding," and the book's real theme lies in its treatment of fundamental human values and conflicts.[73]

In 1978 prospects for a revival of interest in John O'Hara's work brightened. A scholarly conference on O'Hara was held in his hometown of Pottsville, Pennsylvania, and the first issue of a new scholarly publication, the *John O'Hara Journal*, appeared shortly thereafter. The first issue published papers presented at the conference, including pieces by O'Hara stalwarts Matthew J. Bruccoli and Charles W. Bassett, a reminiscence from O'Hara's *New Yorker* days by B. A. Bergman, and an account of the reconstruction of O'Hara's study at Penn State, where O'Hara's papers are housed, by Leon J. Stout.[74] In a brief but tantalizing analysis of O'Hara's use of language, Raymond K. O'Cain examined words and phrases O'Hara uses in *Appointment in Samarra* against the supplement to the *Oxford English Dictionary*.[75] It is lamentable that O'Hara's writings, long hailed for their accuracy in rendering colloquial American speech, have yet to be studied from a purely linguistic point of view.

In its second issue the *JO'HJ* performed a signal service to O'Hara students by devoting the whole issue to Charles W. Bassett's biographical study, "John O'Hara—Irishman and American."[76] Bassett wrote the first doctoral dissertation on O'Hara at the University of Kansas in 1964.[77] Shortly after O'Hara's death he wrote a series of articles for the *Pottsville Republican* on "O'Hara's Roots," and these articles formed the basis for the extended study published in the *JO'HJ*. Bassett provides the most complete analysis yet of O'Hara's family background, particularly his grandfather Michael O'Hara and his father Dr. Patrick Henry O'Hara. He discusses the larger social milieu of Pottsville and the anthracite region that informs O'Hara's fiction. Bassett seeks to defend O'Hara against the charges of some critics that he failed to exploit his own Irish-Catholic ethnicity in his fiction. According to Bassett, O'Hara's "experience in the Pennsylvania anthracite region reflected his family's emphasis upon assimilation, upon individualistic success in the American tradition."[78]

The *John O'Hara Journal* served as the primary vehicle for articles about O'Hara, and during its brief life it published several interesting and valuable essays, two of which are included in this volume. Articles of specialized interest in the *Journal* include accounts of O'Hara's reception abroad in Germany, Poland, and Hungary.[79] Bibliographical study of O'Hara was advanced by my two compilations of addenda and corrigenda to Matthew J. Bruccoli's standard *John O'Hara: A Descriptive Bibliography*. I also uncovered a hitherto unnoticed piece by O'Hara published in the Stalinist *New Masses*.[80]

Despite the efforts of the *Journal*'s editor, Vincent D. Balitas, there was simply not enough interest in O'Hara to sustain the publication. Journals devoted to single authors are usually shaky operations at best, and while there seems to be a devoted contingent of O'Hara fans, the *JO'HJ* ceased publication after five years.

A particularly interesting issue of the *John O'Hara Journal* was a special double issue published in 1980 for which the editor solicited statements on O'Hara and his work from a wide variety of writers and critics. In a short commentary for this special issue, Guy Davenport, whose own modernist fiction bears little resemblance to John O'Hara's, but who has written several extremely favorable reviews of O'Hara's books, offered the following prediction. "O'Hara's concerns will be tabulated by the scholars. I can imagine dissertations on ambition in O'Hara, on ingratitude in O'Hara, on the rapacious male, the unfulfilled woman, on status consciousness, on character deterioration, and so on. No one has as yet made a clear statement as to what he achieved. I think he is as accomplished as Henry James, and is something like a James for our time. Instead of James' subtlety and refinement he had a boldness (perhaps bluntness) and accurate articulation of the vulgar tongue."[81] Davenport's expectations of future scholarly attention to be devoted to O'Hara's works have yet to be fulfilled. His comparison to Henry James would no doubt strike many as simply fatuous. William Dean Howells would probably seem the more fitting analogue to most people, but Howells has secured an enduring niche in the American literary canon, partly because of his influential critical role as a champion of realism.

A serious author who has produced as substantial a body of work as has John O'Hara deserves greater critical attention. Davenport's laundry list of potential topics contains suggestive clues for fruitful areas of investigation.

Many of the familiar elements in O'Hara's fiction have not been fully explored. One example in his use of sex. The sexual revolution has made O'Hara's once provocative use of sex in his fiction seem almost quaint. Yet clearly he was a pioneer in the more accurate rendering of human sexual instincts. Despite the important role he accords to sex, there has not been much extended critical analysis of his use of sex in his fiction or of how he views the sexual impulse in men and women. His later works pay increased attention to homosexuality, particularly lesbianism. Irene Thompson's "Homophobia in the Heartland" focuses on O'Hara's attitudes toward lesbianism as it is displayed in *The Ewings*.[82] Clearly there are possibilities for more critical investigation in this area.

O'Hara's interest in lesbianism is no doubt part of his broader interest in female sexuality. In an essay on *Appointment in Samarra*, John Updike has written that "the repeated offense O'Hara gave to Mrs. Grundy lay mostly, I think, in his insistence on crediting his female characters with sexual appetites—with sturdy and even sweaty bodily and psychological existences independent of male desires."[83] In a long review of *Selected Letters of John O'Hara*, Updike had earlier praised O'Hara for his creation of women characters. "O'Hara's ability and willingness to portray women has not been often enough complimented. He became, in such late stories as 'The Women of Madison Avenue' and 'Sunday Morning,' virtually a feminist writer. Throughout his fiction, women occupy the same merciless space his men do, with an equal toughness. 'I hate *them*,' concludes one of the unfaithful wives of 'Mary and Norma' to the other; 'It isn't only them hating us.' The disadvantaged position of women and the strength of the strategies with which they seek advantages are comprehended without doctrine, and without a loss of heterosexual warmth."[84] Updike's comments suggest that scholars interested in gender studies and the relations between the sexes might find valuable material in John O'Hara.

O'Hara has been accused by some critics of not possessing a comprehensive view of humanity, of being content merely to record surface characteristics and events. The clarity of his writing and the wealth of detail he presents do tend to mask his larger vision. Sheldon Grebstein has pondered the difficulties of discerning O'Hara's analysis of human character.[85] Clearly this is another area to which critics could devote their attention. With the ready availability of the necessary scholarly tools such as biographies, bibliographies, and manuscript collections, and with the passing of his literary generation now giving scholars the valuable perspective of time, a modest resurgence of critical interest in the work of John O'Hara may yet come to pass.

The aim of this volume is to present a comprehensive selection of reviews and critical articles published on John O'Hara. I have included a rather generous sampling of book reviews, and this in part reflects the relative paucity of criticism of O'Hara in scholarly journals. But John O'Hara was an enormously popular author in his lifetime, and despite his assertion that "critical reception does not really affect the general reception of my books,"[86] contemporary reviews of his books did play an important role in establishing his literary reputation. Distinguished literary critics who often gave O'Hara scant attention in their books or in the scholarly journals did pay attention to O'Hara from time to time in their book reviews. As Sheldon Grebstein has observed, "They have not always spoken well of him, but at least they have spoken."[87] The reviews are the best way to see the controversies over such perennial questions as O'Hara's use of sex, his ear for dialogue, his eye for detail, or the relative value of his short stories as opposed to his novels. As a best-selling author, O'Hara was reviewed regularly and widely. The value of most of these countless reviews is negligible except in suggesting the widespread attention given to his books and the kind of response they received. There are numerous reviews, however, that contain insightful comments on O'Hara's work and offer suggestions for further investigation. Consider, for example, Hayden Carruth's comment that O'Hara's "stories are embedded in the condition of life at exactly the same depth as the reader, which is why the reader, in order to appreciate John O'Hara's genius, must extricate himself, momentarily and at considerable effort, from that condition of life."[88] Or consider Robert Taylor's suggestion that snobbism is not the key to O'Hara's work but rather "his sensibilities as a lapsed Catholic."[89] I have endeavored to include a sampling of such reviews, not just from the New York press, but from newspapers around the country.

Two essays are published here for the first time, and both are examples of critical forays into areas that could bear further study. O'Hara's debts and similarities to other writers have often been mentioned, but seldom discussed in any great detail. Therefore it is useful to have Charles Bassett's comparative study of O'Hara's Gibbsville and Sinclair Lewis's Gopher Prairie and Zenith. *Appointment in Samarra* emerges as a bleak study of futility in a doomed society.

John O'Hara took a certain pride in the fact that the techniques he used in writing his novels and stories were invisible to the average reader. His style is so plain and straightforward, however, that these techniques have often escaped critics as well, thereby enabling them to dismiss his books out of hand. Thomas P. Coakley offers a valuable corrective in his essay on O'Hara's manipulation of point of view, particularly his use of the interior dramatic monologue. Coakley's elucidation of O'Hara's skill as a literary craftsman helps explain the compelling readability and believability of O'Hara's works.

In *O'Hara: A Biography*, Finis Farr suggested that O'Hara's "achievement was so great that it may take a while for us to realize its extent, as a mountain lifts above the shoreline in the eyes of travelers putting out to sea."[90] Farr's simile may have been merely the optimistic hope of a devoted O'Hara friend and fan. It probably would be far-fetched to suggest that a literary revival of the kind enjoyed by Herman Melville, Henry James, or F. Scott Fitzgerald will someday propel O'Hara's reputation to new critical heights. The literary canon is ever changing, however, and there is no doubt a grain of truth in

Farr's prediction, because O'Hara and his fiction were so closely identified with a particular time. As the O'Hara years recede into the more distant past, the unique contribution of his fiction in presenting "the way people talked and thought and felt"[91] during the first half of the twentieth century may yet secure him a firmer niche in the American literary pantheon. But O'Hara's appeal to future readers will not be based solely on his skills as a social historian, for he felt that his time was too important to be left "in the hands of the historians and the editors of picture books."[92] His strength lies in his artistic ability to render life itself in all of its dimensions. John O'Hara left a vast literary legacy that the literary critics have only begun to explore in depth.

Notes

1. *Selected Letters of John O'Hara*, ed. Matthew J. Bruccoli (New York: Random House, 1978), 459.

2. *The Cape Cod Lighter* (New York: Random House, 1962), x.

3. Prescott had written a critical review of *A Rage to Live* for the *New York Times*. Beginning with *Ten North Frederick* in 1955, O'Hara began his custom of publishing on Thanksgiving day. See Matthew J. Bruccoli, *The O'Hara Concern: A Biography of John O'Hara* (New York: Random House, 1975), 228.

4. Arthur Mizener, "Some Kinds of Modern Novel," *Sewanee Review* 69 (Winter 1961): 156–58. In 1963, when he saw the Signet Classic edition of *Appointment in Samarra* with an afterword by Mizener, O'Hara was enraged and wanted to have the whole edition withdrawn from circulation.

5. *The Horse Knows the Way* (New York: Random House, 1964), vii. Albert Erskine, "Introduction" to *The O'Hara Generation*, by John O'Hara (New York: Random House, 1969), x–xi. At least three reviewers made the mistake: Adrian Mitchell in the *New York Times Book Review*, 29 November 1964; Stanley Kauffman in the *New York Review of Books*, 17 December 1964, and James Meagher in the *National Observer*, 30 November 1964.

6. *Selected Letters of John O'Hara*, 286.

7. *Selected Letters of John O'Hara*, 286.

8. Bruccoli, *O'Hara Concern*, 158n.

9. Sheldon Norman Grebstein, *John O'Hara* (New York: Twayne Publishers, 1966), 17.

10. Grebstein, *John O'Hara*, 19. For a discussion of O'Hara's relationship with the literary and historical currents of the 1930s, see Deborah A. Forczek, " 'He Told the Truth about his Time': John O'Hara and the 1930's," *John O'Hara Journal* 2, no. 1 (Winter 1979–80): 46–65.

11. *Selected Letters of John O'Hara*, 77.

12. Grebstein, *John O'Hara*, 22.

13. Dorothy Canfield Fisher, Review of *Appointment in Samarra*, *Book-of-the-Month Club News*, September 1934, n.p.

14. Henry Seidel Canby, "Mr. O'Hara, and the Vulgar School," *Saturday Review of Literature* 11 (18 August 1934): 55.

15. Sinclair Lewis, "Nostalgia for the Nineties," *Saturday Review of Literature* 11 (6 October 1934): 157.

16. R. P. Blackmur, "The Morality of Pointlessness," *Nation* 139 (22 August 1934): 220–21.

17. John Chamberlain, review of *Appointment in Samarra*, *New York Times*, 16 August 1934, 15.

18.   Fred T. Marsh, review of *The Doctor's Son and Other Stories, New York Times Book Review*, 3 March 1945, 17.

19.   Clifton Fadiman, Review of *Hope of Heaven, New Yorker* 14 (19 March 1938): 79.

20.   *Selected Letters of John O'Hara*, 129.

21.   Robert van Gelder, "O'Hara's Portrait of a Night-Club Singer," *New York Times Book Review*, 3 November 1940, 5.

22.   Edmund Wilson, "The Boys in the Back Room: James M. Cain and John O'Hara," *New Republic* 103 (11 November 1940): 665–66. Wilson's essay was reprinted in his *Classics and Commercials: A Literary Chronicle of the Forties* (New York: Farrar, Straus, 1950).

23.   Lionel Trilling, "Mr. O'Hara Observes Our Mores," *New York Times Book Review*, 18 March 1945, 1.

24.   Irving Howe, "Fiction Chronicle," *Partisan Review* 16 (October 1949): 1047.

25.   A. C. Spectorsky, "Portrait of a Woman," *New York Times Book Review*, 21 August 1949, 4.

26.   Morton Fineman, "O'Hara Proves His Mastery," *Philadelphia Inquirer Book Review*, 21 August 1949, 2.

27.   Brendan Gill, "The O'Hara Report and the Wit of Miss McCarthy," *New Yorker* 25 (20 August 1949): 64–65.

28.   Milton Rugoff, "Masterly Portrait by John O'Hara," *New York Herald Tribune Book Review*, 27 November 1955, 18.

29.   Saunders Redding, "Book Review," Baltimore *Afro American*, 3 March 1956, magazine section, 2.

30.   Stanley Cooperman, "A Flat Sort of Realism," *Nation* 181 (31 December 1955): 580.

31.   Alfred Kazin, "The Great American Bore," *The Reporter* 19 (11 December 1958): 30–33. Reprinted in Kazin's *Contemporaries* (Boston & Toronto: Little, Brown and Co., 1962).

32.   Arthur Mizener, "Something Went Seriously Wrong," *New York Times Book Review*, 23 November 1958, 1, 14.

33.   Robert Kirsch, "O'Hara's Latest Held Magnificent," *Los Angeles Times*, 7 December 1958, part V, 6.

34.   Charles Poore, Review of *From the Terrace, New York Times*, 25 November 1958, 31.

35.   John Chamberlain, "'Passions Spin the Plot' in O'Hara's Novel of a Tragically-Flawed Man," *New York Herald Tribune Book Review*, 28 February 1960, 3.

36.   William May, "O'Hara's Latest," *Newark Sunday News*, 28 February 1960, section 3, E7.

37.   *Selected Letters of John O'Hara*, 380.

38.   Phoebe Adams, Review of *Sermons and Soda-Water, Atlantic Monthly* 206 (December 1960): 120.

39.   George Steiner, "Winter of Discontent," *Yale Review* 50 (Spring 1961): 425.

40.   John O'Hara, *Sermons and Soda-Water* (New York: Random House, 1960), 1:x

41.   Benjamin DeMott, Review of *The Cape Cod Lighter, Harper's* 226 (January 1963): 91.

42.   John Portz, "John O'Hara Up to Now," *College English* 17(May 1955): 493–99, 516. The quotation is from page 493.

43.   Portz, "John O'Hara Up to Now," 499.

44.   Edward Russell Carson, *The Fiction of John O'Hara* (Pittsburgh: University of Pittsburgh Press, 1961).

45.   Grebstein, *John O'Hara*, 146. John Updike made a similar point about O'Hara's prose in his laudatory review of *Selected Letters of John O'Hara*. See *Hugging the Shore: Essays and Criticism* (New York: Alfred A. Knopf, 1983), 185–86.

46.   Grebstein, *John O'Hara*, 147–48.

47.   Charles Child Walcutt, *John O'Hara* (Minneapolis: University of Minnesota Press, 1969). Reprinted in *American Writers: A Collection of Literary Biographies*, ed. Leonard Unger (New York: Charles Scribner's Sons, 1974), 3:361–84.

48. Walcutt, *John O'Hara*, 46.

49. Robert Emmet Long, *John O'Hara* (New York: Frederick Ungar Publishing Co., 1983).

50. Long, *John O'Hara*, 155.

51. Long, *John O'Hara*, 173.

52. Jesse Bier, "O'Hara's *Appointment in Samarra*: His First and Only Real Novel," *College English* 25 (November 1963): 135–41.

53. Scott Donaldson, "Appointment with the Dentist: O'Hara's Naturalistic Novel," *Modern Fiction Studies* 14 (Winter 1968–69): 435–42. The quotation is from page 441.

54. Charles W. Bassett, "Naturalism Revisited: The Case of John O'Hara," *Colby Library Quarterly* 11 (December 1975): 198–218. The quotation is from page 218.

55. John L. Cobbs, "Caste and Class War: The Society of John O'Hara's *A Rage to Live*," *John O'Hara Journal* 2, no. 1 (Winter 1979–80): 24–34. The quotation is from page 31.

56. Rex Roberts, "On *Ten North Frederick*," *John O'Hara Journal* 2, no. 2 (Summer 1980): 69–87. The quotation is from page 70.

57. James W. Tuttleton, *The Novel of Manners in America*. (Chapel Hill: University of North Carolina Press, 1972), 184–206.

58. Tuttleton, *Novel of Manners in America*, 206.

59. Gordon Milne, *The Sense of Society: A History of the American Novel of Manners* (Rutherford, NJ: Fairleigh Dickinson University Press, 1977), 227.

60. Lee Sigelman, "Politics and the Social Order in the Work of John O'Hara," *Journal of American Studies* 20, no. 2 (1981): 238.

61. Charles W. Bassett, "John O'Hara," in *American Short-Story Writers, 1910–1945, First Series*, ed. Bobby Ellen Kimbel (Detroit: Gale Research Co., 1989), 199–222.

62. Nancy Walker, "'All that you need to know': John O'Hara's Achievement in the Novella," *John O'Hara Journal* 4, no. 1 (Spring / Summer 1981): 61–80. Edgar McD. Shawen, "The Unity of John O'Hara's *Waiting for Winter*," *John O'Hara Journal* 5, nos. 1 & 2 (Winter 1982–83): 25–32.

63. Kathryn Riley, "The Suburban Vision in John O'Hara's Short Stories," *Critique* 25 (Winter 1984): 101–13.

64. Charles W. Bassett, "John O'Hara's 'Alone': Preview of Coming Attractions, *John O'Hara Journal* 5, nos. 1 & 2 (Winter 1982–83): 25–32. George Monteiro, "All in the Family: John O'Hara's Story of a Doctor's Life," *Studies in Short Fiction* 24 (Summer 1987): 305–8.

65. Finis Farr, *O'Hara: A Biography* (Boston & Toronto: Little, Brown and Co., 1973).

66. Matthew J. Bruccoli, "Focus on Appointment in Samarra: The Importance of Knowing What You are Talking About," in *Tough Guy Writers of the Thirties*, ed. David Madden (Carbondale & Edwardsville: Southern Illinois University Press, 1968), 129–36.

67. Bruccoli, *O'Hara Concern*, xvi.

68. Bruccoli, *O'Hara Concern*, 345.

69. Matthew J. Bruccoli, *John O'Hara: A Descriptive Bibliography* (Pittsburgh: University of Pittsburgh Press, 1979).

70. *"An Artist Is His Own Fault": John O'Hara on Writers and Writing*, ed. Matthew J. Bruccoli (Carbondale & Edwardsville: Southern Illinois University Press, 1977).

71. Frank MacShane, *The Life of John O'Hara* (New York: E. P. Dutton, 1980).

72. *Selected Letters of John O'Hara*, 480.

73. MacShane, *Life of John O'Hara*, 224.

74. Charles W. Bassett, "John O'Hara and the Noble Experiment: The Use of Alcohol in *Appointment in Samarra*," *John O'Hara Journal* 1, no. 1 (Winter 1978–79): 1–12. *See also* Bernard A. Bergman, "O'Hara and Me," 13–17; Matthew J. Bruccoli, "Out of Life," 18–28; and Leon J. Stout, "The John O'Hara Study," 35–37 in this issue.

75. Raymond K. O'Cain, "Dictionaries Consult Me!'" *John O'Hara Journal* 1, no. 1 (Winter 1978–79): 29–34.

76.   Charles W. Bassett, "John O'Hara—Irishman and American," *John O'Hara Journal* 1, no. 2 (Summer 1979): 1–81.

77.   Charles Walker Bassett, "The Fictional World of John O'Hara" (Ph.D. diss., University of Kansas, 1964). Other dissertations in whole or in part on O'Hara include: Robert Pierce Sedlack, "Manners, Morals, and the Fiction of John O'Hara" (Ph.D. diss., University of Notre Dame, 1965); John Lewis Cobbs, "The Pennsylvania Novels of John O'Hara" (Ph.D. diss., University of North Carolina at Chapel Hill, 1975); Kathryn Louise Riley, "The Use of Suburbia as a Setting in the Fiction of John O'Hara, John Cheever, and John Updike" (Ph.D. diss., University of Maryland, 1981); Thomas Patrick Coakley, " 'O'Hara Country' Revisited: A Study of Regionalism, Theme, and Point of View in the Work of John O'Hara (Ph.D. diss., Pennsylvania State University, 1983); and Ann Bryant Cramer, "Patterns of Imitation and Innovation: O'Hara, Marquand and Cozzens and the Victorian Novel of Manners," (Ph.D. diss., University of Chicago, 1988).

78.   Bassett, "John O'Hara—Irishman and American," 72. One critic who has argued that O'Hara's apparent antipathy toward the Irish damages his fiction is Joseph Browne. See his "John O'Hara and Tom McHale: How Green Is Their Valley?" *Journal of Ethnic Studies* 6, no. 2 (Summer 1978): 57–64.

79.   Thekla Zachrau, "The Reception of John O'Hara in Germany," *John O'Hara Journal* 2, no. 1 (Winter 1979–80): 1–12; Yurek Kutnik, "O'Hara in Poland: A Letter," *John O'Hara Journal* 2, no. 2 (Summer 1980): 22–30; Zsolt Viragos, "John O'Hara in Hungary," *John O'Hara Journal* 5, nos. 1 & 2 (Winter 1982–83): 38–42.

80.   Philip B. Eppard, "Bibliographical Supplement: Addenda to Bruccoli," *John O'Hara Journal* 2, no. 1 (Winter 1979–80): 41–45; "Bibliographical Supplement: Addenda to Bruccoli," 4, no. 2 (Winter 1981): 59–61; "John O'Hara in the *New Masses*," 5, nos. 1 & 2 (Winter 1982–83): 33–37.

81.   Guy Davenport, "(On O'Hara)," *John O'Hara Journal* 3, nos. 1 / 2 (Fall / Winter 1980): 76.

82.   Irene Thompson, "Homophobia in the Heartland," *John O'Hara Journal* 5, nos. 1 & 2 (Winter 1982–83): 11–17.

83.   John Updike, *Odd Jobs: Essays and Criticism* (New York: Alfred A. Knopf, 1991), 220–21.

84.   John Updike, *Hugging the Shore*, 185. In the original version of Updike's review of O'Hara's letters, he had written, "Compared to the women of his fiction, Hemingway's are mere dolls. Indeed, if there is an American male author who has set a greater variety of believable women on the page, or as effortlessly projected himself into a female point of view, I haven't read him." "The Doctor's Son," *New Yorker* 54 (6 November 1978): 213.

85.   Sheldon Grebstein, "John O'Hara: The Mystery of Character," *John O'Hara Journal* 2, no. 2 (Summer 1980): 14–21.

86.   *Selected Letters of John O'Hara*, 286.

87.   Grebstein, *John O'Hara*, 20.

88.   Hayden Carruth, "O'Hara's Best: A Joy to Behold," *Chicago Daily News*, 23 Nov. 1963, Panorama, 9.

89.   Robert Taylor, "John O'Hara at the Top of His Form," *Boston Sunday Globe*, 3 March 1985, A11.

90.   Farr, *O'Hara*, 282.

91.   O'Hara, *Sermons and Soda-Water*, 1:x.

92.   O'Hara, *Sermons and Soda-Water*, 1:x.

Appointment in Samarra

◆

[Review of *Appointment in Samarra*]

WILLIAM SOSKIN

John O'Hara's first novel, *Appointment in Samarra*, is too good to be true. Ever since I finished it I've gone around knocking on wood and saying please don't let this man go wrong, make him write more novels that are hard and sensuous and elegant reporting of what critics call the American Scene. Don't let him get bored with people and hate and love and the things people do and don't let him run off to proletarian or other movements. Keep him a writer. There are so few of his kind, people who know their subjects and are not pushed over by them.

Appointment in Samarra is a story of a Pennsylvania anthracite town, of the boys, girls, husbands, wives, racketeers, automobile dealers, grass widows, country club dances, torch singers, speakeasies, romances, roads, filling stations, lecheries, introversions, drunks, parked cars, inflations, depressions, traditions, village hamlets, grace-under-pressure Hemingway yokels, small captains of industry, fakes, frauds, phonies, lovely, patient, passionate wives and drinking, hopeless mates, stuffy parents, light and nasty adulteries, adolescents, crooks, practical jokers, cads and all the other human items that go to make up a community which has a country club with a golf course as well as a flock of roadhouses in which the respectable males sometimes indulge in extra-domestic flights.

Reprinted with permission of Harry Ransom Humanities Research Center, The University of Texas at Austin, The New York Journal-American Morgue, The Hearst Corporation. From New York *American*, 16 August 1934, [17] Copyright © 1934 by The Hearst Corporation.

The town John O'Hara describes plays the chief role in his novel, just as surely as the city of Paris is cast for the leading role in Jules Romains' more ponderous work, *Men of Good Will*. But whereas these experimental and socially conscious writers try to depart from the basis of character development and story development, the essential constituents of a good novel, O'Hara in a simpler fashion tells us the story of a man, a solid individual around whom the community exists.

Julian English, the protagonist, would have said nuts if he heard himself described as a sort of Hamlet of the country clubs; but that is what he is— a poisoned, introverted organism deliberately destroying the things and the people he loves most, and driven by some deathly destiny that hangs over his life, over the cheap, hollow civilization that surrounds him.

The title of this novel suggests its irony. It refers to the Somerset Maugham fable in which a servant, jostled by Death in the market place of Bagdad, races off to Samarra to avoid his fate. And Death, questioned regarding the reason for startling the servant, says: "That was not a threatening gesture . . . it was only a start of surprise. I was astonished to see him in Bagdad for I had an appointment with him tonight in Samarra."

I don't want to give the impression that *Appointment in Samarra* is a pretentious allegory. Its meaning emerges just as meaning is evolved in life— through the accidents and the turgid, opaque texture of events. As a matter of fact, very little happens in the book. Julian throws his drink into the face of a red, vulgar and boring Irishman who is an important financial figure in the town of collapsed incomes and businesses.

That simple event, done half consciously and under the influence of liquor and tedium at the country club party, serves to stir the small prejudices, the careful social pretenses, the hidden passions, the jealousies, the strange alliances of underworld and top-dog, the lusts and scandals of the town.

Before O'Hara is through with his landscape, we have gone back into the lives of Julian and his gallant wife, Caroline, seen the boyhoods and girlhoods of typical small city people and the origins of some of their complex troubles, seen the pretensions and hopelessly stuffy ideals of their parents. The language O'Hara uses, whether he is giving us the vernacular of Moronia in a speakeasy, or the clipped, deadly rattle of gangsters' talk, or the deliberately unromantic but aphrodisiac syllables of the modern young man and woman in their more intimate moments, or the hard-boiled ding-dong of the locker room conversation—the language is invariably accurate and carefully recorded.

A quality which most novels of American life lack is very much present in *Appointment in Samarra*—that of careful reporting of the minutiae of daily existence. When O'Hara describes the games, the fantasies, the activities and superstitions of a small boy in a small city he captures a whole era and an entire environment through the simple expedient of good, specific memory and discriminating reporting. In that he resembles Sinclair Lewis at his best, but he combines an emotional sensitivity with that reporting which the author of *Main Street* often lacks. The O'Hara novel has some of the social photography which John Dos Passos pursues so assiduously, but it also has a well disciplined, carefully organized story back of it—a matter which Dos Passos frequently neglects.

There will also be talk of Hemingway and of James Gould Cozzens in relation to this book—but what of all these resemblances? O'Hara exists in his own right now.

A Morality of Pointlessness

R. P. BLACKMUR

Mr. O'Hara's first book is highly readable and grossly entertaining; and it has the advantage of belonging to the most popular of present schools of the novel, the school which includes Hemingway more or less complete and such recent books as "The Postman Always Rings Twice" and "Brain Guy"; it is the school which gives provisionally permanent expression to the attitude which produces a weekly *New Yorker* and a monthly *Esquire*. Thus the dedication is to F. P. A., and the title—which means an appointment with inescapable and sudden death—is explained in an epigraph drawn from an unpublished play of Somerset Maugham's.

Because the school, not only in the content of its productions but also in its public relations, is, so to speak, becoming tough and domineering in terms of its positive but limited virtues, Mr. O'Hara's book deserves examination at a certain length. It is a segmentary novel, occupying Christmas Eve, Christmas, and the day after Christmas, 1930, in the city of Gibbsville, Pennsylvania, with various cut-backs and two postscripts. It contains a telescopic history of Gibbsville and exhibits a segmentary view, as a segmentary novel should, of many of its citizens, most often in a sexual or alcoholic but always evidently normal posture: all these in terms of the characterization above.

The protagonist is Julian English, aged thirty, of the aristocracy, who loves his wife but drinks too much. On Christmas Eve he throws a highball in the face of Harry Reilly, who is self-made, Irish Catholic, and a bore, and to whom Julian owes $20,000. This occurs at the Lantenengo Country Club. On Christmas night he gets drunk, and because his wife refuses to keep a date with him in their parked car, he takes the mistress of Gibbsville's leading bootlegger out of a roadhouse into somebody else's parked car. This occurs in front of his wife, some of his friends, and one of his employees. The day after Christmas is a bad day for Julian, with his servants, his wife, and at his office. So he beats up a one-armed friend and a Polack lawyer or two at the Gibbsville Club. This happens in front of the club steward. Then he drives round the country to cool off, back to town, and finds his wife coming out of her mother's house. When he tells her the latest she tells him she is through and calls off

R. P. Blackmur, "A Morality of Pointlessness," *The Nation* magazine © 1934. The Nation Company, Inc. Reprinted with permission.

the big party they were to have given that night. Julian goes home, sets to work on the liquor for the party and on the female society reporter who calls for the guest list. Then, at the safety point of alcoholic stupor, he kills himself in his garage by carbon-monoxide poisoning.

The book also contains the life histories of Julian, his wife Caroline, his father the doctor, Al Grecco the bootlegger's runner; short sketches of Harry Reilly, Monsignor Creedon, Ed Charney the big shot, Luther Fliegler the normal American salesman; and thumbnail sketches or characteristic anecdotes of a score of others. Luther Fliegler, the normal man, opens and closes the book and is the only chorus for its climax. He is, I think, the author's only ironic representation, but he has no integral part in the action. Al Grecco, whose history is given at the next greatest length to that of Julian, has no integral part either; although, like Fliegler, he is apparently to suffer because of Julian's actions. Fliegler and Grecco are not so much subordinate as parallel characters. The quality of agency so far as the main story goes is reserved to Julian alone. The other characters are interesting as lookers-on and innocent bystanders, affected or injured by Julian's private and inexplicable explosion.

It is characteristic of this school of writing that its crucial gesture is inexplicable. The man kills himself without having once, before that day, thought of death as a solution, and without ever having felt death's lag or its magnetism. We are told only, early in the book, that his grandfather killed himself after having embezzled considerably. Julian is in debt, but not, with his family resources, inextricably. He kills himself, apparently, because his wife does not immediately forgive his drunken stupidity. He kills himself, so far as I can see, either pointlessly or out of back-handed good-will, out of gruff, tough, sentimental loyalty to a code itself pointless.

Part of this pointlessness is due to the segmentary character of the novel. The different groups of characters in the book, their motives and objects, are segments fitted one after another. They do not grow together, nor, I think, are they meant to. They achieve a kind of specious unity by being printed in sequence and by interrupting each other, and they further comprise a patch-work background. It is true that both Fliegler and Al Grecco act in some part as mirrors or reflectors in which we get images of Julian as a real guy, but they are not otherwise even apparently made to work into the main action. However interesting they may be in themselves, and they are interesting, as agents of this novel they are incredibly wasteful and meretricious. In short, although the book is dramatic in the sense that it is exciting, is vivid and written at high speed, is accurate and often penetrating, it is not a well-designed drama, in the sense that its parts do not supplement, bind, and enforce each other. Much of it might exactly as well be in some other novel.

But the book would no doubt repeat that it meant to be pointless and fragmentary. That is the way things are thought to happen ever since Hergesheimer became Hemingway: they are poignantly pointless to the point of sentimentality. Only, to make a book, they have to be tough and exciting about liquor and women. With these stipulations, we have the kind of craft which makes a good detective story good reading: a craft of particulars, and surfaces, and anecdotes, covering a highly artificial convention of reality: an exciting craft to appreciate while the story lasts.

In other words, however immediate and however great the claim to reality, to authority, such a book makes, we are actually reading a romance, which can have as its best merit that it entertains and thrills. The romance I mean is that defined by Henry James as experience liberated, cut loose from our sense of the way things ordinarily happen. The only fault with this sort of writing is that it pretends not to cut loose where it cuts the sharpest: where it makes a morality of pointlessness, and an action out of intoxication.

It may be, of course, that Mr. O'Hara is right. Certainly his first novel has the vigor of conception, the ear for speech, and the eye for effect that make good writing; and he has, more valuable, the facility for the immediate aspects of character. The fault of romanticism I find may be merely a failure to combine his merits with the persuasive force of style. The pointlessness may be right, at least in the legitimate field of sex and liquor. But it is certainly not a new vocation.

[Review of *Appointment in Samarra*]

Dorothy Canfield Fisher

If you are one of those people who feel uneasy unless you "keep up" with what is going on in the world, you will appreciate being told that such a book as this has been written. It will be widely read and widely discussed. Those who like it greatly (there will be many of them) will affirm that it is a "swell job of writing." It will make a good many other people physically sick. The point is, I think, that it is one of those books with no great inherent importance which sum up a literary tendency. Ever since the war, one school of fiction has been pushing farther and farther towards what they call honesty. "Honesty" for them is a denial of any important springs of human action except alcohol and sex, and the use of a bald outspoken vocabulary (partly eighteenth century English, partly contemporary gangster argot) in calling attention to the usually not-mentioned functions and organs of the human body. Mr. O'Hara has, with great verve and considerable skill, carried the use of this sort of honesty about as far as it can go. The setting is any American city of about twenty-five thousand. The characters are the local Country Club gang, with a background of a gang of bootleggers, roadhouse hangers-on and garage men. The description is well done in the sketchy manner of Burnett or Hemingway. The characters (treated in the same manner) are drawn clearly enough for temporary reality. The plot moves from the moment when Julian, the hero, throws his fateful highball, to the time when (drunker still, if that is possible) he sets his car to making carbon monoxide in his locked garage. On the first reading it gives an impression of capable workmanship, and to some extent that impression endures. Having set himself to write objectively, Mr. O'Hara resolutely refrains from sentimentalizing his tragedy. He keeps clear of any philosophic generalizations or any ideas, whatever. One cannot even be sure whether he realizes his hero for the rotter he is. Other elements do not stand up so well on re-reading. What seemed at first, life-like, almost witty conversation, proves to consist mostly of drunken foul-mouthed insults, and of intimate talk between husband and wife on the level of what may possibly be the tone of a low-class brothel. Well, why go on? This is enough to tell you what the tone of the book is. It will be called a picture of life, and so it is, a jazzed-up picture

Reprinted from *Book-of-the-Month Club News*, September 1934 by permission of the Book-of-the-Month Club, Inc. All rights reserved.

of a singularly dull and unimportant section of life. As I said at the start, its real importance is that it seems to sum up all that is possible in the direction of this sort of "honesty." Perhaps it will be the end of the movement, and may start a landslide back towards Victorianism.

The Doctor's Son and Other Stories

◆

Mr. O'Hara's Stories

Edith H. Walton

Acclaimed by Dorothy Parker, Ernest Hemingway, and other old masters of the hard-boiled school, "Appointment in Samarra" made an immediate sensation. Since it, too, summarizes an attitude, it may even become a landmark novel like "This Side of Paradise" and "The Sun Also Rises." From the moment of its publication six months ago Mr. O'Hara was blurbed as a significant writer. Up till then, though he had been writing short stories well and prolifically, he had not attracted any general notice.

Those stories, many of them antedating his novel, have now been collected in a book. Due partly to the fact that the majority appeared in The New Yorker, sharpness and brevity are their distinguishing characteristics. Trenchant all of them, usually ironic, often a little cruel, they display precisely the same qualities as "Appointment in Samarra." The chief difference is a widening of range. Instead of confining himself to wastrels of the country club crowd, Mr. O'Hara has included some lesser folk among his bitter vignettes.

Only one of his tales departs from the deft pattern which Mr O'Hara has established. The title story, a longish and hitherto unpublished piece of work, is more solid and more ambitious than anything else in the book. Presumably autobiographical, to some extent at least, it describes the influenza epidemic of 1918 as it affected a mining district in Pennsylvania. The doctor's son, a

Reprinted from the *New York Times Book Review*, 24 February 1935, 7. Copyright © 1935 by The New York Times Company. Reprinted by permission.

boy of 15, drives a car around the countryside for the young substitute who has come to relieve his father. They ladle out prescriptions wholesale to crowds of miners gathered at cross-road saloons; they encounter, in noisome forms, poverty, death and disease; the young doctor shocks the boy by his conduct with the mother of Jim's best girl. It is all a puzzling experience, harrowing, exciting, and, to his youth, a little meaningless.

Not only is "The Doctor's Son" excellent reporting, but it is less slick than most of John O'Hara's work, and has a quality of honest emotion. So, too, have a few of the shorter pieces. One might mention particularly "In the Morning Sun," which records a woman's detached discovery that her son has lived a life at 27; that, however long he may go on, the living part of him is dead. Or "It Must Have Been Spring." Or that dreadful picture of an old man's ignominy with which the book closes.

There are disadvantages to the form in which Mr. O'Hara casts his stories, and to the glibness which it encourages. Sometimes his sketches of the foolish and the forlorn can sting and bite. Too frequently, however, they become thin, trivial, synthetic. After one has learned the knack it is easy to dress up an anecdote and call it a story—to produce such second-rate stuff as "Mort and Mary," "New Day," "Ella and the Chinee," "Master of Ceremonies."

If one sifts out the chaff, however, there are some fine things in the book—apart, that is, from those already mentioned. "Sportsmanship," which has a pool parlor for its background, is a story so ruthlessly brutal that it somehow recalls "The Killers." "Of Thee I Sing, Baby" is as deft a portrait of a chorus girl as one could ask. "The Public Career of Mr. Seymour Harrisburg," "Pleasure," and "Salute a Thoroughbred" show how versatile irony can be. In all his stories, moreover, Mr. O'Hara has an ear for the rhythms of speech which invoke the banal yet inevitable comparison with Lardner.

To criticize "The Doctor's Son" adequately one would have to embark on a lengthy discussion of the hard-boiled school. Certain virtues Mr. O'Hara possesses which not all of its disciples share. He never is sentimental, in the manner of Dorothy Parker at her work; he never indulges in a secret sob in the throat; he never wastes a word nor strikes an attitude. He is, always, a superbly gifted observer, shrewd, savage, merciless and apparently fertile in ideas. That he seems sometimes a little monotonous is due possibly to the fact that he has no viewpoint to offer, that he records instead of judges, that he synthesizes characters and situations instead of ferreting out their depths.

Butterfield 8

◆

Appointment in Park Avenue

George Stevens

John O'Hara has done it again. His new novel is as slick, as tough, as readable as "Appointment in Samarra"—and that means you can't put it down. Of course there'll be some who can't keep it down.

Because he is laconic and factual, because he writes about people who have too much money and too much alcohol without moralizing about them, John O'Hara has been called a reporter. This would place him, according to the ranking system of our democracy, several degrees below the status of novelist. Now it happens that the story of "Butterfield 8" is similar, in outline and in some detail, to a story which ran in the metropolitan press a few years ago; a story which held the front page for several weeks; a story on which half the reporters in New York got a chance to try their skill. Well, John O'Hara makes all those reporters look like candidates for the *Harvard Crimson*. If he's a reporter, some city editor should offer him a by-line and twenty cents a word.

The newspaper story concerned a young woman who was found drowned, supposedly murdered, on a beach near New York. Like so many newspaper stories, it began at the end. It proceeded backwards without regard to continuity. Occasionally a fact would come out: the victim had been a party girl; she had been to a good school; she had, according to certain testimony, been subjected to precocious sexual experience. But as the weeks went by, these

From *Saturday Review of Literature* 12 (19 October 1935): 14. Reprinted by permission.

items remained isolated. The story went off into a fog, and even the tabloids eventually dropped it.

The data mentioned in the preceding paragraph are all characteristic of Gloria Wandrous, the heroine—for want of a better word—of "Butterfield 8." But John O'Hara tells it straight, with the logic of cause and effect, with characters so well drawn that they explain themselves, with a background of speakeasy New York and country club Long Island unrivalled for accuracy. It is not a pretty story; it may not be literature, lying as it does somewhere between Dostoievsky and Tiffany Thayer. But it is certainly not journalism. Not only is it better than journalism—it is different. In the opinion of this reviewer, and contrary to an opinion previously expressed in this magazine, John O'Hara is a satirist. One sentence will prove it—from a speakeasy scene: "Kitty Meredith, the movie actress, came in with her adopted son, four years old, and everybody said how cute he was, what poise, as he took a sip of her drink." The whole book is written like that. It doesn't parade itself as satire, but it's satire just the same. The speakeasy customers who came from the Butterfield 8 telephone exchange—the Park Avenue region in the 70s and 80s—give Mr. O'Hara a pain. And he knows exactly how they behave in all the typical circumstances of their lives.

So John O'Hara, whose first novel ran away with the carriage trade last year, has done it again. But that's not a hundred per cent compliment. "Butterfield 8" is too much like "Appointment in Samarra." Gloria Wandrous in the new novel is the female counterpart of Julian English in the first novel. Both of them, following their early experiences, become more or less pathological narcissists; both of them are left with a deep conflict which makes them run away from Damascus only to find death waiting at Samarra. And the other characters all come from the same background; rich drunks are very much alike whether they live in Pottsville or New York. "Butterfield 8" is as readable as "Appointment in Samarra" but not quite as good. Gloria Wandrous is harder to handle than Julian English. And the book is more diffuse. There are two unnecessary characters; and there are a few pages of irrelevant reflections—one paragraph of which concerns Shakespeare—which shouldn't have got beyond the galley proofs. Mr. O'Hara is not an essayist. But he is a novelist. And it would be interesting to see what kind of novel he would write if he happened to meet some attractive people.

Hemingway Mixed with Hearst

Malcolm Cowley

John O'Hara's new book has two not inconsiderable virtues. In the first place, it depicts a brief period and a narrow sector of American life more accurately than any other novel. It is futile and more than mildly scabrous, but so too were the daily lives of the speakeasy people, the girls on the loose, the husbands about town; any honest book about them would have to be shocking. In the second place, it is easy to start, it is hard to lay down before reaching the end, and this is more than can be said for a great many books that were written and discussed more solemnly. It often seems to me that critics, in their concern with social purpose and artistic probity, are likely to forget that an essential aim of any novel is to get itself read.

They could find plenty of social purpose in "Butterfield 8" if they looked hard for it. At the very least they could find a deeply felt, almost inarticulate indignation against the business and personal standards of people in the Social Register. The title, by the way, is the name of the telephone exchange that serves upper Park Avenue, and is thus a Manhattan equivalent of "Vanity Fair." More debatable than the author's purpose is the question of his artistic probity. The critics have been troubled to explain just how and where his book falls short of an ideal that he might have set for himself.

Many of them have objected to the general depravity and dullness of the characters. It is indeed true that the people John O'Hara describes are as limited in sensibility as so many shellfish. Born into prosperous families, educated at good universities, elected to the right clubs, their only personal achievement has been to drink and dawdle themselves into a state of practical anesthesia, a state in which their response to any human stimulus—love, friendship, death, no matter what—is less than human and even less than that of the lower vertebrate animals. They are confined to four interests in life: getting money, getting drunk, going to bed and going to the bathroom. Some of them have the glamor of youth and wild high spirits—like the heroine, Gloria Wandrous, whose career resembles the life and death of Starr Faithfull. But the middle-aged characters—like Gloria's lover, Weston Liggett—are presented without redeeming qualities; they have boorish man-

Reprinted from *New Republic* 85 (4 December 1935): 108–109.

ners and the morals of a pink-nosed Chester boar. Apparently the critics are justified in their objection.

On the other hand, it is easy to remember novels, some of them great novels, in which the principal characters are equally depraved. I am aware of no law that obliges novelists to deal only with strong or affectionate or otherwise admirable people. John O'Hara's real mistake is that he has not dealt with such people at all. His real mistake is that he has given us too close a view of his pub-crawlers, without ever stepping back from them, without ever introducing characters or incidents that would offer a perspective on their lives. He writes as if from the inside of a speakeasy, without opening windows to clear away the smoke.

This is a criticism that involves merely his judgment. As for his integrity as a novelist, there is only one scene that reflects on it: the scene of Gloria's death. Here we ought to be reaching the climax of the story, for Gloria is an appealing character and a real one. All her acts ring true, even if the author seems to be giving a false explanation of them when he tells how she was twice corrupted during her childhood by middle-aged men; there were plenty of girls who acted like Gloria without this excuse. At any rate she does symbolize her age, in spite of what the novelist says about the folly of looking for symbols. She has the right to die tragically, as the result of some conflict or some deliberate choice. But Mr. O'Hara denies her that right and makes her die by accident, fall off a steamer because she chose to walk in the darkness on the top deck, and because the "City of Essex" had a low guardrail. It is this slovenly handled death scene that changes the story from drama to melodrama, from Hemingway at his best to Hemingway mixed with Hearst.

Hope of Heaven

◆

[Review of *Hope of Heaven*]

JOSEPH HENRY JACKSON

There is, as the publisher suggests on the jacket of this book, only one John O'Hara. That is, unless you count James M. Cain.

What the publisher didn't intend, however, was that his remark about Mr. O'Hara's singular quality should be read with the word "unfortunately" in front of it. Put it that way, "Unfortunately, there is only one O'Hara," and you'll see what I mean. Because, by the time he has published a third novel there should be (I can't help feeling) another O'Hara—an O'Hara bigger and better than the first one. What I am trying to say is simply that "Hope of Heaven" is O'Hara just exactly as he was when he wrote "Appointment in Samarra." And I sincerely believe that in that first novel he showed a promise that he has not, so far, fulfilled.

This is not to say that "Hope of Heaven" isn't a splendidly written, rapidly told story. Where story is concerned, and in his command of a sort of terse, angry shorthand that is a cross between what his characters say what they mean, Mr. O'Hara is thoroughly up to his best level here. Consider the yarn itself.

His hero is a Hollywood writer who tells you what he is like on Page One when he explains that he wears $35 shoes, $7.50 socks and has a $2200 car. This clever gentleman loves a clerk in a Hollywood bookstore, finds

Reprinted from the *San Francisco Chronicle*, 25 March 1938, 11. © *San Francisco Chronicle*. Reprinted by permission.

himself in the middle of an ugly family situation and involved indirectly in murder. What he does with these two circumstances makes the story. Before you are done with it you have a pretty miscellaneous assortment of (a) drunken scenes, (b) hangovers and (c) sex entertainment of a varied type. You have also a group of O'Hara characters including a none-too-convincing rascal of a father, a thinnish character in the son, a not-more-than-fairly delineated heroine and a weak young good-for-nothing who is nevertheless the most credible individual in the book, in spite of the fact that you see him only disconnectedly and jumpily, in occasional glimpses. There are other people, too, of several sorts; none of them important.

All of these characters are put through their tricks in the typical O'Hara manner. And O'Hara is very good indeed at his ringmaster's job, as you'll know if you have read him. In addition to his astonishing knack at clipped, curt conversation, Mr. O'Hara has a curious talent for making any given scene seem ten times as significant when you first come to it as it is when you look back at it. Given these two aptitudes, Mr. O'Hara can make a story loop the loop until the reader is dizzy. He has done it before and he does it again here. It's his specialty.

But you arrive, still dizzy, at the end of his yarn and put the book down, you experience a strange reaction—the kind of thing Mr. O'Hara is so apt at describing in his characters in their hangover moments. Your head clears and you begin to wonder just what Mr. O'Hara has told you. And you don't know. You just don't. You've been fascinated, drugged by the writing tricks the author has at his command—and he has them, no doubt of that. You have been doped, just as you're doped by the screen, into thinking for the moment that just because the people you're looking at move and act in a lifelike manner they have done something. And then you realize they haven't. They have simply been moved about in a limited space by a man who has the talent for moving people about in a way that will make them appear to have performed for themselves.

To be sure, there is some merit in this. In itself it is no small accomplishment. It takes talent, and a lot of it. To write as Mr. O'Hara writes, to direct as a good motion picture director does it, to photograph as an expert cameraman can take pictures—all these things take ability of no mean order. But after all it is fair to wonder why the possessors of such ability don't do more with it.

That is all I'm wondering about Mr. O'Hara. And all I'm hoping is that one of these days he will use his really remarkable gifts to better account. I should like to see him do a novel of which his publisher could find something better to say than "There is only one O'Hara," and (as he does later on the jacket) "The California setting is something new in the work of O'Hara." It is a melancholy thought that a man of O'Hara's unquestioned brilliance can be recommended on no more solid ground than that he has used a backdrop he hadn't used before.

Files on Parade

◆

[Review of *Files on Parade*]

Mark Schorer

In a brief preface to his new collection of stories, John O'Hara lists his favorite short story writers. They include, predictably, Lardner, Hemingway, Dorothy Parker, and Scott Fitzgerald; if you add O'Hara and his imitators (of which there are many) to these, you have what is practically a tradition. Lardner is the grand old man to whom all of them went to school and from whom all of them learned something—not the whole thing, usually. O'Hara, in turn, without becoming quite another Lardner, has taken one or two things from each of these and put them back together, and these things give his work its characteristic accents.

From Hemingway, of course, comes the attitude—the hard-boiled, sporting point of view, the expectation that the winner takes nothing—and the trick of the dialogue, the compression of situation and the rapid pace. From Dorothy Parker comes a particular kind of caricaturing detail (of speech, of dress, of manner), the sharp types, and the occasional faked ending. And from Scott Fitzgerald comes most of the subject matter—country clubs, cafes, night clubs, Hollywood, and so on and the beings who inhabit these glamorous spheres. I do not mean, of course, that O'Hara has "taken" each of these things from each of these writers—no writing is so simple; I do mean that he finds his precedent and perhaps his lesson among them, and thus inevitably associates his work with theirs, and clarifies its parts for us.

From *Boston Evening Transcript*, 7 October 1939, Section 4, 2. Reprinted by permission of the estate of Mark Schorer.

But when you put these parts together again, you have original work, unmistakably O'Hara's, an idiom, almost a level of experience which, limited as both may be, are peculiarly his own. All his stories are very short, very slight, simple in structure, and almost naively direct. This is to say that, unlike Hemingway's stories, for instance, O'Hara's imply almost nothing beyond the immediate situation which is being set forth.

Take even such a fine job as "Lunch Tuesday": two women are lunching together and one discovers that the other is her husband's mistress; the story comes down to nothing more than the shock of the discovery and the fact that the two characters are left embarrassingly together with it. Sometimes, feeling the need of complication, O'Hara gives this basic simplicity of effect a spurious complexity through elaborate and tricky situations. "All the Girls He Wanted" is such a story. Throughout, we are led to believe one thing, and then, sharply, at the end, are told another. "Saffercisco" and "It Wouldn't Break Your Arm" are others.

Certainly these are clever and amusing, but they do not come up to O'Hara's straightforward best—like "Days." This story consists of nothing more than the first step (employing a full-time gardener) in a husband's infidelity; but this much is wonderfully well done, and one feels its truth and importance. O'Hara does not always write so truthfully; sometimes his plots, as I have indicated, falsify his point, and sometimes, with his curious gift (Fitzgerald had it too) for lending glamor to persons who are actually without it, it is simply his style that does it. Even then, he is as entertaining a writer as we have, and most of the time (the four "Pal Joey" letters, "Shave," "Days," "Sidesaddle," "No Mistakes," "My Girls," "Goodbye, Herman," "Gentleman in the Tan Suit," "Give and Take," and half-a-dozen others) he is pretty nearly perfect. His is a slick and smart-aleck art, but, at its best and within its limitations, it is also superb.

Pal Joey

◆

O'Hara's Portrait of a Night-Club Singer

Robert van Gelder

Pal Joey is a night-club singer who is down in the world and has to sing in quite cheap dives partly because he is getting a bit old for his job. He is not worth even a poor unfortunate mouse's time for long because he is such a liar that even a loving woman can't believe anything he says, and because he is so mean and dumb that he double-crosses every one with whom he has contact, and also double-crosses himself even though toward himself he has the best intentions in the world. This book is made up of Joey's letters to a band leader named Ted. Ted is doing very well in New York and Joey is doing very badly in the Middle West.

Out of this unlikely material—Pal Joey and his mice and his bosses, the boys in the band, the punch-drunk doorman, the socialites who act like big-shots on three dollars, the mobmen who back the clubs—Mr. O'Hara has written a minor masterpiece. Tipped a bit this way or that way Pal Joey would have been just a comic character, but Mr. O'Hara renders him so faithfully, with such perfect precision, such absolute accuracy, that Pal Joey stands forth as his own, no-good self, a typical yet arresting figure, with an authentic background.

There is nothing much hidden about Joey. His ignorance is very nearly absolute, and so is his conceit. When people asked him where he went to

Reprinted from the *New York Times Book Review*, 3 November 1940, 5. Copyright © 1940 by The New York Times Company. Reprinted by permission.

school he formerly said Princeton but he never had found out whether or not Princeton was in Philadelphia so he played safe by saying that he had been educated at Dartmouth University, or, rather, Dartmouth U. Once there was a certain mouse who was a banker's daughter and something of a lush and after she'd had a few drinks she'd wonder if she could live without Joey. So for a little while Joey could dream of meeting her family and being offered a place in the bank. Other than that he had few hopes. Mostly there was a new mouse to be met or a sucker to be taken for twenty dollars or so. And Joey had enough to do just getting by.

One night, for example, when the crowd in the night club wasn't big enough to pay expenses, Joey happened to notice the boss looking at him. "He did not say anything. He merely looked. But the way he looked was the way the head man looks on one of those Arctic expeditions after nobody had anything to eat for a week. They are going around barefooted because they have used up their moccasins for scoff. Maybe one of the chaps has gnawed off a nice juicy thumb. But the head man is looking at me. I am the fat one."

Mr. O'Hara's talent, which is great, is forced into rather narrow range by this material and by the aping of Joey's style of letterwriting. Yet he creates with exhaustive apt detail and impeccable phrase a very bright light that clearly illumines Joey and all that he is, and there can be no doubt but that these letters are part of his best work.

Pipe Night

◆

John O'Hara Observes Our Mores

LIONEL TRILLING

John O'Hara occupies a unique position in our contemporary literature. He stands alone not by reason of his literary skill, although that is considerable, but by reason of his subject—he is at present the only American writer to whom America presents itself as a social scene in the way it once presented itself to Howells or Edith Wharton, or in the way that England presented itself to Henry James, or France to Proust.

More than anyone now writing, O'Hara understands the complex, contradictory, asymmetrical society in which we live. He has the most precise knowledge of the content of our subtlest snobberies, of our points of social honor and idiosyncrasies of personal prestige. He knows, and persuades us to believe, that life's deepest intentions may be expressed by the angle at which a hat is worn, the pattern of a necktie, the size of a monogram, the pitch of a voice, the turn of a phrase of slang, a gesture of courtesy and the way it is received. "Cigarettes, there in the white pigskin box," says one of his cinema queens, and by that excess of specification we know the room and the mind and the culture in which the box has its existence.

Our Latin teachers used to take pleasure in explaining that the word *mores* meant not only morals but customs, and not only customs but manners. O'Hara works with the consciousness of this identity of meaning. For him customs and manners are morals.

In this he is of course no different in intention from the social novelists of twenty years ago. But writers like Dreiser or Sinclair Lewis, concerned as they were with Philistinism in the gross, were inclined to see society as a solid, undifferentiated front of respectability against which free spirits beat and bruised their wings. They did not permit themselves to see the details, the infinitely various ways in which the same thing is expressed, the tangle of antagonistic manners of which the social fact is composed; and they always assumed that poor people or really good people lived outside the world of social desires. Dreiser was notoriously unperceptive, even absurd, in his portrayal of manners. Even Sinclair Lewis, for all his great comic success with Babbitt in the bathroom and at the club, did not have an eye for the truths of the social shadings.

A few contemporary novelists have had some measure of O'Hara's gift of observation. Dos Passos, for example, has drawn on a kindred sensibility for some of his best effects. Edmund Wilson's interesting novel, "I Thought of Daisy," is full of sharp social perception, and George Weller's two works of fiction were most promising in this respect. And of course there was Fitzgerald, who in many ways is O'Hara's master. But at the present time O'Hara stands pretty much alone in his devotion to the precise social fact, and at his best he has a great deal to tell us.

He is not always at his best. Of the thirty-one stories of "Pipe Night," the new collection, a few—such as "Now We Know," "Free," "Nothing Missing," "Too Young"—fall into the pit of easy and all too well known sentiment. A larger group takes what value it has—considerable but not finally impressive—from its anthropological accuracy and from a quality of grim, humorous social notation in the good tradition of Petronius. But no less than seven of the new stories, and that makes a fair proportion, are first-rate.

These seven stories—"Summer's Day," "The King of the Desert," "Bread Alone," "A Respectable Place," "Graven Image," "Revenge" and "Lieutenant"—are remarkable if only because they so brilliantly transcend their form. For the very short story, with its well-taken bitter or pathetic point, is getting more and more tiresome, what with its situation so briskly set up and its insight so neatly given and the author skipping so nimbly out of the way, leaving the reader with the emotion on his hands to do with it what he can. Katherine Mansfield bastardized the great Chekhov to create this genre and we have all admired it for two decades while secretly we have been bored with it. O'Hara works more and more in this form, but he does not get easily trapped by the clichés it is likely to generate; he is saved by his passionate social curiosity and his remarkable social intelligence.

O'Hara's insatiable curiosity provides him with the actuality that fleshes his stories and keeps them from being what examples of this genre too often are, stories of pathetic sensibility. His intelligence has taught him how intense and how deep are the emotions which social considerations call forth. He has always been aware, to take but a single and obvious example of his perception, of how secretly profound is the feeling which many modern Americans have about their college lives; it seems to me that no other writer could have projected the story "Graven Image" in which the New Deal bigwig, even at the moment of his greatest power, cannot forget or forgive his exclusion from the Harvard Club he had wanted to make. (It is worth noting, by the way, that O'Hara is the first writer—and even he is a little late—to deal fictionally with the social and emotional possibilities of the New Deal dignitaries.)

Edmund Wilson has referred to O'Hara's sensitivity to social differences as "half-snobbish," and perhaps any close observer of social values must in this sense be a little ambiguous. But O'Hara knows that social judgments of a strict kind are not confined to the upper classes. They are as frequent in the poolroom as in the club lounge. And he knows that in the poolroom as elsewhere they are deeply involved with other vital considerations; in "Lieutenant" dim class loyalties are mixed up with intense feelings about age and virility to make one of the best comments we have yet had on the social changes the war is bringing.

An emphasis on the accuracy of O'Hara's social sense may seem to imply that a very subtle reporting is the best it can give us. But the accuracy of O'Hara's observation exists for more than its own sake. It allows him to deal with emotion in a specially effective way. Thus the grief of T. K. Attrell in "Summer's Day" is conveyed by a variety of literary devices, but its special poignancy appears through the particular quality of the social intercourse at the fashionable beach, and its hopeless isolation is made manifest by Attrell overhearing a group of half-grown boys speaking with vulgar contempt of his age and of his suicide daughter. That boys might indeed happen to talk with such spiteful cruelty is the kind of thing O'Hara would know.

Again, "Bread Alone" is—after Gertrude Stein's "Melanctha"—the best story that I know about a Negro because the Negro is so precisely seen in all his particularity as a Negro that he wonderfully emerges, by one of the paradoxes of art, as a man and a father.

Yet again, in a writer of the liberal persuasion it required not only a clean conscience on anti-Semitism but also the perfect innocence which knowledge can give, to draw the issue, in "King of the Desert," between two clever Jewish writers from Hollywood and a simple rancher, to show the writers' expert kidding to be ambivalent between affection and malice, to show the rancher's pride in his New England ancestry as a rather nice thing in him, and at last to disclose fully and disagreeably the writers' unpleasant impulse; literature has of late grown very pious and it is a relief to see O'Hara's intelligence being perfectly clear that the particular relates to the general but is not to be confused with it.

O'Hara's stories are getting neater, tighter and more economical in their form, and this, I suppose, constitutes an increase in expertness. But I cannot observe the development with pleasure, not merely because the span, tempo and rhythm of the stories in "Pipe Night" need to be varied to avoid monotony, nor because I have a taste for a more relaxed kind of writer such as O'Hara himself gave us in "The Doctor's Son," but because this increasing virtuosity of brevity seems to tend away from the novel and it seems to me that for O'Hara's talents the novel is the proper form. There is perhaps a specific short story talent which, for those who have it, makes the novel an impossible form. O'Hara may be a writer of such a talent; if he is, then what he can accomplish in the short story is a sufficient justification of his gifts. Still, no one who has recently reread "Appointment in Samarra" can help thinking of O'Hara as a novelist.

Even the incoherence of "Butterfield 8" and the flippant treatment of the almost interesting idea of "Hope of Heaven" do not discourage the promise of "Appointment in Samarra." That first novel was not a great book, nor even a perfect book, but it was an organized book—it organized not only its material but also its author's talents. The quality of the two later novels seemed almost to suggest that the intensity of the vision of explosive doom of "Appointment in Samarra" had damaged O'Hara's ability to think in terms of coherence—that he could handle only the quick, isolated, discontinuous insights of the short stories.

To be sure, the stories taken together are not without their coherence; they relate to each other and add to each other's meaning. But the novel was invented, one might say, to deal with just the matter that O'Hara loves. Snobbery, vulgarity, the shades of social status and pretension, the addiction to objects of luxury, the innumerable social uncertainties, the comic juxtaposition of social assumptions—the novel thrives on them, and best knows how to deal with them.

But it is one of criticism's unpleasant traits to ask for what it thinks we should have instead of finding pleasure in what we do have. And what we have from O'Hara when he is at his best is very good indeed.

Here's O'Hara

◆

[Review of *Here's O'Hara*]

William McFee

This deponent is always ready to depose that, while he hopes never to meet any of John O'Hara's characters, he is prepared to read (and re-read) anything and everything John O'Hara writes. But he must stick to fiction, or there will be no guaranty.

The new omnibus "Here's O'Hara" (Duell, Sloan & Pearce, $3) has a score of O'Hara's short stories and some longer ones; also "Butterfield 8," "Hope of Heaven," a sardonic Hollywood tale, and the now famous "Pal Joey." It is a fine three dollars' worth.

There may be, in fact there are, some who dislike O'Hara's approach to life. His uncompromising truthfulness, his lack of those qualities we find in writers like Thomas Wolfe, Damon Runyon and O. Henry, sentimentality, pathos and a subconscious yearning to make people bigger and better than they are in real life, repels a section of the reading public. O'Hara never philosophizes, never comments beyond the irreducible minimum demanded by the story. He leaves that to his characters, who are nothing if they are not terse. They are often extremely hard-boiled, and polite citizens, whose tradition in literature is classical, feel they are engaged in slumming in the underworld when they read O'Hara.

Reprinted by permission of Scripps-Howard Inc. from the *New York Sun*, 15 May 1946, 25 and also by permission of the General Research Division, The New York Public Library, Astor, Lenox and Tilden Foundations.

This reviewer does not feel that way at all. He regards John O'Hara as an extremely able craftsman and a very important artist in words. The fact that he describes heels and harlots, sophisticated Broadway and Hollywood operatives, has nothing to do with the case. What he does with them is to create works of art, as Ring Lardner did, and William Faulkner does, and Hemingway.

Those whose conception of a good story is a love tale in which they can participate, seeing themselves as hero or heroine of a romance, escaping vicariously into Fairyland, had better keep away from "Here's O'Hara." There is an austerity and an honesty in these stories, even when they dazzle and shock by their technical skill, which makes any concession to Victorian standards unthinkable.

Compare, for example, a story by O'Hara of a triangle situation and the same theme by Dreiser. With all respect for that famous fighting pioneer, Dreiser, in the sense that O'Hara is a writer, never could write at all. In two pages O'Hara can give you, with lightning strokes, not only all that Dreiser would offer in a hundred pages of clumsy prose, but he will give you the very sound of the voices, the whole atmosphere and pattern of the lives. In Conrad's classic phrase, he will make you hear, he will make you feel and he will make you see.

With the very first sentence his characters step into view, in focus too, three-dimensional, alive, cunning, wicked, or just simple and pathetic, and they begin to move around and speak. They may inspire aversion and even contempt, but never indifference or boredom.

Is this art? We think it is. If the reader is skeptical let him try these samples of O'Hara. Let him read, for instance, "Saffercisco," or "Can You Carry Me?" or "I Could Have Had a Yacht." He may remain unconvinced. Some are tone-deaf and color-blind. Some think that only Russians or Frenchmen can write short stories. Neither O'Hara nor this reviewer can do anything about that. But those who know will recognize a first-class writer in this book.

Hellbox

[Review of *Hellbox*]

Charles Angoff

One marvels that so obviously skillful a man as Mr. O'Hara can produce so little in the way of genuine literary effects. He has a superb ear for the talk in the social underworld of New York and Hollywood—the expensive nightclubs and gaudy bedrooms, and the shabby roadhouses where the habitués of these clubs and bedrooms occasionally go when slumming. He also has a fine sense for brevity; no one can say he overwrites. Finally, he has an excellent feeling for dramatic situations and characters. Yet, with all this talent, his stories fail to impress, his people fail to live, and all that remains after a reading of any one of his books is a vast disappointment, a sorrow that so much effort and skill have been put to such piddling use.

Mr. O'Hara suffers from the beliefs of so many writers for *The New Yorker*, to wit: that the crudities and vulgarities of the fancier clubs and bedrooms visited by the "sophisticates" are more real than the quiet, gentle doings of more modest living quarters, that displays of deep affection and consideration for one's fellows are silly and not grown-up, and that the sneer and bang on the nose reveal more of the truth about people than the kiss and the embrace. Needless to say, all these beliefs run contrary to the principles behind the great writings of all times and places. Always great literature has been concerned with great emotions, great love, great pity. This is not to say that hate and

From *Tomorrow*, Garrett Publications, October 1947 (volume 7 No 2). Reprinted by permission of the Parapsychology Foundation.

scorn and despair have been absent from the enduring books, but they have mostly been treated under the aspect of loving kindness and a sympathy for the aberrations of lost human souls—not from the point of view of a bartender or a grasping lady of the night.

Mr. O'Hara, unfortunately, seems to think that the only life with any meaning is that experienced and observed by bartenders, prize-fighters, conniving motion-picture producers, amateur prostitutes, elderly madames, and roving bachelors. There is not a genuine emotion in any one of the twenty-six stories that make up his latest book. A Hollywood mogul goes to a nightclub and arranges an assignation with a chorine whom he's just seen for the first time, suddenly remembers his weak heart—and tries to get out of it; a nightclub frequenter gets a married woman, a friend of his sister, to agree to a brief afternoon affair with him, almost under the nose of her husband—but he backs out at the end, because he had grown "old and cautious"; a successful businessman and a waitress talk over old times, when they did things clergymen of all denominations would have frowned upon; a father and a neighborhood bachelor boatman discuss in a roundabout way, on the very day of the daughter's wedding, the affair the boatman and the daughter had had long ago; a man comes to visit an old flame, whom he hasn't seen for years—he finds she is away, but her stepdaughter seems to be willing to jump into bed with him; a run-down piano player and his run-down wife sit around and bore each other till a couple comes to make use of a spare room they have—and what takes place in the group has overtones of Lesbianism; a schoolteacher is confronted by an old beau who reminds her of an episode in her past she would rather forget; and so on for 210 pages.

There is not one genuine character in the entire book. There is not one situation that has any real meaning. There is not a single phrase that is worth repeating. There is not, in short, a single story that stays in the memory. Worse, the over-all effect is that of having gone a-slumming in the literary world and having learned nothing. Mr. O'Hara, as a writer, is a slum-dweller as surely as James T. Farrell is. The perfumed world he is acquainted with is on a level, artistically, with the submerged world of Chicago that Mr. Farrell knows. Great works of the imagination can be written about the submerged on any level, as Zola and Gorki and George Moore, to mention only those authors who come to mind at the moment, have shown. But setting down conversations among shabby people without insight and pity and imagination is not art. It is little more than tabloid journalism. This is why so many people find the reading of Mr. Farrell's books so unprofitable. It is also why more and more people are finding it unrewarding to read Mr. O'Hara's books. One hopes that Mr. O'Hara will take a new direction. For unlike Mr. Farrell, he has many of the attributes of the real writer—and he reveals a wholesome respect for the English language, alas all too rare in the current American literary scene.

A Rage to Live

◆

[Review of *A Rage to Live*]

JOHN K. HUTCHENS

Here is the most ambitious work of a greatly talented writer, his first novel in eleven years and, from the day it was announced, a major event of this new season.

That kind of event can, of course, go on from there to success or failure, taking its chances like any other. To this inspector it seems that John O'Hara's "A Rage to Live," published on the fifteenth anniversary of his memorable "Appointment in Samarra," succeeds impressively—that it has the notable virtues of his short, brilliant work, and then something more: the weight and depth of the big novel into which have gone many lives, taking with them the long, slow accretion of living, the experience of time and change that no little story, however fine, can fully convey. It might as well be noted at once that there are going to be a lot of arguments about it, ranging from the laments of the squeamish to some reasonable criticism relating to the insistent role that sex plays in it. The important thing is that the real values of "A Rage to Live," and of Mr. O'Hara as a writer, should not somehow get lost in an uproar that might start at any moment and probably will.

What he has achieved is a social history of a Pennsylvania city in the last years of the nineteenth century and the first twenty years of this one, a history told in terms of a seignorial family and, especially, of its only daughter who

Reprinted from the *New York Herald Tribune*, 16 August 1949, 19. © 1949, New York Herald Tribune Inc. All rights reserved. Reprinted by permission.

is later the dominant member of the house. It begins in 1917, as the fourteen-year marriage of Grace Caldwell and Sidney Tate is apparently about to break up; goes back beyond the turn of the century to the childhood and adolescence of Grace; comes down to 1917 again, and moves a little beyond it into the post–World War I era.

It is long, solid and subtle, and when you have finished it you will know Mr. O'Hara's Fort Penn (Harrisburg, it would seem) somewhat as you know the town or city in which you grew up—and for the same reasons. You will know its politics, newspaper, clubs, courts, marriage and funeral customs and sexual mores. Above all, you will know its delicate social gradations based on time, money and family.

Some of this you will get from Mr. O'Hara writing almost as straight as a historian, or a reporter filing a descriptive story from the immediate scene, and this is finely done: no novelist now functioning can do so much with a set of apparently simple facts, building them into a social pattern that lives and moves and is not simple at all. But this is also a book that lives in terms of people, and so you will get even more from Mr. O'Hara as a creative writer with an ear uncannily sensitive to the shadings of speech, an eye whose honesty takes him into strange, dark places.

The strange, dark places are chiefly in the marriage of Grace Caldwell and Sidney Tate—the daughter of the supreme local family and the well-to-do outsider from New York who can never quite make himself accepted in this rich, long-settled Pennsylvania-Dutch country. They love each other. Sidney Tate is a gentleman, with a decent ideal about the marriage relationship. Grace is kind, tolerant, courteous—and oversexed. Early in the book you have seen how and why she became so. Sidney, naturally, has not. A marriage evaporates in wounded pride.

It is, of course, the double standard operating in reverse, this time with the wife saying—as the husband has said immemorially—that whatever happened outside has nothing to do with the marriage as such. The moralists will, one suspects, be as unrelenting toward Mr. O'Hara's Grace Caldwell as they have been to all the lost ladies. If, on the other hand, you look at Grace as the author does, as a person driven by her nature and not as a symbol in a didactic lesson, then her story becomes a personal and poignant tragedy. However, the reader who contemplates casting stones had better not embark on "A Rage to Live" in the first place.

But the reader who takes Mr. O'Hara's novel as it is written will find it fascinating on a number of counts. Through the extraordinary O'Hara ear he will hear, time and again, a whole relationship come to life in a few sentences, will see a whole era revived in a word or an allusion. He will listen in on the local politicians, watch the gentry at a wedding, meet the local business men, and in general enter into a scene assembled with a naturalist's documentary skill. But (and this could be a major aspect of his development) the O'Hara eye and ear go beyond documentation. The almost absolute precision with which they function does not merely describe. They create something that goes beyond technical efficiency or the admiring surprise you feel at the perfect rendering of a fact or an object. And the result is a story told with overtones of compassion outside the limitations of the naturalistic novel. Mr. O'Hara can be merciless, here as in his flashing short stories. He can also respect a tragedy by declining to get maudlin about it.

It may occur to you that no given group of people are likely to be as absorbed, from moment to moment, by the adventures of the bed as many of Mr. O'Hara's people are, a prepossession suggesting that they don't think about anything much. This is, I should say, a valid point, in the sense that that insistence slightly mars the final effect of a generally objective work. But only slightly. This is a true novel, capacious and real, that moves under its own power.

[Review of *A Rage to Live*]

BRENDAN GILL

"The present volume is a progress report from a case history study on human sex behavior." So, bumpily but with a certain grandeur, begins the first chapter of the Kinsey-Pomeroy-Martin whodunit, "Sexual Behavior in the Human Male." Translated into less gravelly English, this quotation from last year's romantic best-seller would make a pretty accurate description of what will probably be one of this year's best-sellers, the enormous new novel by John O'Hara, entitled "A Rage to Live" (Random House). The parallels between the Kinsey Report and the O'Hara Report are unmistakable. The authors not only share a major theme but have a similar interest in determining the extent to which the various classes in our society can be distinguished from one another in terms of what they do about sex and then in terms of what they *think* about what they do about sex. Dr. Kinsey is perhaps the leading professional student of this subject and as such has had the advantage of having numerous assistants, as well as the financial backing of the Rockefeller Foundation. Dr. O'Hara, our leading amateur, has had to go it alone, at his own expense. On the other hand, O'Hara has long been one of the most prominent figures in the profession of letters, while Kinsey, an old gall-wasp man, is a taxonomist first and a literary craftsman second.

Granted that Kinsey has the edge in statistics and O'Hara in style, the layman's immediate response to "A Rage to Live," as to the earlier, pioneer work, is likely to be one of uncritical admiration for the amount of scholarly research involved. This feeling is soon displaced, however, by one of depression, and eventually of suffocation, for the reader who begins by being ashamed of having paid so little heed to the true nature of the human condition ends by being convinced, half against his will, that the investigation of sexual practices had better be left, as it always used to be, not to the expert but to the young. It was predicted last year that the Kinsey Report would open our eyes and jolt us into a lively awareness of the complexity of our sexual problems; now it appears that the Report put more people to sleep than it awakened, and numbed our minds instead of jolting them. The recurrent passages of maudlin sexuality in "A Rage to Live," complete even to so worn a stencil as the

Reprinted from the *New Yorker* 25 (20 August 1949): 64–65. Reprinted by permission; © 1949, 1977 The New Yorker Magazine, Inc.

prostitute with a loving heart and a high I. Q., may have the same effect. If so, it will be all the sadder, because the author has plainly intended to do more than out-Kinsey Kinsey; he has intended, indeed, to write nothing less than a great American novel.

There was reason enough for this ambition. "A Rage to Live" is O'Hara's first novel in eleven years and comes exactly fifteen years after "Appointment in Samarra," which was, and is, an almost perfect book—taut, vivid, tough-minded, and compassionate. In the period between "Appointment in Samarra" and "A Rage to Live," O'Hara published two other novels—the successful "Butterfield 8" and the inconclusive "Hope of Heaven"—and five volumes of short stories, many of which are as good as anything in the language. Within the tight framework of these stories, apparently so small in compass but nearly always so explosive in force, O'Hara was able to take the measure of an astonishing variety of subjects, describing for us, with or without sex but with every appearance of authenticity, the customs of such dissimilar outposts of civilization as Hollywood, Stockbridge, Washington, D. C., and Hobe Sound, as well as half a dozen New Yorks—Wall Street, Jackson Heights, the Village, Fifty-second Street, Beekman Place, Riverside Drive. But it is an unbreakable convention of our time that a man who has written novels goes on writing novels, and perhaps partly for this reason, but surely for other deeper and more compelling reasons, O'Hara sat down and doggedly accumulated "A Rage to Live," which must be about as long as his three previous novels put together and which bears little or no resemblance to any of them.

A sprawling book, discursive and prolix, ranging in time from 1877 to 1947, and full of a multitude of semidetached characters and subplots, what "A Rage to Live" *does* resemble is one of those "panoramic," three-or-four-generation novels that writers of the third and fourth magnitude turn out in such disheartening abundance. Dr. O'Hara's handy guide to healthy sex practices has been tucked inside the disarming wrapper of the formula family novel, and one result of this odd combination is the loss of the old sure-fire, ice-cold O'Hara dialogue. Here, for example, is Sidney Tate addressing his wife, Grace Caldwell Tate, the heroine of the novel, on the subject of her affair with a cheap, lower-middle-class Irish contractor:

[Y]ou see, in this world you learn a set of rules, *or* you *don't* learn them. But assuming you learn them, you stick by them. They may be no damn good, but you're who you are and what you are because they're your rules and you stick by them. And of course when it's easy to stick by them, that's no test. It's when it's hard to obey the rules, that's when they mean something. That's what I believe, and I always thought you did too. I'm the first, God knows, to grant that you, with your beauty, you had opportunities or invitations. But you obeyed the rules, the same rules I obeyed. But then you said the hell with them. What it amounts to is you said the hell with my rules, and the hell with me. So, Grace—the hell with you. I love you, but if I have any luck, that'll pass, in my new life.

Now, if this sounds like something out of an old *Redbook*, one is prepared at first to account for it on the ground that Tate is a Yale man, but no, he is the closest thing to a hero in the novel, and his ethics appear to be those of the author. That passage is, in fact, the intellectual high point of the book, and from there it grinds slowly downhill, through Sidney's death and a few more love affairs for Grace, to a sinister postlude, in which we learn that all the surviving characters have turned more or less physically into swine. In "Appointment in Samarra," there was nothing about Julian English that we did not know and want to know, but Grace Caldwell Tate is a fatally uninteresting woman, and her rage to live rarely amounts to more than pique. It is hard to understand how one of our best writers could have written this book, and it is because of O'Hara's distinction that his failure here seems in the nature of a catastrophe.

People Look Like Animals in O'Hara's Spyglass

Theodore M. O'Leary

Reading the opening pages of John O'Hara's first novel in eleven years is likely to be an exciting experience for his admirers. At least, they will feel the man has chosen a subject worthy of his talents, has utilized his tremendous ability and written the major American novel toward which his previous books have pointed. But after that, disillusionment will set in. The realization will come that once again the reader has been blinded by O'Hara's surface brilliance, that the O'Hara promise still is unrealized, that the man with the keenest eye and the most acute ear among living American writers, still is that, and little more.

Disillusionment, however, will not be accompanied by apathy, for at the outset it should be emphasized that "A Rage to Live" is thoroughly engrossing from start to finish, no matter how far it falls below one's ultimate hopes for its author.

In scope and subject "A Rage to Live" undoubtedly is O'Hara's most ambitious undertaking. It is an attempt to portray the various aspects of the society of a dynamic, quickly changing American city in the years just before, during and immediately after World War I. The city is called Fort Penn, but in the usual prefatory note, pointing out that none of the characters is real, O'Hara, in a characteristically sardonic way, leaves no doubt that he is writing about Harrisburg, Pa., and that he knows quite a lot about that city as a result of first hand observation.

As a first hand observer, John O'Hara has no peer. By telling you the pattern of a man's necktie, describing the car he drives, what he eats and drinks, he can often tell you more about his characters in a sentence than a less observant writer might do in ten pages. His ear for the spoken word is far more sensitive than that of the more widely publicized Ernest Hemingway. For verisimilitude O'Hara's dialogue is unsurpassed (note in this book the realistic manner in which his characters misuse the words we and us).

In short, O'Hara seems to know everything about people except the one

Reprinted from the *Kansas City Star*, 24 September 1949, 14. Reprinted by permission of the *Kansas City Star*.

thing the reader wants to know most, which is not *how* they behave, but *why* they behave the way they do. O'Hara seems unaware of any human motives other than the sexual, and to a lesser extent, greed for money and power. And having made up his mind that human beings are fundamentally animals, and can be expected to act like animals, O'Hara assumes a true Irish belligerence in support of his contention, which is why in "A Rage to Live," as in his other novels, the overall impression is of the author truculently defying his readers to deny that the O'Hara theory of human behavior is correct. In fairness to O'Hara it should be acknowledged that possibly his theory is correct, and that the tendency on the part of the reader to challenge it may be due to its unpalatability.

Although O'Hara touches on the political, commercial and journalistic life of Fort Penn, his main concern is with the wealthy and powerful Caldwell family, and particularly with the Caldwell daughter, Grace, who marries Sidney Tate, a socially impeccable and reasonably rich New Yorker, with whom she goes to live on the Caldwell farm outside of Fort Penn.

Grace is at once domineering and kindly, provincial and worldly wise. She is beautiful and strong willed, independent in thought and deed, usually willing and strong enough to take the consequences of her often impetuous acts. Also, she is incapable of being content with one man, although she is far from promiscuous. When she yields to a strong instinct and has an affair with Roger Bannon, a political building contractor, it ends her marriage in the true sense of the word, if not in fact.

Later, when the same instinct leads her to attempt to enter upon an obviously impossible relationship with a young newspaper man, the consequences, with a touch of irony, become more than even Grace can cope with and the Caldwell dominance of Fort Penn comes to an end, with Grace fleeing to New York, leaving her idler brother, Brock, to carry on the Caldwell tradition, which he has neither the inclination nor the energy to do.

Aside from Grace's parents, who are on the whole admirable (which makes Grace's behavior even less clearly motivated than that of most of O'Hara's people), Sidney Tate is about the only one of O'Hara's many characters who has much decency about him. Sidney has a code and he lives up to it; he expects other people to do the same. When they don't, he is disappointed and ceases to be interested in them. Sidney is virtually the only character drawn with much subtlety, the only one who seems to have sufficient complexity about him to make the reader long to know more about him. His life suddenly becomes a tragedy when he learns of Grace's unfaithfulness. The reader sympathizes with him; toward the rest of the characters one's main feeling is that they get about what they deserve.

Although the total effect of O'Hara's book is negligible because of its preoccupation with the surface of life, somewhat paradoxically many of its parts are impressive. This is a devastatingly truthful book, to the extent that O'Hara is capable of getting at the truth. As far as he is able to go, he is uncannily perceptive and observant. He is not the sort of person you would want hanging around town if you had anything to conceal. Very little in Fort Penn escapes him.

Technically, O'Hara is superb. The economy with which he writes is emphasized in what he calls a "postlude" to "A Rage to Live." Here, in six pages and a few snatches of dialogue, he covers twenty-seven years in the lives of Grace, her two children, her brother and her best friend, with an effectiveness that is remarkable. Developing according to the O'Hara theory of human behavior, the lives of all concerned have moved along inevitable lines and in each case the result is desolation, waste and emptiness.

It could be that at heart John O'Hara is supremely a moralist.

The Farmers Hotel

♦

Violence in the O'Hara Country

ELIZABETH JANEWAY

There was a blizzard last November in the O'Hara country which is as definite a part of the geography of the United States as is Faulkner's Yoknapatawpha County. On that night Ira Studebaker opened the Farmers Hotel in Rockbottom, Pa. It was Ira's first venture in hotelkeeping—he had retired from the wholesale fruit and vegetable business after the death of his wife—but it was merely a reopening for the Farmers Hotel, which had seen people come and go for many years. Six guests stopped at the hotel that night, caught in the blizzard. This is the story of what happened to them and to Ira, to Mrs. Fenstermacher who did the cooking for him, and to Charles Mannering, Negro, Ira's general factotum and friend. Dr. Graeff, who lived next door, and a state trooper played a part in it too.

O'Hara has certain great talents. One is a kind of richness and thickness of important detail: his books are embedded in the solidity and reality of life. Another, perhaps a development of the first, is his ability to fascinate us with ordinary people; or rather with people who, in O'Hara's hands, reveal beneath their ordinary exteriors a magnificent individuality. Neither of these talents is lacking in this book. O'Hara, reporting in his deceptively simple style on the way things work, touches on half a hundred facets of experience: on how to run a hotel, on the wholesale vegetable business, on the kind of alibi that can save an unmarried couple in need of one ("She's here but you can't talk to her," lies a faithful friend, "she's passed out"), on the historical reasons for the peculiarities of the Pennsylvania road system, to cite just a few. He introduces us to members of the upper and middle classes, to a trio of strolling players on their way to a Legion smoker, to a tough truck-driver and, best of all, to Charles Mannering in whom there exists the potentiality of a picaresque hero as good as Conrad's Nostromo. But in spite of O'Hara's talent, the book is unsuccessful.

The fault, it seems to me, is one of structure. Prepared as we should be for the violent end, we are not prepared *enough*. Coincidence plays too large a part in the death which overtakes two of the six guests of the Farmers Hotel. The train of events leading to this dénouement—as the guests arrive, meet, quarrel, make up, eat together, entertain each other and quarrel again—is simply not strong enough to support the shock of the ending.

Now violence runs through O'Hara's books as a persistent theme. And since violence itself is ambivalent—being sometimes self-induced or self-provoked and sometimes external and coincidental—it is impossible to blame O'Hara for treating it ambivalently. In his best books, notably "Appointment in Samarra," the violent end is self-provoked. Fate operates through the character of the hero and the classic form of tragedy purges and satisfies the reader.

We must certainly not blame O'Hara, indeed we must honor him, for attempting to subdue to significance the other form of violence, the sudden thunderclap which destroys a man or a city, the accident that strews death about at random. The attempt to interpret such violence and to relate it to life is a hard and noble task closely related to the old effort of philosophy and religion to deal with the Problem of Evil. But perhaps it is an impossible one. At any rate, in "The Farmers Hotel," O'Hara has not been able to turn coincidence into Fate. The deaths which end the book do not enlarge its reach, nor cast a light on earlier pages to throw them into a more meaningful perspective.

Rather the book is disrupted and the reader left puzzled and inclined to discount what has gone before. We are given merely a bewildering episode to ponder: this is less than we have a right to expect from O'Hara—just because he has given us so much more in the past.

Sweet and Sour

◆

The O'Hara Swath

SAMUEL T. WILLIAMSON

These 1,400-word chapters were first turned out for Sunday editions of The Trenton (N.J.) Times-Advertiser. Novelist John O'Hara says a fourteen-page contract stipulated that he should write as he pleased but mainly about books and authors. One crippling specification was that he must really read the books he wrote about. He got around that by not writing about many books.

It is an O'Hara boast in "Sweet and Sour" that he's the only columnist who doesn't pose as an intimate Hemingway friend. He "never called him Papa, Pops, Hemingstein or anything but Ernest." Then follow three or four paragraphs of scorn poured upon chit-chatterers, name-droppers and other latchers-on who attach themselves like barnacles, or "pilot fish," to Hemingway. He prays eloquently that the Great Man might be deprived of five years of postage stamps and telegraph blanks with which to communicate with this gaggle of gagglers.

Most of these sketches read as though they were written off the top of the O'Hara head, and when he blows his top, he's good mental relaxation. He's a long-practiced workman in terse, hard-bitten prose. And he's far more enjoyable when he's butting his head against something—or someone—than when he tries to be nice, which, fortunately, is seldom.

He likes Red Smith and Thurber, John Hutchens, and Pegler when he

Reprinted from the *New York Times Book Review*, 17 October 1954, 30. Copyright © 1954 by The New York Times Company. Reprinted by permission.

is writing about bums and gamblers. Also Charlie Poore, beside whose puns O'Hara's are feeble. He doesn't like people who call him "John" on first acquaintance. He works up a lively hate against blurbs and "casual" photos of authors on book jackets. (See blurb and O'Hara picture on jacket of "Sweet and Sour.") He's fed up with novels about Time editors and writers. He hasn't any use for Pegler or Winchell as statesmen, his views of J. Donald Adams and Orville Prescott are somewhat misty, and he wishes Cecil Beaton would throw away his pen and stick to his camera. He scoffs at claims that writers write for art and not for money.

"Sweet and Sour" has the informality of a relaxed conversationalist with feet on the coffee table, base of spine on the davenport and right elbow bent. The sweet is no more sugary than a whisky sour, and there's considerable maraschino in the sour. John O'Hara may pose as a crab, but he's a soft-shelled one.

Ten North Frederick

♦

An Old Pro at Work

Leslie A. Fiedler

I should like to say first of all what there is about Mr. O'Hara's book that pleases me, but I do not find this task very easy. Surely, it is not the subject matter: still another family history which is also the history of a town, a patiently documented exposé of Gibbsville, Pa., that can only reveal finally the secret shouted from the housetops through the last 75 years of fiction: *trouble in bed*! This is a bore, as are most of the characters. Joseph B. Chapin, the man who wanted to be President of the United States and died of cirrhosis and a broken heart, is not imagined but carefully reconstructed out of old newspaper items and sociological surveys: a sort of unsuccessful Republican version of F. D. R., rendered statistically as a fact of history rather than of the imagination. And yet I found pleasure as well as tedium in the novel; for it contains a certain quality—modesty and competence are the words that occur to me—which has become rare. *Ten North Frederick* has, that is to say, certain old-fashioned virtues as well as other more apparent old-fashioned weaknesses. It is pre-eminently the work of a "pro," put together efficiently and with a kind of honesty that has nothing to do with its philosophy or its feelings, an honesty of craftsmanship.

It is important, I think, to distinguish the professional writer from the professional entertainer—Mr. O'Hara, say, from Mr. Wouk; for the former

Reprinted from the *New Republic* 134 (9 January 1956): 16–17. Reprinted by permission of THE NEW REPUBLIC, © 1956, The New Republic, Inc.

produces certain standard items in accordance with tried and trustworthy techniques, while the latter forges slick (and bowdlerized) facsimiles of those items. It is, perhaps, because I have been recently engaged with *Marjorie Morningstar* that I have turned with special relish to *Ten North Frederick*. There is in Mr. O'Hara none of the pretentiousness of the counterfeiter; as there is in him none of the pretentiousness of the amateur: the proud-shy proferring of inexpertness as a guarantee of honesty. I recall, in this connection, Norman Mailer, whom I have also just finished reading. Mr. Mailer is just as much the prisoner of certain obsolete conventions of the novel as Mr. O'Hara, but he keeps thinking that by inventing Hemingway all over from scratch he is making something quite new. Mr. O'Hara claims only to be performing well, and this in itself is a pleasurable relief.

There are, of course, real limitations to professionalism, however modest, and of these I am well aware. Not only does this sort of competence imply a reworking of already established models, a kind of academicism (for academic Mr. O'Hara is, despite a frankness which his blurb writers hope we will find "shocking"), a preclusion of invention and experiment; it leads also to the mechanical. It is dangerous to emulate too closely the precision of the machine; when the guildsman has reached the ultimate pitch of such efficiency, there is no longer any reason not to substitute for him the actual machine, which is, after all, even more efficient. In quite the same way as the camera inherited the job of academic realism in painting, an analogous machine seems bound to take over in writing. I am sure that even now there is being put together in the cellar of some half-mad inventor a device which will replace the academic realist in fiction. By denying imagination and poetry, such novelists as Mr. O'Hara have cleared the way for their own extinction.

Here, for instance, is Mr. O'Hara establishing in accordance with his principles the "reality" of a certain neighborhood: "The Johnson's neighbors in the 100 block were a railroad engineer, two railroad firemen, a young chiropractor, a Civil War veteran and his maiden nieces, a pharmacist, two salesmen for clothing stores, an insurance adjuster, the manager of an absentee-owned bakery, a state forestry official, a freight clerk for the Pennsylvania Railroad, and a newspaper man."

One could not ask an I. B. M. machine to do better—or worse! One does not doubt the minimal "truth" of such observations, any more than one doubts the "truth" of the phonographically recorded dialogue which fills most of the space between such chunks of data; they are merely not true enough—and they are finally irrelevant. This is "solidity of specification" turned into "hypertrophy of information." The same confusion of insight and fact, which made a large part of the more respectable public think of the participants on *Information Please* as sages, has produced this sad impasse in the novel.

Nearly 50 years ago, certain more advanced writers, become aware of the threat posed by the statistical novel, sought to defy the pressure of science and the retreat to statistical truth. But of the whole "stream of consciousness," symbolist adventure, Mr. O'Hara has deliberately remained unaware. It is not, I think, that he has chosen to bypass Joyce, but that he has never felt his impact at all, never listened to any protest that the truth of art is not the truth of fact and figures, the reality of art not the reality of the newspaper or the caseworker's report. Mr. O'Hara feels dimly that there is some difference between fiction and "straight history," but he does not know what that difference is; and one finds him apologizing in a brief foreword for having told us in the novel that Joe Chapin's grandfather had been Lieutenant Governor of Pennsylvania before that office had in fact been instituted. At first, I tried to read this apology as some elaborate Twainian jest; but I have had finally to accept it as a quite straight-faced plea for pardon: the final betrayal of the silliness of Mr. O'Hara's aesthetics—and an ultimate indignity he is willing to endure for its sake.

Yet no one, I am sure (beyond certain professional fact-hawks, who search works of this kind for "slips"), would continue to read Mr. O'Hara if his work were *merely* a cold and rigorous attempt to trap "truth" in a web of observations about the exact height of pushbells from the ground, the exact percentage of luncheon guests who take pills before eating, the exact date the word "bore" became current at a certain level of provincial society, etc. On the other hand, there are real O'Hara devotees, dedicated fans like the boy I once met in a bar, who insisted on telling me over and over again through an interminable evening how his life had been redeemed by reading *Butterfield 8* eleven times! What appeal do such addicts find in fiction which denies all imagination and poetry? Certainly, it is not Mr. O'Hara's neat workmanship which thrills them.

It is rather, I suspect, the profound sentimentality into which he lapses from time to time, when the burden of icy exposure grows too great. I use the word "sentimentality" only for lack of a better one, to stand for a certain kind of ersatz poetry: the poor man's poetry of those who think they believe only in a poor man's science. Mr. O'Hara's more maudlin moments are usually connected with sex, which is for him (in a distressingly simple-minded way) the single root of all joy and sorrow in life. He has toward it what seems superficially a no-nonsense air, a resolve to insist upon the mechanical facts of copulation behind the superstructure of romantic love; but one finds that his insistence upon the physical nature of passion has left quite untouched in his mind all the Victorian clichés about love at first sight. There is no more doubt about what he means by "living happily ever after" than there is about what that phrase means to the most conventionally romantic schoolgirl.

His softer banalities are buttressed with a certain tougher sort of wisdom largely gleaned from the sexual mythology of the streets: that cold looking women are always the hottest ones in the clinch; that upperclass ladies invariably dream of being raped by unshaven roughnecks, etc.; but the central dogma of his creed is the notion that real passion—the blind reaching out of lonely souls for mutual physical relief—goes sour in marriage. The main fable of *Ten North Frederick* concerns Joe Chapin's slow extinction inside a world defined by the sexuality and ambition of his wife; but there is a bitter-sweet up-ending before his final dissolution into a lush and "leading citizen"—a climax which finds him in bed with the beautiful and passionate young girl who is the room-mate of his nymphomaniac daughter.

The falsity of this quasi-incestuous flight from the arms of mama to those of sis is compounded by a ladies' magazine aura of self-sacrifice, in which the two improbable lovers (yes, love did come at last to Joe Chapin!) agree to separate at their moment of bliss, one to live and one to die. I feel in this resolution as egregious a loss of nerve as in, say, the hoaked-up conclusion of *Great Expectations*. O'Hara finally betrays his own conception to gratify the maudlin wishes of his readers. By all the logic of plot and character up to the very moment when O'Hara relents, Joe Chapin should have been too bound in the prison of habit and reserve to have declared himself at all; or if he had managed to blurt out a confession of his love, the girl should have found him an old goat, half pitiful, half absurd—to be milked for an expensive gift or to be rejected out of hand.

Here the book buckles and is lost; for only a dedication to imaginative truth is a protection against the sentimental falsification which neither the craftsmanship of the professional, nor the realism of the journalist can withstand.

In the Broad Stream

JOHN CHAMBERLAIN

John O'Hara is a serious novelist who wishes with a great deal of yearning intensity to be taken seriously. The perfervid quality of his desire sometimes makes him extremely self-conscious. He is apt to press for attention, particularly in his statements about other writers. His sexual passages sometimes scream at the reader; it is as if he were saying, "Look, I'm the only honest writer about sex in America." But in *Ten North Frederick* (Random House, $3.95) O'Hara is disciplined beyond his former wont. This is well-rounded fiction, relaxed and mournful even in its most unpleasant realism. As a story, it is filled with a sense of a whole community, but it is also intensely personal. The skeletons shake and rattle in the boarded-up attic closets of the Chapin house at 10 North Frederick Street, Gibbsville, Pa. Gibbsville is, of course, a thinly disguised version of Mr. O'Hara's home town of Pottsville, a community which contains just about everything in its mixed middle-class and proletarian microcosm.

In *Ten North Frederick* Mr. O'Hara takes an extremely long view. This is a three-generation story, and at times it assumes the quality of a parade of horrors. The first of Mr. O'Hara's Chapins, Ben and Charlotte, had the bad luck to produce a couple of stillborn babies, one of them obviously a monster. This naturally served to warp Charlotte's relationship to Joe Chapin, her only normal son, and it set Ben, her bewildered husband, to haunting a red light district in Philadelphia for his lugubrious satisfactions. Joe Chapin had better luck than his father, for his plain wife, Edith, believed with an unspontaneous solicitude in making her marriage a planned and charted success. The trouble with Edith was her possessiveness, which drove her to crazy lengths (and a silly revenge) in the effort to own her husband completely. In the end Edith's selfishness betrays her; she alienates both her husband and her children, Ann and Joby.

Mr. O'Hara chronicles the glacial drift of the Chapins' years with a Hardyesque attention to the gloomy irony which seems to be the single indulgence of the President of the Immortals. O'Hara is an utterly disenchanted writer whenever he looks at life in terms of decades. Fortunately for the reader,

Reprinted from *National Review* 1 (1 February 1956): 26–27. Copyright © 1956 by *National Review*, Inc., 150 East 35th Street, New York, NY 10016. Reprinted by permission.

there is another O'Hara—the O'Hara of the enchanted moment. Though time runs on to a dreary beat over the decades, both Joe Chapin and his daughter Ann manage to snatch at sweetness. Ann's first marriage to a piano player in a name band is broken up by her misguided parents. But it was beautiful and magical while it lasted, a thing of Cheshire-cat smiles and excruciatingly happy tears carried out to the lilt of "Sweet and Lovely." Even though it ends badly, with a family-dictated abortion and an annulment, it deepens Ann's perceptions to the point where she can forgive her father and love him all the more for his mistake about her welfare.

As for Joe, the father, he has the dignity that comes to all men when they learn how to meet failure without losing self-respect. Joe is played for a sucker by Pennsylvania politicians who take his money and then turn him down for the lieutenant governorship. He goes toward his death in a state of armed truce with his wife after both of them have engaged in momentary infidelities. Joe utters no complaints; he is not one to indulge in self-pity, unless a heightened consumption of whisky is a form of self-pity. Nor is Ann a whimperer when her second marriage goes on the rocks.

The thing that makes this O'Hara novel something more than a dull and sordid chronicle of second-rate lives is the author's sense of the absurd intermixtures that go to make up any life. O'Hara writes about young love with an eye and ear for wonder in the commonplace that recalls Arthur Davison Ficke's sonnet: "I only know our first impassioned kiss / Was in your cellar rummaging for beer." He can distill the glory of a moment by mentioning a snatch of song or by evoking a vagrant memory of Dan Moriarty's famous speakeasy. O'Hara is a true child of popular culture, which he works into his prose with all the appropriate rhythms. The preoccupations of teenagers, the foibles of country club life, the problems of young married couples moving into the Age of the Children, the inevitable capitulations of middle age—all of these things carry no great tragic weight when taken in isolation. But glimpsed against the procession of the decades in Gibbsville they seem somber and at the same time piercingly nostalgic.

Has O'Hara, then, the true tragic sense of life? He hasn't quite reached that state of illumination. What he seems to lack is a feeling that life is something to be accepted as a supreme gift even though it must end amid the sadness of failing powers, the loss of friends who are gone forever. O'Hara doesn't accept consciousness as a miracle raised from dust which is in itself a miracle.

To put it succinctly, he lacks the Schweitzer touch of reverence. His people have a rage to live; but the rage is never consistent with humility or the glad heart, or with such a thing as delight in skills, tastes and excellences. O'Hara likes to write about Pennsylvania families, but his choice of subject never includes one of those close-knit Pennsylvania family groups that can produce an Emily Kimbrough and her two ebullient and fantastically energetic daughters, or a talented tribe of Kellys running from oarsman-contractor John to the enchanting Grace.

The important thing about O'Hara, however, is that he is still growing in his middle-to-old age as a novelist. In a period which makes novels out of the tidy room in Bedlam or seeks universality amid the parochial disturbances of futile artists' colonies, O'Hara sticks to the broad stream. On the basis of *Ten North Frederick* he may be expected some day to do something truly good.

From the Terrace

♦

Something Went Seriously Wrong

Arthur Mizener

In his novel, "From the Terrace," John O'Hara tells the story of Raymond Alfred Eaton, who was born and raised in affluent but unhappy circumstances in Port Johnson, Pa., a town not very different from Gibbsville, Pa., and not far from it. Alfred Eaton visits Gibbsville and knows Julian and Caroline English of "Appointment in Samarra" and Joe and Joby Chapin of "Ten North Frederick." "From the Terrace" is about the same Pottsville-Tamaqua-Scranton people as are O'Hara's other books. We follow Alfred's life in minute detail from his birth in 1897 to the time, shortly after World War II, when something has gone seriously wrong: he is a completely defeated man.

Alfred goes to an obscure prep school and to Princeton, marries and has three children, becomes at 35 the youngest partner in an important New York financial house, makes $3,000,000, is divorced by his wife, becomes Assistant Secretary of the Navy under Roosevelt, marries the love of his life after she has been his mistress for years, and, in his fifties, goes to pieces.

Something, too, has gone seriously wrong with the John O'Hara of the Thirties, who was a good writer. Perhaps the O'Hara of the Thirties was good because he had not forgotten what it felt like to be one of an Irish doctor's eight children, to have flunked out of a couple of obscure schools and been unable to go to Yale because his father died and there was not enough money.

Reprinted from the *New York Times Book Review*, 23 November 1958, 1, 14. Copyright © 1958 by The New York Times Company. Reprinted by permission.

Something certainly gave him his astonishing alertness to the fine social distinctions of American life, that half envious but wholly understanding and acutely observant curiosity which is the source of his early work.

O'Hara's feeling for the ironic discrepancies between people's socially determined selves and their essential, human nature was so intense that his early work, like Hemingway's, is hardly an act of the discursive intelligence at all. "I haven't got a good thinking brain," says Jim Malloy in "Hope of Heaven," "but I have sound emotions." Jim Malloy is "the doctor's son" in O'Hara's story of that title and the nearest thing to a self-portrait in O'Hara's work.

The early O'Hara held what Lionel Trilling has called "his exacerbated social awareness" wholly under the control of these "sound emotions" which, if they were not profound, were shrewd and generous. They gave his work human purpose. There are dozens of short stories like "By Way of Yonkers," "Pardner" and "Over the River and Through the Wood" (a veritable *selva oscura*) which create whole lives, in all their strangeness and pathos, with a few pages of luminous description and wonderfully perspicuous dialogue. And O'Hara's wry sympathy for the human spirit within Al Grecco the gangster, Luther Fliegler the homely Dutchman, and Julian English the self-destructive gentleman gives his first novel, "Appointment in Samarra," a unity of feeling and an orderliness of form that none of his later novels have.

That something had gone seriously wrong with this O'Hara began to be evident with "A Rage to Live" (1949), his first novel in over ten years. When it was published O'Hara said, "The earlier books were special books about specialized people, but this is the big one, the over-all one." They have been getting bigger, or at least fatter, ever since, until, with "From the Terrace," they have become monstrous. O'Hara's "thinking brain" is quite as bad as Jim Malloy's and is a hopelessly inadequate substitute for the sound emotions it has more and more replaced since O'Hara began to give us his views.

As social commentary, "From the Terrace" is a simple-minded "U. S. A." for the upper classes, a history of American society in the twentieth century, in which the hero is a thoroughly nice, rich guy, not brainy, of course, but attractive, successful in business and fundamentally a man of integrity and ideals. The contrasting character is Tom Rothermel, a poor boy from Port Johnson, whom our hero has helped through Penn State, where some Commie professor turned Tom into an envious hater of the rich. Tom works for T. V. A. and then the C. I. O., but is in the market and cynically ready to sell labor out if he can make money doing it.

O'Hara's social awareness is as acute as ever, and there are scenes in "From the Terrace" that have all his old brilliance, but the book stretches out to its incredible length partly at least because it contains so much merely mechanical detail about the social past, detail that is controlled by nothing much more than the popular social historian's easy nostalgia. O'Hara is even beginning to slip up about small details as he never would have in the past (he has Yale's supporters in 1915 sitting on the wrong side of Palmer Stadium, for example) and he is also beginning to play frivolous literary tricks (Alfred Eaton's wife goes off one evening with Newton Orchid of Films Par Excellence, a character out of Fitzgerald's "The Great Gatsby," and at another point Alfred explains a song from "Pal Joey").

Even more destructive of the book's interest is what has happened to O'Hara's attitude toward sex. O'Hara has always made the act of sexual intercourse a divine transaction. In his early work this extravagance was harmless enough, a primitive and naïve version of the older romantic habit of idealizing love because, for the romantic, "the divine is life at its intensest." Like so much else about O'Hara, this feeling, too, began to go wrong with "A Rage to Live."

In "From the Terrace" sex has become a boring absurdity. The book is filled with textbooky descriptions of how women are made to feel and to act, and we are given ludicrously solemn discussions of "goosing" and a number of other tricks available to both sexes for attacking strangers in public. Gay backchat between Alfred Eaton, the alleged Princeton gentleman, and his supposedly gentle wife consists largely of off-color jokes and various witty and ribald fancies.

The pity is that somewhere beneath this kitchen midden of insignificant social detail and the dreary minutiae of sex, there is still a feeling about experience. It is just possible to detect that what moves this older O'Hara is a sense of the waste and futility of life. Alfred Eaton is meant to be—and occasionally is—what Joe Chapin of "Ten North Frederick" more often is, an essentially simple man of some charm, given principles by the discipline of upper-classes life, whose final anguish it is to discover that all human feeling fails.

Alfred's marriage ends in hate and then indifference; he loses the love of his children; his lifelong friend becomes a middle-aged lecher and a bore. His ambition for business success dies, leaving him with nothing to work for; and his devoted second wife, seeing him no longer a serious man, comes to pity his weakness and to hate him for depending on her to conceal it from him. But where the "sound emotion" in O'Hara's early work gave life to every sentence, this emotion is barely discoverable beneath the nearly 900 pages of lifeless detail in "From the Terrace."

O'Hara's Biggest, Best Novel: The Disintegration of a Tycoon

GERALD KLOSS

On page 890 of this 897-page novel—the longest, the richest and the best that John O'Hara has written—the hero of the story concludes a telephone conversation in which he has been as incisive and positive a man as at any time in his successful business and governmental career.

On page 891, he is a weak, pitiable person and, worst of all, ignorant of the vast change. Never again will he speak to people in the old manner; never again will people react to him in the old way. He will live out his years graciously, as a New York clubman and honorary chairman of various worthy committees, until in a terrible moment of accidental self-examination, he will see the truth of what has happened, and very likely commit suicide.

This is just one example of why "From the Terrace" demands more from the reader than any of O'Hara's previous novels. You cannot skim this book. Buried in a page of straight dialog there may be a question or response that entirely alters the reader's attitude toward a principal character or course of action. Skip that page and you've lost something; O'Hara is not a man to repeat.

The hero is Alfred Eaton, son of a steel mill owner in Port Johnson, Pa. That's O'Hara country, familiar to readers of "Appointment in Samarra," "A Rage to Live" and "Ten North Frederick," but examined here more thoroughly than in the previous novels.

We follow Alfred's life from his birth in 1897 through prep school, Princeton, naval service in World War I, marriage, a brilliant Wall Street career in the 1920's and 1930's and his years as a forceful assistant secretary of the navy in World War II. We probe the customs and morals of every level of society that Alfred becomes involved in, and there are times when the reader may mutter, "Okay, O'Hara, that's enough. Let's move on." But O'Hara will not let you go until the surgery is completed to his satisfaction.

He is clinical, too, in his treatment of love and sex, and if the reader is shocked by the many intimate scenes, it is not through salacious description

Reprinted from the *Milwaukee Journal*, 30 November 1958, Christmas Books, 3. Reprinted by permission of The Milwaukee Journal.

but by the author's cold-eyed, dispassionate manner. In his striving for thoroughness, O'Hara sometimes substitutes a report on the salt content of tears for the novelist's real function of telling why the tears flow.

There is also the matter of O'Hara's dialog, famed for its realism. It is swift, direct and pleasing to the ear, although there are times, because of a lack of sufficient "he saids" and "she saids," when the reader has to track back half a page to learn who is saying what.

But this crisp style often defeats the larger purpose of reflecting the character and manner of the person who is talking. Not all the people in the book are swift of mind or direct of heart, but that's the way they talk. The old Eaton groom grasps the nuances of a conversation with the skill of a trained diplomat, and he knows, from what has *not* been said, that he is being fired after decades of faithful service.

All this is beside the main point, which is that "From the Terrace," for all its demands on the reader, abundantly rewards him. The sudden change in Alfred's whole manner of living from page 890 to 891, for example, has been carefully prepared. But you don't recognize that until you have read page 891. You then recall that in Alfred's most powerful era, as a millionaire banker and high government official, the little flaws were present that eventually led to his collapse.

Does it really require 897 pages to tell this story? Another novelist— one less analytical, less interested in description of things not directly concerned with the central theme—could tell it in half the space. O'Hara himself could have done it, as he has demonstrated in earlier books. He tries a larger project here, with vastly greater chances for failure—and succeeds.

O'Hara's Latest Held Magnificent

Robert R. Kirsch

In most novels the reader is a spectator. He may become enmeshed in the events and fascinated by the characters but essentially the story unfolds itself before him. In the work of John O'Hara and a handful of other novelists the reader is given entry directly into the world of the novel. It is as though he stands in the very center of the action; things go on around him, even as they do in life. He may look off to the side and view an incident or hear a whisper behind him or watch for a moment a subtle and revealing nuance in the background. This is the essential impact of John O'Hara's latest novel, FROM THE TERRACE (Random House: $6.95), which evokes the total life of Alfred Eaton, second son of a Pennsylvania steelmaker, and portrays the complex, textured world which molded and shaped him.

This novel may or may not be the best novel O'Hara has ever written. There will always be those among his enthusiasts who will argue for "Appointment in Samarra" or "Butterfield 8" or "A Rage to Live" or "Ten North Frederick." But one thing is certainly beyond argument: few novelists can point to such an imposing body of literary work. From the very beginning O'Hara has resisted the fads and fashions of the novel. He has matured and developed in his craft, writing on the basic assumption that his readers are intelligent enough to understand without facile interpretation or special psychiatric theory. The result is that more than any other American novelist he has both reflected his times and captured the universal, the unique individual for the generations to come. In this sense FROM THE TERRACE is a magnificent piece of work and I predict it will endure.

When you pick up this book you will see what I mean. It represents a blending of the social and psychological novel which is one of O'Hara's most important contributions to 20th-century fiction. No one will quibble with describing O'Hara as a social novelist, a chronicler of periods and places, of classes and types. But he goes beyond this to study the interplay of individual and group, of the single man and society. Alfred Eaton is an excellent example of this. He is a product of O'Hara country—Port Johnson, Pa., not far from Gibbsville—and of O'Hara class—the well-to-do, socially elite families with

From the *Los Angeles Times*, 7 December 1958, Part V, 6. Copyright 1958, Los Angeles Times. Reprinted by permission.

connections in Philadelphia, New York and Boston. He is a product of the times—his life spans the events and developments of 20th-century America, the two world wars, the depressions, the booms.

Yet, Alfred Eaton never becomes merely a type. He is an individual, the product as well of a specific family environment and relationships which act on his character and personality. His father, Sam Eaton, a tough, self-sufficient man incapable of giving any affection to Alfred, molded the boy. When Alfred's handsome older brother dies of spinal meningitis, Sam regards his second son as a poor substitute. Alfred's mother, Martha, is ineffectual and weak, gradually seeks love in illicit affairs and solace in drinking. She ends as an incurable alcoholic.

Love and guilt become the central themes of Alfred's life. They are rooted in each other. The first girl he loves, Victoria, is killed in an automobile accident, and Alfred feels the sense of responsibility because she went on that ride only as a rebellious reaction to his request that she not go. The second girl, Norma, an older girl who introduced him to the world of physical love, dies in a suicide pact and again Alfred feels that it is because he has failed her. His marriage is a failure almost from the start and his relationship with Natalie, the mistress he marries after a long illicit affair, seems also doomed to another kind of failure. The question then is whether Alfred is capable of love at all. Certainly, he is incapable of communicating his deepest feelings to any other person. "Hence his fear, his fears and his terror, made worse by his inability to release some of it in an expression of his guilt and alarm to another living person."

Ironically, his outward life is successful for a long time, in business, in government, in society. He is a respected man but a lonely man, a man who lives in a world of acquaintanceship but not friendship. So great is the power, the incremental effect of detail and situation, that we are for the duration of the novel part of Alfred Eaton's life and granted a kind of understanding which is the result of only the best in fiction, that truth which goes beyond the truth of generalities and case studies.

Only one further comment in the form of a prediction. It may take several years but I want to put it on record that John O'Hara more than any contemporary American writer deserves the Nobel prize and I have a strong hunch that he will get it.

Ourselves to Know

◆

A Desperate Detour to Destruction

DAVID BOROFF

John O'Hara, for some time now, has had an ambiguous status in American letters. At the age of fifty-five, he is regarded, somewhat implausibly, as the grand old man of social realism. But realism has been unmodish of late—so rapidly do literary fashions obsolesce. (By no means extinct, it flourishes in the dingy sub-literature of paperbacks.) Certainly O'Hara has been his own man, disdainful of the ukases of the literary mandarins, stubbornly creating his own body of work. He has been indifferent to what has been described as "the symbolist adventure" of our time, preferring to follow his own course of painstaking and acute social documentation.

His latest novel, "Ourselves to Know," does not open new vistas, but it puts a seal on the author's extraordinary knowledge of the social topography of small-town Pennsylvania—that well-chosen country of his middle age. This is a shapelier novel than its recent predecessors—not even half as long as "From the Terrace"—written with economy and austere control.

We meet Robert Milhouser in 1927, an old man with the commanding dignity of the doomed, enduring a death-in-life some twenty years after he has murdered his nineteen-year-old wife. The novel is a penetrating reconstruction of the crime and of the circumstances that precipitated it, as told by Gerald Higgins, a young man who is fascinated by Milhouser's mortuary calm.

Why did Robert Milhouser kill his beautiful young wife? He had come

From *Saturday Review* 43 (27 February 1960): 23, 29. Reprinted by permission.

to love late in life. Earlier he had been emotionally maimed by his mother, a charming but dominating woman. Liberated by her death, he was caught up at the age of fifty-one in a tempestuous love affair with a wilful eighteen-year-old schoolgirl, "his lifelong loneliness changed into an angry thing."

Life glowed for him but all too briefly. His young wife, whose curious sexual pathology O'Hara probes with clinical sobriety, betrays and humiliates him. Milhouser feels a simple, irrevocable obligation to destroy her. He does so with the heavy recognition that in her death he has entombed his own life. However, he is given only a light sentence (O'Hara anatomizes small-town justice with mordant skill) and the broken man lives out his curious twilight existence in the "comfortable monastery" of his large house.

Again, O'Hara projects a bleak and desperate vision of life's emptiness and moral anarchy, redeemed only by the calm courage with which his heroes face their destruction. Milhouser is a decent man, epitomizing all that is viable in upper-class America. But in the end, life's implacable malevolence— embodied in a woman—triumphs. Only a woman can dispel the grayness that suffuses existence, but in the end she crushes life's frail joys.

O'Hara captures the stark and terrible beauty of the sexual drama. In his universe, it is sex alone which can irradiate and fulfill. Yet love, like friendship, always fails. And in the failure of love there is destruction. There is a chilling coda in the last sentence of the book, when Gerald Higgins, overseas in the Navy, contemplates the old man's death in 1943 and remarks: "I often tried to think of things like that to take my mind off Frances [his own wife] and the stories that had got back to me."

John O'Hara is a major writer working in the grand tradition of the novel. He has a compelling sense of how the present issues from the past, and he lays bare, with stunning accuracy, the fabric of society.

I am at a loss to understand how his work can be dismissed by critics as "phono-photographic," or its tough, solid bulk characterized as "elephantiasis." His novels are not random exercises in fact-grubbing but, rather, cunningly contrived mosaics of fact and insight, the prose always judicious and neat. In the end he creates a cosmos which is no less a world of the imagination for illuminating our own society so mercilessly.

John O'Hara, egregiously undervalued by many critics, is, in my judgment, among the few great writers of our time.

O'Hara in a Descending Spiral

David T. Bazelon

Since John O'Hara started writing novels again in 1949, the continuity in his work has been a preoccupation with the concept of the gentleman in America, and what (God help us all) certain kinds of women can do to them. Even here the theme of adultery predominates, or is pivotal, as in much of his writing. But in his second career—after the Hollywood dunking—the idea of the American gentleman has been nagged and worked to death. His fascination with this character-type is truly awesome. Reading any of the four big novels he has done in the last decade, or viewing them in tandem, one wonders just what he has been trying to get at with these portraits of his dullish gentlemen. Salts of the earth, noble Romans, principled stoics, washed-out bridges between the prewar worlds and the modern, they are finely-carved wooden figures that never really get up and move. They are nothing like the vital images in his beautiful and elaborate gallery of women (most of whom are not very gentle).

Julian English, for example, the hero of his first novel, *Appointment in Samarra* (1934), was well-born, upper-classy, and so on—but a wild drunk who destroyed himself in short order. Joe Chapin, the principal figure in the later *Ten North Frederick*, also drank himself to death—but at an advanced age, and in a quiet, calculated, reasonable way. Something had happened to O'Hara: His own wildness disappeared from his personal life and survived in his fiction almost solely in his women. The result, for the men, has been gentlemanliness—and for O'Hara a value found in the restraint of principled men who are the moral force holding society together.

Ah, but the women! His imagination has suffered no hardening of the arteries regarding them. They swish across the pages of his later works, the darlings, in uninhibited profusion. If anything, the encyclopedic range of female types and propensities in O'Hara's vision has broadened and lengthened. There are agate-efficient social lionesses, middle-aged ladies competently prepared for life's later romantic opportunities, bulldog mothers, dirty little girls, ideal ingénues, madams and whores and kid-sisters, and a full Sears, Roebuck assortment of wives—any size, shape, or class, and in all states of spiritual disrepair.

Reprinted from the *New Leader* 43 (4 April 1960): 22–23. Reprinted with permission of The New Leader, April 4, 1960.

We have Grace Caldwell Tate of *A Rage to Live* (1949), a small-town aristocrat and fallen demi-goddess, containing an awe-inspiring force of sexual love—one of the most compelling portraits of a fully alive, sexual woman in our modern fiction. Then Edith Chapin, the killer-wife of *Ten North Frederick* (1955), a brilliant characterization, both powerful and subtle, of the possessive woman; and Kate Drummond of the same book, the unreal ingénue who gladdens a gentleman's autumn. In *From the Terrace* (1958) we are presented with the most interesting of the later O'Hara gentlemen—most interesting because drawn at greatest length and most ambivalently—and a complete convention of female types, including Alfred Eaton's two wives, the first of whom grows into a very exciting, rapacious and mature sensualist, the second of whom never really grows at all.

And now we have *Ourselves to Know*, with the dullest gentleman of them all, situated in the smallest Pennsylvania town O'Hara has yet written about and with the dirtiest little heroine in the entire O'Hara gallery. Another way of introducing this new book would be to say that John O'Hara has finally written a whole novel about a man who remained a virgin until the age of 27. The story, briefly, is focussed on the gentleman, Robert Millhouser, who shoots and kills the dirty little girl, who was his wife, because she had been adulterous. He kills her for the same reason that he married her at an advanced age— because he had waited too long for love, because he had incurred too deep a debt of loneliness, because his character required the punishment of isolation. There is considerable psychological insight in this portrait of a disastrously lonely man: The author evokes some of the real quality of the coldness and emptiness of that inner abyss.

Hedda, the dirty little girl, is well-drawn, vital and thoroughly believable: O'Hara makes her sexual evil a concrete human quality. (She is a descendant of Gloria Wandrous of *Butterfield 8* who was ruined at an early age by Dr. Reddington—"within a month he had her sniffing ether and loving it"—but Hedda has no saving graces, and she manages to do all of her own corrupting.) The gentleman's mother is a standard O'Hara woman-of-strength, which means excellent. The depiction of the system of power in a small town is fascinating and has the usual aura of authenticity—not as good as the high quality of the political scenes in *Ten North Frederick*, but still very good, especially in the legal aspects of the crime (better, by far, for instance than anything in Cozzens' *The Just and the Unjust*). And there is also a detailed and surprisingly sympathetic portrait of an Oscar Wilde or Ronald Firbank litterateur, a *fin de siècle* homosexual.

The structure of this novel is more involved and artificial than any of the previous works: a young man, the first-person narrator, serves as Millhouser's foil in telling his story. Because of this interview-confession device, the story is told in a rather disconnected fashion and, like *Ten North Frederick*, begins at a point closer to the end than the beginning. For most of the telling, the first-person narration is either baldly abandoned or irrelevant; it functions chiefly, when at all, to let the author project the quality of a detective story or a psychoanalysis, or just to be self-conscious about the process of reconstructing a life-story. If one recalls a more successful use of the creator's self-consciousness as part of the narration—say André Gide's *The Counterfeiters*—he sees immediately the reason for O'Hara's relative failure. In Gide the self-consciousness was integral because he was writing a novel about a novel-writer writing a novel. O'Hara is not, and the self-consciousness never really becomes more than a mere device.

But apart from its ill-advised structure the book contains a great deal of value and interest, as does all of O'Hara's work. Though this is the least successful of his recent books, it reveals again that his median level is very good indeed, and has been consistently so over a 30-year career.

Ourselves to Know will be reviewed badly by the highbrows not because it is the least successful of his recent novels, but just because it is one of them. I cannot think of any important contemporary American writer treated quite so shabbily and with such consistent tastelessness by the "better" critics. (The chief exception is Lionel Trilling, who appears to have been wearied by his thankless, uphill effort to induce the highbrow audience to stop disgracing itself in this matter.) But it does seem obvious now that since *Ten North Frederick*, O'Hara is not improving. *From the Terrace* was not the book its size would have led one to expect and the present effort is even less successful. Regrettably, O'Hara seems to be repeating himself in a slowly descending spiral, and reaching too far for birds he cannot catch.

Sermons and Soda-Water

♦

The Middle Depths

Time

This collection of three related novellas is John O'Hara's best work in years. The stories remind one strongly of the author's early novels, and not only because the suicide of Julian English, the hero of *Appointment in Samarra*, is an offstage incident in one of them. The prose has the great clarity of all of O'Hara's writing, and an economy of expression that he has seemed afraid to trust in such vast recent novels as *From the Terrace* and *Ten North Frederick*.

ATTRACTIVE RETICENCE

In his preface, O'Hara mentions the weight factor in bookselling and hopes that readers will not apply the heft test to his small volumes. He need have no fears; done up in a slipcase, the novellas are not only handsome but hefty, and the publisher is able to ask as much for about 60,000 words of text as he does for 260,000. Regrettably, O'Hara also reports that he is working on his heftiest novel yet (previous record: 897 pages in *From the Terrace*), apparently ignoring the fact that his jumbo works are not as good as his short ones. The outstanding qualities of these stories are matchless dialogue and—since there

Reprinted from *Time* 76 (28 November 1960): 98. Copyright 1960 Time Inc. Reprinted by permission.

is much that dialogue cannot express directly—an attractive measure of reticence.

They are narrated by Jim Malloy (who appeared in earlier novels), an O'Hara-like man who has been a reporter and pressagent and who, in middle age, is a successful novelist. In the first volume, *The Girl on the Baggage Truck*, he is a major character, a young publicity man who avoids, mostly by luck, becoming the pet poodle of an aging actress. Malloy is an observer in the next book, *Imagine Kissing Pete*, concerning an adulterous marriage that worked better than expected. There is a hint in this one of sentimentality, a quality to which the 20th century reacts as the 19th did to sex—with outward shock masking secret delight—and in O'Hara's hands the flavor is pleasant.

THE FINAL CONDITION

The third story, *We're Friends Again*, is elegiac; Malloy is moved by the death of a meddlesome woman to reflect forbearingly on his own life and that of his acquaintances. At the end of the book, the woman's husband, Malloy's closest friend, tells him that he loved his wife deeply. "On my way home," the narrator relates, looking into the middle depths. "I realized that until then I had not known him at all. It was not a discovery to cause me dismay. What did he know about me? What, really, can any of us know about any of us, and why must we make such a thing of loneliness when it is the final condition of us all?"

As this statement suggests, Novelist O'Hara is not one of those few who can function in the ooze of the soul's floor; he works best at middle depth, and in a story composed mostly of dialogue, that is where he must stay. It is not a bad place for any writer.

[Review of *Sermons and Soda-Water*]

Granville Hicks

In his foreword to "Sermons and Soda-Water" (Random House, 3 vols. boxed, $5.95) John O'Hara observes that each of the three novellas could have been made into a full-length novel. He chose the shorter form, he says, because he wanted to, which is a good reason. In the second place, he explains, he is a child of the twentieth century and it is his ambition "to record the way people talked and thought and felt, and to do it with complete honesty and variety." So, while he is preparing to write another hefty novel, he has, as he puts it, "written these novellas from memory, with a minimum of research." Remembering his recent novels, I am grateful for his decision.

The title comes from Byron: "Let us have wine and women, mirth and laughter, / Sermons and soda-water the day after." All three of the stories are told from the point of view of the day after. That is, the narrator, Jim Malloy, is looking back from the sober present to the not so sober past. Malloy, whose career closely parallels O'Hara's, has an active part in each of the narratives, but he is primarily the observer, the man who keeps his eyes open, the man in whom others confide. And now, as he tells his stories, he is the man who knows how it all came out and can evaluate the failures and the successes.

The novellas cover considerable territory. "Imagine Kissing Pete," the story of a marriage that in the long run turned out better than anyone could have expected, is laid in Gibbsville, the Pennsylvania city that was the scene of O'Hara's first novel, "Appointment in Samarra." Much of the action of "The Girl on the Baggage Truck" takes place in New York night clubs and in the Long Island home of a very rich family. "We're Friends Again" moves from New York to Boston to Washington. The time ranges from the late Twenties to the present.

As always, the two things that O'Hara is interested in are money and sex, with sex well out in front. Two of the stories deal with unhappy marriages, and all of them are full of infidelities. There are also inexplicable but irresistible attachments, for O'Hara can be romantic as well as clinical. Long before Kinsey began his study, O'Hara was making his own researches into the sexual habits of Americans, and his findings are an important part of his contribution to social history.

Reprinted with permission from *Saturday Review* 43 (10 December 1960): 18.

"We're Friends Again," which involves several love affairs, seems too complicated, but the other two move rapidly and surely. The great value of the form for O'Hara lies in the fact that it compels him to omit most of the documentation that is his pride and the despair of many of his critics. No one has a better eye for the significant detail than O'Hara, but as a rule, not trusting that detail to do its work, he backs it up with a mass of trivia. Here, as in some of his early work, he makes a little count for a lot. He is not a master of the novella; these are, as he admits, condensed novels. But the condensation is skilfully done. It has been some time since I have enjoyed anything of O'Hara's as much as I have these novellas, and I do not expect to take the same sort of pleasure in that "longer, longest" novel he promises.

Five Plays

◆

A Novelist in the Wings

Howard Taubman

In a fighting mood, John O'Hara has sanctioned the publication of five plays. Since Broadway has not seen fit to produce them as he wrote them, he has reached out to the public—and it is large—that his books have cultivated. In a sense he is appealing over the heads of the producers, directors and other Broadway characters who have, for one reason or another, voted No, on these five scripts. In a foreword he says, speaking of "Pal Joey" and "Appointment in Samarra" and no doubt referring to these five titles as well, "I always have to wait, and while I'm waiting, I work." The plays were written while he waited—and, presumably while he waits for their recognition as theatre-worthy, he writes, possibly, further plays.

How good are these five unproduced scripts ("The Farmers Hotel," "The Searching Sun," "The Champagne Pool," "Veronique" and "The Way It Was")? Must we judge them as dialogue to be spoken by actors? Or as writing to be read and appreciated by the reader in the study?

Since they are available in the bookshops and not in the theatre, let us examine the second question first. Mr. O'Hara's gift for placing people under his microscope, for making them talk, act and feel, illuminates his plays as it does his novels. Like Hemingway, he has forged a tight, deceptively transparent style that glints with surface sharpness and humor and that carries a powerful undercurrent of emotion. He tells his stories with concentration and tension.

Reprinted from the *New York Times Book Review*, 20 August 1961, 4. Copyright © 1961 by The New York Times Company. Reprinted by permission.

As a story, "The Farmers Hotel" (which has already appeared in short-novel form) is the most arresting of the five pieces in this volume. Set in a rustic hotel in Pennsylvania during a winter storm, its meaning will be enigmatic to some readers—but it fascinates and provokes. It contrasts credulity and cynicism, good and evil in a combination that shocks. It is an allegory that reverberates with a variety of implications.

The other plays, though plainer in content, also reflect the author's preoccupation with men and women who are hard, bitter, weak and defeated. In "The Searching Sun" he considers an acting couple fighting to arrest a decline in their careers. In "The Champagne Pool" he deals with a playwright, a flamboyant actress and one of those "creative directors" whom he evidently despises. In his foreword he intimates that his refusal to give in to this breed because "I know of no director whose writing talent I respect" has had a lot to do with the failure to get his manuscripts produced. Yet he is artist enough to treat the director in "The Champagne Pool" with a relish for his vital, if angry and dominating, personality.

Mr. O'Hara is not far from show business in all of these plays, but "The Champagne Pool" is saturated in the milieu. "Veronique" purports to recover a sense of what Greenwich Village was in the Twenties, and it captures a good deal of its spirit of drift and aspiration. "The Way It Was" is another evocation of the Twenties, with its story of an unfulfilled love of a proud, almost inarticulate pair from the wrong side of the tracks.

As a story on the printed page "The Way It Was" comes closest to "The Farmers Hotel" to being a satisfying experience; it is told with an economy and accuracy that mirror the bitter-sweet mood the author wishes to convey. One suspects that "The Way It Was," supported by an imaginative score, would have a fine chance in the theatre. A composer with a talent for the blues might catch the note of despair and yearning and help to make the sardonic ending viable on Broadway. (Mr. O'Hara meant the play to have music, and he approached Irving Berlin. A young Gershwin or Rodgers would not be amiss either.)

If "The Way It Was," with the right composer and lyricist, would work effectively in the theatre, as "Pal Joey" did, what of the other four pieces? No one, of course, can predict precisely how a script will emerge on the stage—but this much can be said. To one who sat through some offerings on Broadway last season that were an insult to an adult it is difficult to see why some of Mr. O'Hara's pieces were by-passed. "The Searching Sun," for example, is incisive and theatrical. "The Farmers Hotel" may be both too tight and too ambiguous. For all its good things, "The Champagne Pool" peters out in a conventionally happy ending—and "Veronique" arrives at one that changes the focus of the play. (Mr. O'Hara has no patience with the producers who want a last act changed, but even producers sometimes are right.)

As a writer, whether for the printed page or the stage, Mr. O'Hara is essentially a dramatist. His subject-matter is often disturbing and violent. "Pal

Joey," his one theatre contribution to reach Broadway, at first put people off because it was not pretty. But the heels are still around, and so are the hard, lacquered, self-indulgent women, and this author still writes about them with an irony that reflects a streak of sentimentality as well as honest anger. He is no philosopher, but he is a shrewd observer. Without worrying over how these plays would fare on the stage, one finds them amusing and stimulating in book form.

Assembly

◆

The Flaw in O'Hara

IRVING HOWE

Were mimicry the soul of art, O'Hara would a master be. Not many writers know as much as he does about the social surface of American life, nor are as committed to so inflexible and ingenuous a belief in its significance. O'Hara's prosperity has enabled him to keep mobile and avoid those academic jobs that confine so many other writers, while his tastes have led him to a beguiled absorption in the ways of the upper middle class.

O'Hara's new book contains 26 stories, of which I judge four to be successful, a good rate for any writer; but even in his failures there is something to be learned, particularly about that segment of the new rich that has lately been showing signs of wishing to constitute itself as a self-made gentry.

As always in his stories, O'Hara has an eye for the details of the physical setting in which civilized relations are enacted: he knows about *things* and believes in their fetishistic power. His ear is still very keen, though he has become somewhat vain about it, with the result that patches of dialogue stand out as displays of expertness breaking the line of his stories. He builds these stories with the uninspired conscientiousness of a good carpenter who trusts more to measurement than imagination, and this is not always so great a fault as some modern readers are likely to suppose.

Yet O'Hara is not a first-rate writer, and the main reason is that he does

Reprinted from the *New Republic* 145 (27 November 1961): 16–17. Reprinted by permission of THE NEW REPUBLIC, © 1961, The New Republic, Inc.

not have a first-rate mind. Writers possessed by a vision, like Faulkner, can for a time dispense with the ordinary uses of intelligence; but writers like O'Hara, who depend mostly upon observation of daily life, need the kind of intelligence that enables them to move beyond the bric-a-brac of what they observe. O'Hara's mind, however, is imprisoned in the kind of small-spirited and skeptical materialism which in this country tends too often to be mistaken for worldliness. It is a leaden, literalistic and insistently mundane mind, and it has an embarrassing way of sliding from pseudo-masculine coarseness to whiskey sentimentalism.

Time after time O'Hara brings together fresh material but is unable to do anything except present it. Because he has serious literary ambitions and has pushed his craft as far as he can, he knows by now that something more than mere presentation is needed. He therefore falls back upon devices of shock and melodrama—a plot switch, a gimmick, a radical drop in tone—to gain the imaginative coherence he has not really earned. Yet even this fault, grave as it is, might not be so hopelessly damaging were it not that his intellectual weakness is reinforced by an unattractive temperament. O'Hara is a peculiarly unwinning writer: a mood of heavy truculence hangs over his work like smog in California.

Still, one learns something here, for his stories, unlike much current fiction, are about the public world and can at least offer news. In this latest group he observes that as a result of several decades of prosperity there is forming in the United States a new gentry which consists of people whose money is fresh, who have no particular family tradition they care to proclaim, who show little concern with the substance of culture but a close alertness to the nuances of cultivation, and who are determined to make for themselves a style of life in which there will be some built-in mode of validation, a validation not apart from but emerging out of their social pleasures. I put this, unavoidably, in abstract terms, but it is a decidedly interesting matter and O'Hara has a good deal to say and show about it.

The literary purposes to which he puts this knowledge are, however, severely constricted, and just how constricted will be clear to anyone who compares his work to the better fiction of Edith Wharton. She too was a portraitist of the social surface, she too had close involvements with the class she described, but because of her personal culture and temperament she brought to bear upon her material an enlarging standard of humane values and civilized reflection. It is precisely such a standard that one looks for and seldom finds in O'Hara, some sense of that critical detachment from his world which keeps the writer from being merely identified with it.

In O'Hara's new stories there are some new faults, both touching and amusing. He has become pedantic, inserting passages into his stories which boastfully set other writers straight about those points of information that seem to him a key to truth. He has also become interested in wisdom, and there are sudden flat sentences of comment and psychology embarrasing for what they say though moving when one considers his need to say them. His prose is no longer as terse as it once was, suffering at times from *New Yorker* spread. And when he writes in the first person, through his literary shadow Malloy, he affects a tone of gentlemanly *savoir faire*, as if he were Captain Marlow returning from the heart of American darkness. All the while, however, one detects in him a great earnestness: I entirely believe the statement in his preface that his feeling about writing is "practically religious." It is as if he were hoping to find a way to break through that surface perception to which he seems doomed, a way of grasping that imaginative largesse he so much admires in Scott Fitzgerald.

Still, four good stories. "The Weakness," written in his earlier style of harsh economy, shows a prize-fighter reaching the end of his career, getting himself into trouble with a woman and returning bleary and pugnacious to his wife. "The High Point" is a chilling notation on ugliness in marriage, "It's Mental Work" on ugliness in small business. Best of all is "The Old Folks," a quiet account of two middle-aged people who are fond of each other and nervously go off on a weekend to see whether they can build a marriage for their late years. This beautiful piece of work leads one to speculate on the writer O'Hara might have been if he had not stiffened into the limitations on which his reputation so securely rests.

The Big Laugh

♦

Heelprints on Hollywood and Vine

Arthur Marx

This seems to be the type of fare that major novelists sometimes dash off between major novels, either in pursuit of a "fast buck" or merely to satisfy reader and publisher demands that they turn out books at regular intervals, regardless of the quality. But whichever is the case here (and I seriously doubt if it's the former, since at last count Mr. O'Hara had taken well over a million dollars out of the movie business, which he so callously knocks in this novel), it is quite apparent that "The Big Laugh" isn't one of his major efforts.

In "The Big Laugh" O'Hara tells the story of Hubert Ward, the handsome but slightly caddish son of a New Jersey bank embezzler, who rises from obscurity to movie stardom by capitalizing on his biggest asset—ruthlessness. He has some acting talent too (although the character as Mr. O'Hara paints him is so hazy you can't be sure), but it's his penchant for being an unmitigated heel that gets him to the top. Through blackmail he coerces a director into giving him his first acting job on Broadway. After that it's just a question of time and some fancy scene stealing before Hubert winds up in Hollywood, where he eventually becomes a full-fledged movie star. But do success and maturity change Hubert Ward? Certainly not. Hubert Ward remains the same selfish heel of old, double-crossing business acquaintances by day and seducing best friends' wives by night. Indirectly, in fact, he is even responsible for the death of one of his good friends, a movie tycoon. Nevertheless, remorse

From *Saturday Review* 45 (7 July 1962): 29. Reprinted by permission.

doesn't set in until Hubert falls in love with Nina, a beautiful society girl from the East, who tames him, marries him, and makes him into a model husband. In fact, Hubert turns into such a paragon of respectability that Nina becomes bored with him and runs off with someone else, which is, I suppose, the irony of it all.

The trouble with "The Big Laugh" is not that its central character is a heel. After all, "Pal Joey" was about a heel, and the book was delightful. What hurts this narrative is that Hubert Ward never comes to life. None of the characters do, for that matter, but it is more noticeable in the case of Ward, perhaps because he is an actor. To reach the top of their profession, actors must have a certain amount of verve and personality that add up to a thing called charm—even if it's a phony charm. And in order to write about them successfully, one must be able to convey this to the reader. This O'Hara fails to do. In fact, he seems to have little or no insight into an actor's character. It isn't enough to make Hubert a heel. God knows, plenty of movie stars are heels. But plenty of heels aren't movie stars. And that's what's mainly wrong with "The Big Laugh." Ward's a cipher, whom you never get to know or understand. And no matter how often O'Hara refers to him as a successful actor, you don't for a moment believe that this colorless figure could be successful on the stage, or on the screen, or even in a bedroom, where he spends a great deal of time, as do most O'Hara heroes.

Another of the book's shortcomings is O'Hara's handling of the Hollywood background, which seems curiously old-fashioned and cliché ridden. Granted, the main part of the narrative takes place in the Thirties. But even in the Thirties, when Hollywood was in its most Rabelaisian period, there was more to the picture business than drunken orgies at Malibu, illiterate producers and agents, and nymphomaniac actresses. There were quite a few serious-minded, talented people working in the studios as well, including Mr. O'Hara, who ought to have a better memory.

The Cape Cod Lighter

◆

From Tiny Details, the Big Truth

ROBERT GUTWILLIG

Like all good writers, John O'Hara is a collector and a gossip. He collects both the relevant and the apparently irrelevant details of our society, and is absolutely compelled to tell us everything he knows. He is, of course, interested in the minutiae of our lives for its own sake, but beyond that he is a student, critic and lay analyst of our foibles and failures. He views society as a living organism with its own cruel and perplexing laws and customs. Perhaps no one recently, not even F. Scott Fitzgerald, James Gould Cozzens or John P. Marquand, has seen more clearly the subtle but violent struggle between the individual and society in this country.

In nothing Mr. O'Hara has written previously is this struggle presented any more forceably or poignantly than in the long story "Pat Collins," which now appears in his new collection of stories, mysteriously titled "The Cape Cod Lighter." Pat Collins came to Gibbsville, Pa., during the nineteen-twenties, and his and his wife's involvement with the town and with Whit and Kitty Hofman over the years is rendered not only with attention to details of speech and manners but also to personal involvements—particularly sex, a subject that never seems to operate successfully or meaningfully in O'Hara's long novels.

Perhaps "The Cape Cod Lighter" is not so fully satisfying a collection as

Reprinted from the *New York Times Book Review*, 25 November 1962, 1, 16. Copyright © 1962 by The New York Times Company. Reprinted by permission.

last year's "Assembly." Still, it is fiction of a very high, if not the highest, order. Following a foreword as ill-advised as it is ill-tempered, in which Mr. O'Hara takes on critics in general and one in particular, the author has collected 23 stories written during the last two years. Some of these stories originally appeared in The New Yorker: the majority are published here for the first time and five or six represent O'Hara at the top of his form. In fact, as the author himself states, since 1960 he has been writing even better stories than ever before. For those of us who still remember "The Doctor's Son," "Are We Leaving Tomorrow?", "Summer's Day," "Do You Like It Here?" that is saying a great deal.

Mr. O'Hara has been turning out his hand (not machine) tooled, polished (but not slick) interpretations of his own and our experience for the last 30 years—with a regrettable 11-year interruption during the nineteen-fifties, while he devoted most of his time to writing long novels—and within his limitations (some of his own choosing, some of nature's) I know of no better record or more accurate interpretation of those 30 years.

Here is John O'Hara on the short story: "The short story is such a different art form [from the novel] that an author simply must not have the same approach to a novel that he has to the short story. The author must say to himself that this is to be a short story; he must say it over and over again so that he conditions himself before setting words down on paper, until the habit of thinking in short story terms is re-formed. Obviously he must make all the words count, obviously he must set space limits ahead of time. But at the time he is preparing himself to compress, he must also bear in mind the fact that this may be the only thing of his that some reader will ever read. In other words, the artistic conscience must be functioning."

The flatness, the clarity, the declarativeness, the repetitiveness of those phrases are immediately and unmistakably O'Hara, as unmistakable as any line in any O'Hara story. His is a style, manner, tone, point of view uniquely suited to the short story, the long story or short novel (i.e., "Appointment in Samarra," "Pal Joey," "Sermons and Soda Water"). It is over the longer haul that I believe this author's manner and his method let him down, for both his prose and his viewpoint are geared to exposés not revelations, to crises not developments, to statements not persuasions, to sentiments not emotions.

After all this time, John O'Hara's dialogue is still a marvel. The patterns and accents of our speech have undergone enormous alterations and outright obliterations in 30 years; but in "The Father," "Justice," "The Nothing Machine" and other stories in this collection, here is O'Hara bang on, prodding on his characters to illuminate and destroy themselves in their own pithy accents. And his eyes are still as sharp and penetrating as his ears. As Lionel Trilling wrote some years ago, "The work of no other American writer tells us so precisely, and with such a sense of the importance of the communication, how people look and how they want to look, where they buy their clothes and where they wish they could buy their clothes, how they speak and how they think they ought to speak."

"The Cape Cod Lighter" also illustrates Mr. O'Hara's great range of both subject matter and time—a range that has been generally ignored. We are all by this time as familiar with a hundred years of Gibbsville history as we are with the fabulous past and present of Yoknapatawpha County, but Mr. O'Hara is equally at home on Broadway, in the West Seventies, the Bronx, Hollywood, Middle Atlantic suburbs and exurbs, Quogue and the Hamptons, in speakeasies and country clubs, coal towns and club cars, in the scrupulously observed interiors of the old and new rich and the evocatively recaptured mountains and woods of his Pennsylvania boyhood. And the range of characterization is even broader. Actually, the author's expanding facility with older characters, as demonstrated in his last two collections, suggest both an enlargement and deepening of his talent.

If, as many people seem to think, John O'Hara has always been writing what has been called "The New Yorker formula" short story, it must also be acknowledged that the "formula" and we ourselves have altered in the last 30 years more than we've noticed.

The New Yorker story has been defined and re-defined as a short, semifictional examination of various but not varied aspects of urban and suburban upper-middle-class life here and in England in which more is suggested than rendered, more is implied than the action seems to justify. In this story far less is going on than meets the eye, particularly since the story invariably terminates abruptly and without resolution, or just when the writer and his characters appear to be getting down to the business of living and communication. Like most subliterary definitions, this one is cheerfully pejorative, aimed at the lowest common denominator, and accounts rather more for failure than success. It certainly does not measure or even explain the achievement and the diversity of—to list just a few—Cheever, Nabokov, Thurber, Frank O'Connor, Irwin Shaw, McCullers, Pritchett, Stafford, Welty, Salinger, Elizabeth Spencer, Updike, Roth. Or O'Hara.

Any magazine that can print in one issue (as The New Yorker did last month) stories of the first order by John Cheever and Philip Roth deserves our attention and our gratitude. Similarly, any writer who can produce more than 50 stories of the first order, as Mr. O'Hara has done, deserves our attention and our gratitude, despite what we may think of several of his later novels.

In "Mrs. Stratton at Oak Knoll" (published in "Assembly"), Evan Reese, a painter, discussing his talent and his limitations with his wife, is made to say, "But I've always been interested in the near-misses. Understandably, I'm one myself." Clearly, that is how O'Hara sees himself. Placed beside the bullseyes of Faulkner, Fitzgerald and Hemingway, whose finest achievements may, in time, also be seen as their shorter fiction, O'Hara is indeed a near-miss. Yet, in a sense, literary archery is a depressing game, and, in the end, destructive and feckless.

What impresses one most about John O'Hara is his high level of consistency over three decades and, finally, his professionalism. In a time when so many of our best and our worst writers have closed their minds, their hearts, their eyes and their ears to everything but their own problems and their own voices, it is good to have someone around like O'Hara who has the interest and the courage to attend the rest of us. In a period when amateurism seems to be overtaking everything, including the creation of fiction, it is damn nice to have a professional in good working order among us.

John O'Hara's Stories Strangely Moralistic

Irving Malin

John O'Hara is a social historian. He captures the way "high and low" people in New Jersey towns and Gibbsville, Pa. drive their cars, drink, light their cigarettes, and speak. Because he is so interested in social tone, he spends little time on individual psychology. His people are often representative; they repeat class errors—drinking excessively, committing adultery. We know as soon as they display their "manners," that they will do certain nasty things.

But we should not dismiss O'Hara as only a hardboiled reporter. In an odd way he is a religious writer. His people are "sinners." Not only do they flirt with Catholicism—many are lapsed Catholics—but occasionally they *believe* in it. They sense that they are falling, hurting themselves and God. Does O'Hara believe in sin? The question is difficult to answer. Perhaps the easiest answer is that like his people he sees some Higher Cause—not entirely social—in life; he wants to embrace it as he combats it.

The most compelling stories in "The Cape Cod Lighter" are those which glimmer with hints of sin and destiny. "The Butterfly," "Your Fah Neefah Neeface," and "The Engineer" are good examples.

These three stories deal with ordinary people (in spite of their wealth or lack of it) who are suddenly confronted by the grotesque. Incest, homosexuality, and gratuitous cruelty come to the social surface, distorting it. It is too easy to claim that O'Hara is merely sensational. Here sex is monstrous and tempting—it destroys the conventions of daily life, right reason, and community. But its satanic ugliness enlightens O'Hara's people: it shows them that although they live by social appearances, they cannot cope with their own mysterious bodies. Sex is an agent of some obscure, just Cause.

From *Courier Journal*, 23 December 1962, Section 4, 5. Reprinted by permission of the author.

Elizabeth Appleton

◆

More of the Same from an Old Pro

Hayden Carruth

John O'Hara is the old pro *par excellence*, as everyone knows. He can turn out a novel easier than most people can write home for money. Which, for that matter, comes to about the same thing.

The lingo he has running in his head! It's too much, really. One boggles at the brilliance. Everything from the shoeshine boy to the college president, all in their appropriate accents, tones, and rhythms. In fact, Mr. O'Hara has carried the realistic reproduction of dialogue, which Mark Twain said was his chief interest in writing "Huckleberry Finn," about as far as it can go.

The story this time concerns the lady for whom the book is named, Elizabeth Appleton. Daughter of a wealthy and socially prominent New York family, Elizabeth spends her childhood and adolescence in the manner acceptable to her class and station. That is to say, private school in winter, tennis and boating at Southhampton in the summer.

Then, however, she falls in love with John Appleton, a young history professor at a small college in Pennsylvania, and with her father's blessing and her mother's contempt, she marries him and goes with him to live in Pennsylvania, far from the gilded circle. She spends the next 20 years and something like 300 pages finding out which of her parents was right.

As one might expect, both were right, though the father was more right

From the *Chicago Daily News*, 5 June 1963, 37. Reprinted with permission from the *Chicago Sun-Times*, © 1993.

than the mother. Elizabeth pursues her investigations by way of a strenuous course in adultery and an equally strenuous course in matrimony, from which strenuosities she emerges the vanquished but grateful wife.

The novel is, in fact, a highly moral tale, even if some of the episodes are not what you'd recommend to your grandmother from Cedar Rapids.

Elizabeth is surrounded by a good many interesting types. The college campus is a standard game preserve for novelists these days, of course, but Mr. O'Hara brings down his quarry with keener shots than most, even if his bag contains the same old partridges. Here they are: the smooth but incompetent president, the cigar-smoking trustee, the lecherous old psychology professor, the ambitious professor's wife, etc. They are caricatures, every one of them, but that doesn't mean you won't find them walking, talking, and more or less living in any college town you care to visit.

"Elizabeth Appleton" is a fast, hard novel in the O'Hara tradition; in other words, a good piece of work. Yet devotees of the old O'Hara are likely to be disappointed. In spite of the keen dialogue, much of the style in the new book is limp. There are too many places where a trite phrase could be replaced by a crisp word. One has the impression that Mr. O'Hara is turning it out these days at a prodigious rate without bothering to reread what he has written. Or perhaps he leaves the editing to his secretary.

And then there is the question of the professionalism. Mr. O'Hara can whip a novel like a top, but when a top spins fast enough it looks as if it were standing still. He has his technique pat. He gives us the present in the first chapter, then backtracks for 300 pages to bring us up to the present again. But it is too slick; the first chapter is built up so tightly and urgently that we resent being thrown back 20 years and told we must read 300 pages to learn the outcome of the dilemma posed in the first 10 pages. And besides, we are sick to death of this technique anyway.

Nevertheless, Mr. O'Hara has his virtues. If his style sags a bit and his form is too smooth, he still puts together a clear, driving story, he still catches the social tone of a group or a city with remarkable economy, and he still writes about women in terms which lack the faintest trace of femininity, making them all the more believable on that account. These are not distinctions to be lightly set aside.

The Hat on the Bed

◆

O'Hara's Best: A Joy to Behold

Hayden Carruth

This book of 24 new short stories is John O'Hara's best work; which is, without doubt, an extraordinary observation. Mr. O'Hara has been going for close to 30 years, and has published something like 30 previous books, to say nothing of movie scenarios, documentations, and all manner of trivia and trash. Very few writers, after such a fierce spell of activity, can hope to maintain the quality of their best earlier, work, let alone surpass it.

It is possible to say, as a rule of thumb, that this kind of staying power is one sign which distinguishes the genuine artist from the frips and frumps?

Perhaps. And another rule may be that the work of the genuine artist tends somewhat to conceal itself. Certainly this is the case with Mr. O'Hara.

There is the question, for instance, of his professionalism. Any other writer who reads these stories is bound to be struck with admiration for Mr. O'Hara's skill. The five pages, in the first story, which wrap up the whole life of a thrice-married woman—not many can manage it so economically. Compression in itself, of course, is no virtue; any police officer making up a dossier has the knack. But compression which leaves no suggestion of anything omitted or oversimplified, compression which does not violate our humane and instinctive sympathy for the fictional character—who is, of course, the underdog in the author-character relationship—such compression is a virtue. And Mr. O'Hara knows how to do it.

From the *Chicago Daily News*, 23 November 1963, Panorama, 9. Reprinted with permission from the *Chicago Sun-Times*, © 1993.

Or consider the question of dialogue. No one writing in America today has a keener ear than John O'Hara's for the shades of distinction in colloquial speech. Other writers give us the speech of one regional or racial minority, perfectly reproduced; but Mr. O'Hara skips from The Bronx to Oyster Bay to Bucks County to Chicago to Malibu, and then back again, with a hundred stops between. He makes mistakes, naturally. But not many, and most of his writing, considered linguistically, is a joy to behold.

Nevertheless, these signs of professionalism are just what we have been taught, with some justice, to reprehend. In an age like ours, when the experimental impulse has died and the pressures of academicism have become powerful, slickness and technical virtuosity usually betray a fundamental dilettantism. Hence we have come recently to believe that serious writing must be rough, ragged, hyperbolical, or otherwise extreme, and this is the sense in which, at first, Mr. O'Hara's professionalism conceals his artistry.

There is another and more basic sense, however. The reader is likely to find these stories unimportant. Moving and real, yes—they are certainly that. But nothing much happens in them, and they are not loaded with symbols intended to recall history's great cultural and moral issues. These stories seem too simple. And at this point the reader casts his mind back over the great short story writers of the past, Maupassant, Chekhov, Katherine Mansfield.

The truth is that nothing much happened in their stories either, nor were they loaded with symbols. Then why are they important? Because they evoke, with great economy of means and depth of vision, the civilizations which produced them.

"A-ha," the reader says to himself, "this is where O'Hara falls down. His stories have no cultural or social significance." But what kind of nonsense is this? As ten minutes' study will prove to anyone, these stories are embedded in the condition of life at exactly the same depth as the reader, which is why the reader, in order to appreciate John O'Hara's genius, must extricate himself, momentarily and at considerable effort, from that condition of life.

Thus his stories, like a number of other books that have come upon us recently, force us to reverse some of our previous concepts, precisely those concepts of modern literary understanding which we have been at such pains to acquire. Or is it that we have reached a stage in cultural development which demands a reversal of sensibility simply as a consequence of dynamic inner change, without regard to what books may come along?

No matter. The point is that two reversals are needed here. We must, first, look upon Mr. O'Hara's virtuosity as a useful implement of genius. Second, in order to perceive his importance we must cultivate a point of view which is not more contemporary in nature, but less so. There are other necessary reversals as well, too intricate for discussion in a book review. But the second reversal mentioned here is enough to merit our scrutiny.

Contrast John O'Hara, for example, with the Southern short story writers. Contrast his richly unexceptional characters with the outlandish persons of

Southern literature, Faulkner's Popeye or Flannery O'Connor's one-legged girl. Do not these Gothic types from the South attract our attention precisely because they are outside our condition of life? Which view of the world, Mr. O'Hara's or the Southern, will be more revealing to the reader who examines them fifty years from now, when our condition of life will be excruciatingly remote?

In any event, the reader who makes the effort to discover John O'Hara, an effort so unapparent that at first the reader scarcely realizes it need be made, will find in this new book some particularly beautiful specimens of American writing. Not simply a few, either. This is a thick book—Mr. O'Hara's productiveness lately has been extraordinary—and of the 24 stories included in it, something like 17 or 18 are first-rate.

Only a Few Trips from His Small, Tidy Realm

Edmund Keeley

According to John Hutchens (in his introduction to the Modern Library Giant edition of O'Hara's stories, quoted on the dust jacket of this latest collection) John O'Hara is a "master" in the old, dignified sense of the term because "knowing just what he is doing, and doing it with precision, authority and ever-increasing range and insight, [he] has created through the years a body of fiction not equaled by any fellow countryman of his now living."

The publishers suggest that this year's volume "gives additional authority to Mr. Hutchens' judgment." Since this reviewer agrees with Mr. Hutchens that "they toss that word master around pretty easily these days," he feels compelled to test both the term and the judgment with reference to O'Hara's current work.

One should begin by acknowledging the large measure of truth in Mr. Hutchens' claim: O'Hara does seem always to know what he is doing: most of the stories in this volume are the work of a precise craftsman; and some of the stories reveal a shrewd, honest insight within the range of experience that they explore ("How Can I Tell You?" "The Public Dorothy," "The Twinkle in His Eye," to name the first that come to mind).

But this acknowledgement raises certain questions. Is it enough for a "master" to know what he is doing, or should he always be doing something significant, something that challenges his talent and thereby serves to extend the borders of his art? What of the precise craftsman who fails to select the good from the merely perfunctory, the merely routine, in the work he creates? Can you call any craftsman a master if he so limits himself to outworn forms and familiar subjects that he has nothing to teach an aspiring apprentice who might approach him for guidance, as the masters Joyce and Lawrence and Kafka, or Hemingway and Fitzgerald and Faulkner have taught and guided younger writers in recent times?

Perhaps one asks too much; but the label "master" presses us to look at O'Hara on the highest level, to question his accomplishment in these terms, and on the evidence of this volume, he has not yet earned the title, the stature, claimed for him by his most generous critics and readers.

From *Washington Post Book Week*, 1 December 1963, 8. Copyright © 1963, The Washington Post. Reprinted with permission.

It is time to be specific. Though there is no story in this collection that can be called totally uninteresting, over half of its 400 pages satisfy an interest that is hardly more literary, more imaginative, than gossip in a New York club—the Princeton Club, say. Too many of the stories are mere anecdotes, sketches, portraits, and the experience in reading them is very much like that of browsing through somebody's family album.

Yet if it is a world beyond the reach of most, it is all too familiar nevertheless—familiar from our reading in O'Hara's other voluminous works. The few stories that succeed in rousing more than the pleasures of gossip or anecdote are exactly those that stray beyond—below is more accurate—this restricted yet thoroughly photographed territory: a car salesman contemplating suicide, a college instructor contemplating the murder of his wife, a cub reporter rescuing a whore from a smalltown jail, etc. Is this evidence of O'Hara's "ever-increasing range" in subject matter? If so, it is confined to a small portion of the book, too small a portion to suggest some imminent excursion into undiscovered country.

But the range in terms of form is even more restricted. Without exception, each of the 24 stories in this collection makes use of an uncomplicated third-person narrator who usually commits himself, in an uncomplicated way, to the perspective of a single character. O'Hara's handling of point of view is less sophisticated than Dreiser's even, and since Dreiser we've had Fitzgerald and Dos Passos and Faulkner. Where has O'Hara been during the long revolution in this area of form that Joyce initiated at the turn of the century?

His reticence, his lack of daring in this regard, is one reason for the flatness of so much in this collection. Another reason is his lack of stylistic daring: there is only one story here ("Our Friend the Sea") that offers anything more than the thoroughly competent, clean-cut, no-monkey-business prose of a high-level reporter (Dreiser again?), and what that story projects to brighten its touching moments is a rather desperate substitute for poetry ("He watched her with an old sense of deity, as God might watch her, and as though she were playing with the wind and the sun as her personal playmates").

A third cause of flatness is O'Hara's proclivity for turning on dialogue—long, sometimes endless dialogue—the second two characters are brought together, as though the author were really a playwright afraid that his audience might walk out on him if he were to let his characters remain silent for a moment when the stage is so bare. Finally, there is little evidence that O'Hara intends to explore modes more ambitious, more experimental, more poetic than that of reportorial realism, the mode that has both served and circumscribed him for these many years.

So much for the volume considered as the work of a master. Those who have come to share this view of O'Hara's limitations will still find entertainment in his latest work, and some superior craftsmanship.

The Horse Knows the Way

♦

The War of Marriage, Observed by a Master

Tom Yarbrough

Never has the war between men and women been more truly reported than in these latest pages by John O'Hara. The title is only a label, but since any collection of short stories has to have a title this is as good as any other. The book consists of 28 stories in the old O'Hara manner, in which he tells about the lives of a multitude of types—people of Gibbsville, P.A., as usual, but also of New York, Hollywood and other alluring places.

The technique is the same, and for that the reader can be grateful, because Mr. O'Hara has developed his talents into a style that comes close to television. He takes the reader right into the room with the characters at hand, and we see them and hear them talking—exactly as they speak and not with phrases manipulated into standard English.

Mr. O'Hara's ear has become famous for its accuracy. Here again are the familiar trademark expressions, "ha' past seven," "something worr'ing you?," and "give me fi' dollars," spellings that remind the reader that he is getting the real article. The reader also gets some precise reporting of fractured grammar, again so real that he is reminded of people he has heard speaking exactly that way.

"This one I want to pay cash," "Jake, you're always telling me those kind of things." "That's a wonderful picture of Gary Cooper and I."

"The War of Marriage, Observed by a Master," by Tom Yarbrough, from *St. Louis Post-Dispatch*, 29 November 1964, 4B. Reprinted with permission of the St. Louis Post-Dispatch, copyright 1993.

Extreme accuracy by ear can be overdone, and Mr. O'Hara just now and then overdoes it. For example, he has a character say, "You should of been a preacher." In normal speech, "of" in this case has a sound no different from that of "have," and no purpose is served in the use of the word "of," except to make the speaker ridiculous.

In selection of striking detail this author has few equals. The focus is sharp in such glimpses as this: "He lit a kitchen match with his thumbnail and slowly revolved the cigar between his lips to get an even light." That thumbnail bit has been used before, but it is still good.

Mr. O'Hara still feels no obligation to plot his stories, and so the endings are sometimes abrupt, leaving loose ends lying about and many problems and questions unresolved. This lets the reader in on the story, free to work out his own denouement. Such absence of clarity is highly rated by some critics of the art of the short story. In the main, however, Mr. O'Hara is clear, above all, in what he writes. Faulkner's blurred ramblings are not for him.

He has a variety of style that is always delightful. In one section we race along with the staccato dialogue that derives from Ernest Hemingway in "The Killers," and in another we encounter granite pages of solid type, unbroken by paragraph, but these have their compensations for slower reading, for they are rich in substance.

If there is a single strand that runs through this fabric, or much of it, it is that of a middle-aged man in earnest conversation with his middle-aged wife—conversation that runs through many pages. Most of the time they are fighting, nagging, each accusing the other and being accused in turn, and now and then the finality is homicide or suicide. What we have in sum is a veritable primer on the strategy and tactics of marital debate. He has used such a scene many times.

Man and wife understand each other perfectly—in the sum of their years together—and Mr. O'Hara understands both. One of the finest qualities of his writing, from the beginning with "Appointment in Samarra" in 1928, has been his ability to place himself in the midst of a great assortment of scenes. He is there. He seems most at home with the well-to-do, and he describes the ornate rooms of their houses, but he does not make the people attractive. Undoubtedly he has found them unattractive.

This book represents a turn in the O'Hara career. "For a while, at least, this will be my last book of short stories," he writes in a foreword. This is no final farewell, for he hastens to call attention to his qualifier, "For a while."

He notes that he received the Award of Merit of the American Academy of Arts and Letters, not for the short story but for the novel, "at a stage in my career when my short stories were being praised and my novels deplored." To me the short stories are no better than the novels, but no worse. The stories are different in structure, of course, but the writing is much the same. It is O'Hara, and it is 99 44 / 100 per cent good.

The Lockwood Concern

◆

O'Hara, Still a Moralist, Is Losing His Compassion

THEODORE M. O'LEARY

One thing that is often overlooked in John O'Hara is that he is a moralist, and he has never been a sterner one than in "The Lockwood Concern," the story of four generations of a deservedly unloved family operating from a base in Swedish Haven, Pa., not far from the capital of the O'Hara Country, Gibbsville.

Strange the misconceptions we get about our important writers. Most people thought that Sinclair Lewis hated America because he satirized and burlesqued it. But he loved it so much he couldn't bear to see it demean itself and play the fool, so he did what he could to prevent it doing so.

To tens of thousands of people John O'Hara writes dirty books. He doesn't. He writes books in which many of the characters misbehave sexually and succumb to materialism and he does not gloss over their misbehavior and their pursuit of false values. But ultimately most of his characters pay for their affronts to morality and their misplaced faith. So O'Hara is in his way an unswerving moralist, fated to be regarded as a purveyor of obscenity by a great part of the public which buys his novels by the thousands largely for their superficial aspects rather than their underlying meanings.

Reprinted from the *Kansas City Star*, 28 November 1965, 5F. Reprinted by permission of the *Kansas City Star*.

As he ages, O'Hara's sympathy for his characters seems to be diminishing. For Julian English of his first and possibly still his best novel, "Appointment in Samarra," O'Hara showed compassion. For the Lockwood men of this latest novel he has none. Perhaps that is because Julian English was weak and the Lockwoods are strong, to the point of arrogance. Looking back on his family, George Bingham Lockwood tells his daughter Tina: "They were opportunists. But I will say for them that they stood off their opposition for a whole century. They made no friends, but they did the next best thing, which was to repel their enemies."

First of the Lockwoods with whom O'Hara concerns himself is Moses, born in 1811, who goes to Swedish Haven and accumulates a fortune of $200,000, gets part of his ear shot off in the Civil War and guns two men to death. The polishing starts with his son Abraham, born in 1840, who goes to the University of Pennsylvania, makes acquaintances in Philadelphia and Washington society, uses marriage as a tactic in building the family's power and increases the Lockwood fortune enormously.

It is Abraham who, borrowing a Quaker term, conceives the idea of a Lockwood "Concern"—an obsessive act or thought, much more than a plan or an ambition. But while the Quakers use Concern in a constructive religious sense, Abraham's design is to insure a dynasty—to have begun with his father and to continue through him, his children and on and on. He wants his family, his dukedom as O'Hara calls it, to be the acknowledged symbol of power in Lantenengo County. He plans for the time when having taught his sons George and Penrose how to take care of their inheritance, "they could remain in comfortable affluent obscurity while deciding which boards to sit on, which ambassadorships to take, what games to play, whose women to sleep with."

Abraham doesn't live to see how his concern works out which may be just as well. Materially his sons surpass almost anything their father could have hoped for. The polishing continues. George, born in 1873 and the central character in this novel, goes to a socially correct prep school and on to Princeton. In the family tradition of secretiveness, he builds a walled estate outside Swedish Haven but his financial interests and power extend far beyond Lantenengo County. Penrose meanwhile becomes a New York financier and comes to a scandalous end.

George is feared, respected but unloved. Like all the Lockwoods he is sexually restless, incapable of a marriage in which the wife is the loved rather than the victim. He finds no comfort or uplift of spirits in his children. Before his own ghastly death he knows that his son is a crook (although a rich one) and his daughter a nymphomaniac married to a half homosexual, a marriage which, knowing the facts, he has encouraged. He also knows that his own second marriage has failed.

It is the measure of George's failure as a human being that this knowledge scarcely distresses him. For such a man it is impossible to feel sympathy or much of anything else except distaste. In varying degrees this applies to all the rest of the important characters in O'Hara's novel. It is his most complete descent into pessimism (it is also one of his most deeply analytical novels), his most relentless exposition of the futility of sexuality and acquisitiveness as the principal aims of life.

But the journey down into a hell fired by the consequences of loveless sexuality and pointless acquisitiveness hardly affects the reader because those resident in this particular hell do not appear to realize that indeed it is hell. But moved or not the wise reader will know that it is hell, and will be warned by John O'Hara—moralist.

Short Stories O'Hara's Forte

Harry T. Moore

John O'Hara is an exceptionally good short story writer who burns for recognition as an important novelist, which he is not. He did write one good novel—his first, "Appointment in Samarra" (1934)—but he has never since been able to master the longer form satisfactorily. He has often beefed when commentators have said this, and in prefaces of his recent novel has scolded the critics for what he considers their failure to place him correctly.

He presents his latest longer fictional effort without any comments on the side. It is a book which has many excellent passages, as all Mr. O'Hara's books do, but it doesn't add up to a novel, at least not to a very good one. The setting is that region of Eastern Pennsylvania often spoken of as the O'Hara Country, the Blue Mountains area, specifically Schuylkill County, which becomes Lantenengo County in the fiction. Mr. O'Hara's home town of Pottsville is Gibbsville in the stories; this place occurs only incidentally in the present book, whose locale is chiefly a smaller town called Swedish Haven.

In book after book, Mr. O'Hara has built up this region so that it exists as a virtual reality in readers' minds, like Faulkner's Yoknapatawpha County in that writer's fabulous version of a part of Mississippi. The main difference is that the people in Faulkner's mythical county are usually far more intense, wilder, more exciting to watch, than those in the O'Hara Country. But the latter mustn't be written off, for they are often compelling American types, especially in the shorter work.

The origins of the Lockwoods who dominate this book are rather misty, apparently beginning in early New England. The Swedish Haven family took its stamp from Moses Lockwood, who arrived there about the middle of the 19th century, where he became a law-enforcement officer known for his quick gun. He laid the foundations of the family fortune.

All this is told in flashbacks from the time of his grandson George, who is in his late prime in the 1920s. Like so many O'Hara protagonists he can balance a mistress against a wife, and he disowns the son who has been kicked out of Princeton for cheating.

From the Memphis *Commercial Appeal*, 19 December 1965, Section 5, 6. Reprinted with permission from the *Chicago Sun-Times*, © 1993.

There is no point in spoiling the story for those who read every part of everything Mr. O'Hara writes; it is enough to say that there is a shock ending that virtually seems to come out of a Gothic novel.

As one reads through the book, however, one notices the lack of growth in the people and the failure of the situations to expand into significant development. And yet one throughout admires the detail—O'Hara knows where people go, which cigarettes they prefer, which kinds of autos were in operation at a certain time, and, above all, he has a keen ear for the nuances of speech, in this book even for some Pennsylvania Dutch idiom.

In going through "The Lockwood Concern" the reader notes again and again how expertly the individual scenes are often handled. Regrettably, when laid end to end, these scenes don't make up a novel, but taken singly they show that deftness of touch, that projection of everyday realism that help make John O'Hara one of the valuable commentators upon the realm of American scenery and manners. But—let it be said this one more time—he belongs to the short story, where he shows an admirable compactness; it is there that he finds his true home.

My Turn

◆

Huff, Puff, and Growl

EDWARD WEEKS

*M*y *Turn* (Random House, $4.95) is a collection of pieces John O'Hara wrote during his employment as a weekly columnist for Harry Guggenheim's *Newsday*. What Mr. Guggenheim thought he was getting when he hired Mr. O'Hara is unknowable; what he got was an inexperienced political commentator whose proclaimed conservatism was seldom enlivened by definite proposals for action. Mr. O'Hara, a Goldwater Republican, disapproved of the Kennedys, income taxes, Mr. Johnson and Mr. Humphrey, the Roosevelts, United Nations diplomats, the Russians, the Chinese, elementary education, the war in Vietnam, and the fact that no university has yet given him an honorary degree. Since he has the fiction writer's tendency to equate opinion and emotion with fact, he never troubled to document any of his complaints.

As a result of these limitations, *My Turn* only occasionally rises above the level of vague disgruntlement. When he gets off politics and falls to reminiscing about Hollywood or denouncing fashionable authors, or damning television, or considering rich men as public servants, or dismissing prizefighting as a subject for adult discussion, he is knowledgeable, tart, and amusing. Mr. O'Hara is such an effective butcher of minor sacred cows that it seems to me a pity that he ever had to mess around with politics.

Reprinted with permission by Phoebe-Lou Weeks from *Atlantic Monthly* 217 (May 1966): 125.

Waiting for Winter

◆

The Darkness Ahead

DAVID MCDOWELL

John O'Hara is probably the most underrated of American writers. Not only is his talent a major one; he has in addition those extremely rare qualities, creative energy and fecundity. Talent isn't particularly hard to come by these days, but such a steady and almost startling productivity most certainly is.

O'Hara, now in his sixty-first year, has published some thirty-odd books, beginning with *Appointment in Samarra* in 1934, and they include at least five major novels. He has also written in the neighborhood of a thousand short stories. Since few writers in any language have worked so hard in that medium, this present collection of twenty-one new stories offers an occasion to speculate a little on O'Hara's accomplishments in it. This is by no means easy. In fact, it is exceedingly hard to pinpoint why one O'Hara story fails and another succeeds. Somewhat the same difficulty is encountered in Chekhov's stories. For a long time I had chalked that up to my being somehow occasionally out of phase with an inscrutable Russian sensibility, but my experiences in rereading O'Hara these past few years have led me to conclude that the cases are similar and that nothing mystical is involved.

The curious thing is that the stories of both writers are so clear, so well made, and, if you like, so professional that they defy any plotting on an esthetic graph. They simply succeed or they don't, for each individual reader—and few readers are in agreement about any except the very, very best.

From *Saturday Review* 49 (17 December 1966): 39–40. Reprinted by permission.

Waiting for Winter has perhaps less range than other O'Hara collections. The title is apt, as O'Hara suggests at the end of his "Author's Note." This is a dark book, full of nostalgia, aging, the end of hope, and death. In tone it is almost completely retrospective and pessimistic. There is no romance in these stories, and even where there is sex or marriage, the specter of infidelity is always in the background whether it materializes or not. And there is no wit or humor at all. O'Hara seems to look upon the process of growing old with as little enthusiasm as Yeats, and with the same compulsion to write about it.

These stories are more uneven, too, than those in the other O'Hara collections I have read. Some end so abruptly that I suspect O'Hara could no longer bear to dwell on such "downward paths to wisdom." For example, "Andrea," a long and beautifully worked out story about a twenty-year relationship between a man and woman, is marred by the absence of any specific motive for the woman's apparent suicide. In "The Pomeranian" O'Hara also develops a wonderful story only to fail to come to terms with it at the end.

But these are minor quarrels. Most writers would be happy with the kind of success O'Hara achieves in "Flight," "The General," "The Portly Gentleman," and "The Way to Majorca." In stories like these we see a completely independent writer plowing his own furrow, and in his "Gibbsville, Pa." populating a countryside as original and as recognizable as Faulkner's Yoknapatawpha County. Surely it is the fault of the literary critics that such creative accomplishments are so often patronized as being out of the mainstream of American letters.

The Instrument

♦

A Tour of O'Hara's Tinsel-Land

SHELDON GREBSTEIN

It is not always easy to distinguish the writer of durable and authentic talent from the skillful and clever entertainer. The entertainer may give greater pleasure and a more graphic sense of life, but his writing is transient. Apart from the temporary sensation and illusion of life any novel evokes, the artist bestows upon his reader the legacy of an imaginative world, a world made permanent once experienced. Such a world is John O'Hara's fictive Pennsylvania, the O'Hara country of Gibbsville and Fort Penn, created in his major novels: *Appointment in Samarra, A Rage to Live, Ten North Frederick*, as well as in dozens of memorable short stories.

This imaginative world has now endured for more than 30 years, an achievement which establishes O'Hara as an artist, although many critics would hardly agree. Unfortunately, his new novel *The Instrument* makes a far better case for those who classify him as an entertainer than for those who see him as an important contemporary American novelist.

The Instrument is a seriously defective book, among the weakest O'Hara has written, but its peculiar faults are not unprecedented. As his readers know, there is a second, minor O'Hara world, a Broadway-Hollywood world full of sexy actresses, unscrupulous producers, shrewd agents and writers in search of their craft and their souls. O'Hara has been fascinated by this microcosm

From *Washington Post Book World*, 19 November 1967, 3. © 1967, The Washington Post. Reprinted with permission.

almost from the beginning, and brought it vibrantly to life in *Pal Joey*. Still, his least successful novels, *Hope of Heaven, The Big Laugh* and now *The Instrument*, are those concerned with this tinsel world.

The protagonist of *The Instrument* is Yank Lucas, a playwright whose near-death serves as the inspiration that transforms his first play into a hit. But Yank recognizes that his success—which includes a passionate affair with the play's star—threatens his work. He escapes to a little Vermont town, unknown, to restore his depleted emotional resources and to write his next play. Eventually he returns to the world of show business, but not until he has finished a new play, and only after bitter events have violated his sanctuary.

Unfortunately, the portrayal of Yank Lucas repeats the same mistakes O'Hara has made before with Broadway-Hollywood people. He probes them to their depths—which lie just beneath the surface. Although Yank Lucas is a potentially resonant and tragic character, his inability to love arouses neither sympathy nor recognition. At best Yank Lucas functions as the vehicle for one idea: that, for the playwright, life is most meaningful as raw material for the stage. In the terms of the novel's title, the playwright is the instrument by which people are shaped into dramatic characters and thereby attain a kind of immortality.

The Instrument has other weaknesses. Its structure is shaky, its action episodic, its dialogues—those justly celebrated O'Hara dialogues—tend to degenerate into lectures and set speeches. Also missing is O'Hara's usual solidity of texture and milieu. Indeed, in no O'Hara novel of recent years is his fundamental talent less visible or his artistic grip looser.

Nevertheless, O'Hara being O'Hara, the faults don't add up to dullness. If *The Instrument* is not art, it is entertainment, better than that provided by professional literary entertainers. And it has its points: flashes of rich, bawdy humor, brisk movement, instructive insights into show business and a number of well-heated bedroom scenes.

As for those readers of O'Hara who want to see his reputation as an artist enhanced, they will not find *The Instrument* very useful to their cause.

And Other Stories

◆

[Review of *And Other Stories*]

GUY DAVENPORT

The horse, from the Bronze Age to half a century ago, reflected its owner's humanity, intelligence and wealth; its successor, the automobile, reflects wealth alone. The replacing of the horse by the automobile coincided with the irreversible point in time at which an aristocracy of money replaced an aristocracy of manners in which civilization had its source. The death of the old aristocracy was watched and recorded by Henry James; the rise and awful flourishing of the second is watched and recorded by John O'Hara, who was born the year of the first city buses and of the first neon sign.

The automobile is a focus of tautologies; its one innovation was a new excuse for idleness, all of its supposed conveniences having been an established part of civilization since the invention of the wheel; and its inconveniences—noise, claustrophobia, carbon monoxide, the corrosion of the city by parking lots, and the death of 750,000 people per year in the United States—are beginning to be absorbed nicely into the normal cycle of calamities of a world exploding into violence. Mr. O'Hara is careful to remind us in his introduction to these stories that much as he likes his Rolls-Royce, he can live without it. Henry James owned a touring car with chauffeur, but never learned to drive. Picasso never learned to drive, nor Ezra Pound, Ray Bradbury nor Harry Levin.

Mr. O'Hara's first story, "Barred," catches a teen-ager in a classic bind,

Reprinted from the *New York Times Book Review*, 24 November 1968, 5, 71. Copyright © 1968 by The New York Times Company. Reprinted by permission.

shunned by the local girls because he has punched a cop in a raid on a whorehouse, and barred from the whorehouse as a troublemaker. We scarcely notice that it was the invisible catalyst of idle mobility that slid him into his troubles. The last story acts as a coda, bidding farewell to the world of the horse and greeting the arrival of the automobile and its new manners. It is about the encounter of a technician of the old aristocracy, a stable handyman, vet and blacksmith, with a horse-fancying member of the new. The encounter comes, ironically, when the handyman is washing an automobile (an activity all but mindless compared to currying a horse) and the horse-fancier has just demonstrated that her sole knowledge of a horse is that it dines on hay and belongs to rich people. Just as horsemanship evolved various codes of behavior, the automobile has its culture. In "The Farmer," a similar encounter brings together a poor man whose life is all work and purpose and a rich girl (she has lost her horse) whose life is utterly empty.

One of the critical platitudes about John O'Hara is that he is repetitious. He is, on the contrary, one of the most varied of writers. The present collection is a cycle of 12 stories on a single theme; the illusion of repetition is in his world—he is not the first artist to choose one locale to spend a lifetime studying. Joyce and Faulkner come to mind.

Mr. O'Hara's latest novel, "The Instrument," was about, among other things, getting rich. These stories are about being rich. There seems to be a philosophical perception underlying money in Mr. O'Hara's mind: one makes money or one lives a life. The two endeavors rarely coincide. One story, "A Man on a Porch," is a dialogue between two rich men trying to understand the village clerk, who is poor, busy and indispensable to the township. He is a mystery to them. The story ends with a routine exchange of expertise about a make of automobile.

Most of these stories are about the misery of being rich; two of them are pictures of the utter squalor that money makes possible. It is not that Mr. O'Hara sees anything inherently evil in money (evil is always in men) or in its basic correlative the automobile; his sharp eyes are on the principle of mobility—money is scope, and scope is the pit into which human frailty wanders. The longest of the stories, "A Few Trips and Some Poetry," is almost a clinical study of how sheer mobility gives a woman the latitude to stir from the depths of her being a chaos which might, in a more settled age, have lain dormant. It is a masterpiece of a story, a kind of rewriting of Henry James's "The Beast in the Jungle."

The adulteries and perversions of Mr. O'Hara's story were simply not convenient to Henry James's characters. Human nature rarely changes, but its choice of moral values does. History will accept these stories, along with Mr. O'Hara's other work, as the most morally sensitive stories of our time. Their clean, strong, accurate style is a dimension of the understanding of humanity that has distinguished their author from the beginning.

Lovey Childs: A Philadelphian's Story

♦

[Review of *Lovey Childs: A Philadelphian's Story*]

Irving Howe

Eight or nine years ago, in a collection of stories called *Assembly*, John O'Hara remarked that his feelings about the writing of fiction are "practically religious." One may well believe him. O'Hara is not the kind of man to drop casual revelations about his inner life, and nothing but some deeply grounded sense of responsibility, a belief that he had been "called" to fulfill a task, could account for the prodigality with which he has kept turning out book after book. Yet even his admirers might wonder how to reconcile this remark about a "practically religious" commitment with the truculent lowbrow image he has chosen steadily to cultivate in public. Here is a novelist who loves to snarl at everything intellectual and "literary," who growls his faith in a redskin mindlessness as against the mystifications of paleface highbrows, yet in his own stolid way seems driven by the consecration to art we associate with a Flaubert or a James. In his public role as novelist-tough guy O'Hara is no doubt reenacting the dumb-ox pretensions of many earlier American writers, those who felt or pretended to feel that their brains would sap their vital creative powers. But something else, quite special to O'Hara, seems also at work here.

The psychology of the boy from the wrong side of the tracks has always

Reprinted with permission of the author from *Harper's Magazine* 240 (February 1970): 114, 116.

been a strong element in O'Hara's fiction. It is an energizing force—a kind of undeclared icy moralism being lowered upon all his characters—in O'Hara's first and best novel *Appointment in Samarra*. A youth breaking out of lace-curtain narrowness into what he regards as the style and largess of the wealthy will be inclined to notice each detail of class bias, each inflection of speech, each setting and locale as he undertakes his journey of ascent. He needs to see things with a hard precision—one mistake can wreck him—that neither the man at the bottom nor the man at the top will bother to develop. And from book to book, both O'Hara and his various surrogate figures have cultivated this knowingness in the ways of the world, this expert capacity at measuring the look and feel of external life. Yet it is a knowledge that remains an outsider's knowledge, and confined to the outside of things. O'Hara has never been truly of the rich as Edith Wharton was, and he has always reported the manners of the upper classes with a glaring overfocus, a visible nervous stress, as if unable to shake off some inner lack of ease. Despite his endless depictions of motel seduction and country-club chicanery, he has kept a kind of innocence, an innocence resting on a behaviorist mystique. In all his work there is a naïve epistemological faith in the transparency of the material, the sufficiency of fact. If only he could pile up the details of American speech, dress, appearance, and manner into a mountain of sorted debris, if only he could diagram all the hidden channels of our social arrangements, then—he seems to feel—he might finally come upon the secret of our life. He might discover the secret of all that moves us and emerge, like his master Fitzgerald, into the blazing light of meaning.

Were mimicry the soul of art, O'Hara would be our greatest master. Not many writers know as much as he about the social surfaces of American experience. He knows about *things*, he writes about them like a woman gone berserk on a shopping trip, he credits their fetishistic power. And if, as I mean to suggest, this is a source of his severe limitations, it is nevertheless closer to the realities of American experience than the assumption of those young writers who feel they need to know nothing about the external world, since by definition it is a locale of corruption.

Trusting more to measurement than inspiration, O'Hara charts with complete reliability the oscillations of power and prestige among the rival strata of our upper classes. In the stories he published about a decade ago, for instance, he began to notice that as a result of some years of postwar prosperity there was emerging in this country a new gentry or at least an ambitious upper stratum aspiring to the condition of a gentry. Its money was fresh, it had no particular family traditions to defend, it showed little concern with the substance of culture though much with the shades of cultivation, and it was determined to make for itself a style of life in which there would be a built-in principle of validation arising directly from its social pleasures. My description of this process is unavoidably abstract, but in O'Hara's fiction it acquired a good deal of vivid authenticating detail.

Surely this is the stuff out of which the novel has traditionally been made: mobility, snobbism, a clash between elite and arrivistes. No one has seen this in recent America as well as O'Hara, and no one written about it so clearly. Yet, once allowance is made for his alertness and care, the fictional result tends often to be disappointing. There is always something constricted even in his most expert social chronicles, and just how constricted becomes clear to anyone who knows the three or four best novels of Edith Wharton. She too was a portraitist of social surface, she too had close connections with the class about which she wrote; but because of a deep personal culture, she could bring to bear upon her material an enlarging standard of humane tradition and civilized reflection. This, however, is precisely what O'Hara lacks: some critical detachment from the world he depicts, some inner resource never to be confused with anything beyond itself.

"Practically religious"—that seems a good way to describe his effort at recording the totality of our customs. But it is a "religion" without a clear object of belief, and in reading O'Hara's stream of fiction one sometimes feels that he is like a man who mumbles a litany without quite grasping the significance of the words. He seems always intent upon breaking into grace— the grace of meaning and vision—through a plunge into circumstantiality. No other writer in our time has staked so much on the hope that finally the exactly recorded fact would shed its contingent dross and light up with a radiant transparency. Most of the time O'Hara has avoided direct statement in his fiction, or even a sharp arrangement of his materials that would force the reader into a certain judgment; yet he must surely have hoped that everything would "fall into place," everything take on shape and significance.

For most serious critics, I suppose, the question of John O'Hara is closed. They see him buried beneath piles of data or imprisoned in an expensive cell of complacence. But anyone with the patience to read O'Hara in bulk—no one, I fear, has the patience to read him in entirety—will discover that he is an enormously talented writer, not merely as social chronicler but also as analyst of moral disturbance. In his earlier work it is the raw sensation of class resentment that gives his work its energy; *Appointment in Samarra* remains a beautifully finished piece of work, for here, as seldom again, O'Hara is writing out of a conception adequate to his materials and his powers. A writer composing a novel needs a controlling idea: he need not be able to articulate it abstractly, he need not have it fully available when he begins to write, but it must be there, informing and shaping his book. This O'Hara had at the beginning, and occasionally toward the later part of his career. In his more recent stories there is again the glimmer of a commanding idea: some notion of the virtues of resignation, a notion of what remains in human life after all worldly and sensual energies have been spent.

Sentiments of this order seem also to motivate O'Hara's most recent book, a short novel called *Lovey Childs: A Philadelphian's Story*. The setting is Main Line; the time, the Twenties into the Depression; the characters, a familiar group of O'Hara rich, as they range from horsey mindlessness to the shrewd toughness of spirit that is the closest anyone in the book comes to intelligence. But there is a new and decidedly intriguing theme—it has appeared in some of his later stories and perhaps (though I can't say) in some of his later novels. O'Hara has become interested in sexual deviation, not as an emblem of sin or a supposed avenue to freedom but simply as a given, one of those facts marking the human condition, must be coped with, perhaps for a time enjoyed, and then subjected to the discipline of maturity. And for reasons I don't understand, O'Hara seems decidedly more interested in sexual deviation among women than among men. In *Lovey Childs* he portrays a wealthy family in which lesbianism first appears in a middle-aged matron who responds to the saucy advances of her daughter's chum during a holiday, and then in the daughter herself, Lovey Childs, who finds intense pleasure in lesbian sex, apparently more than she will ever find in the conventional kind. Later, as the time approaches to settle into family life, Lovey gains the strength to abandon her deviation, and for an adult—I think we are supposed to infer—this constitutes a serious moral act.

Lovey Childs is composed in the short novel form which has given us so many distinguished works in both European and American fiction, but despite the presence here of O'Hara's familiar gifts, it is not a very good book. The theme is interesting—O'Hara has got hold of something important, just as at the outset of his career something important had got hold of him. That civilization depends on patterns of denial neither comfortable nor "natural," that our culture is for good or bad purchased at the price of our instinctual desires, and more particularly, that the rich are allowed a measure of freedom in their personal arrangements which the rest of us neither possess nor can even fully imagine: all this lends itself to the complication of serious writing. But something has gone wrong. O'Hara's prose is flat and toneless, the characters interesting enough only to remind us of earlier O'Hara characters who were truly interesting, and the motivating idea of the book remains inert and unused. O'Hara seems to have reached that point of creative vanity— Faulkner reached it toward the end of his career—where the writer assumes that a mere filling-out of his world, the telling of what happened to a minor figure who appeared in his third novel or a social group he didn't fully portray in his seventh, is going to be of interest, quite apart from the imaginative energy he brings to it. And then there are even some moments when one feels something odd and disturbing in O'Hara's new interest: what is the nature of this pleasure he takes in describing with seeming detachment the way one woman manipulates another sexually?

It is rather troubling, perhaps an equivalent in literature to the psychic costs we pay in our later years for not having confronted problems in our youth. And still more troubling is that a writer who has always prided himself on clarity should now produce a fiction which in its fundamental suggestion seems opaque and out of control.

The Ewings

◆

[Review of *The Ewings*]

JOHN CHEEVER

O'Hara's principal giftedness, as I see it, was a passionate conviction that the writing of stories and novels was a fitting and important task for an adult and virile citizen. There is nowhere in his work any bluff, any hedging, any sleight of hand or archness. He had a prose style like a splendid baritone voice—a persuasive and perfectly pitched organ. The claim that a prose style is determined by its content does not hold for O'Hara. He could describe the most dismal conversations with more authority than some of his contemporaries could describe a storm at sea. It is the voice of a banker, a trust officer, a sometime friend, and it gives a semblance of dignity and interest to the utterly inconsequential comings and goings of an undistinguished family.

These are the Ewings—the subject of O'Hara's posthumous novel (*The Ewings*, Random House, $6.95). Cleveland is their home. The time is from Nineteen Hundred to the end of the First War. This is plainly a dying world, with its Pierce-Arrows, invitation lists, faithful servants and staid clubs. But there is not a trace of nostalgia in O'Hara's range, and he sings of an irrecapturable past without ever once flatting or shifting into the tenor. The scion of the Ewing family meets a young woman at Ann Arbor with whom he falls in love. The courtship is serene and chaste until their wedding night, when it becomes happily ardent. They calculate somewhere along the line that they have fucked seven hundred and eighteen times. They have a son and a

Reprinted with permission of the Estate of John Cheever from *Esquire* 77 (May 1972): 14.

daughter. The daughter dies of diphtheria, but this is about their only acute taste of sorrow. The tragedy of being caught in a clash of social and erotic forces falls to the hero's mother—an able, charming and intelligent woman. Her husband dies when she is fifty, leaving her sexually ardent in a society that little understands her dilemma. She brings off a handjob in a closet, a blowjob on a sofa, two studjobs in Miami, and there is a long description of her sexual engorgements with a younger woman. In the end she settles for women.

O'Hara, through the fineness of his voice, gives to these manifestly dull affairs the stateliness of a dynasty. His voice, of course, is linked to his ear, and I think no man of his time—excepting E. E. Cummings—had such a discerning grasp of the revelations in common speech. In O'Hara's earlier work, sex is a persuasive and a legitimate force, but in this, his last book, where the sexual landscapes are lusher and more mountainous, there is a mysterious element of embarrassment. One is never embarrassed by Burroughs, Miller, Mailer, Updike, etc., but when the fine baritone with the hard-finish suit sings about flagellation and fellatio, one is not shocked, but one has the feeling that perhaps the baritone was. He seems to have got the wrong music. The sexual adventures include Mrs. Ewing's sensible conversion to lesbianism, a man who was debauched by his brother, and a manly homosexual tennis star and soldier who likes to watch his friend mount his wife. There are also two suicides, the death of a child, and a hammer murder. The woman who is beaten to death is promiscuous, and could one conclude from this that the wages of sin is death, and that fornication is sin? Is there some dim and invincible stratum in O'Hara's moral nature that goes back to his Irish Catholic beginnings?

In accepting the Award of Merit Medal from the American Academy of Arts and Letters, O'Hara allied himself to Dreiser, although the most conspicuous alliance would have been to Fitzgerald. O'Hara's boardroom meetings remind one of James Gould Cozzens, although Cozzens' powers of observation are more educated and penetrating. In the same speech O'Hara spoke of his obsolescence, a conclusion that hewed closer to petulance than truth. His readers were enthusiastic and their numbers were vast. When he spoke of his likes and dislikes, one couldn't always be sure of what he meant, but he plainly detested any sort of literary compromise.

This, then, was O'Hara's vision of things, the premise of irony, generated by a ceremonial society and an improvisational erotic life. His disinterest in environment was scrupulous. No virile man will listen to the wind in the trees, and in O'Hara no one ever does. No birds sing, there is no thunder, no lightning, and very little snow. When the chairman of the board gets to his feet, we never hear the creak of his leather chair. Even the bedsprings are still, and there is not a smell in this whole creation. One misses all of this as one misses it in the company of those people O'Hara chose to describe, whose implacable indifference to anything interesting or mysterious in their environment is nearly as important as their money. But the sum of these catalogs, clinical sexual reports, board meetings, and dividend checks is like a passionate and strictly unlyrical epistle to the world in which O'Hara, rather like a lover, found himself involved. One wonders why he should have spent so much time and talent on the Ewings.

He liked them.

The Time Element and Other Stories

◆

Swizzle-Stick Tales

S. K. OBERBECK

John O'Hara was a prolific author, and he peeled off more short stories in the 1940s than there were magazines to publish them. For years, looking down his Dunhill like some suburban, tweedy Henry James, he was a master of The New Yorker short piece, that moody, peckish slice of life—sliced so thin it was almost transparent, but savory with a subtle hint of sage. The 34 stories in this collection (fourteen never before printed, fifteen from his halcyon New Yorker days) seem not so much vintage O'Hara as satisfying flashbacks of camp in which O'Hara probes with a swizzle stick into the distance between boozy, long-married (or much-divorced) couples, the cracks beneath the burnished patina of fastidious clubmen and the fragile angst behind the grinning kissers of sassy college kids.

The least of these stories are like canapés, tasty morsels in cream cheese and chutney prose—character sketches brief as the click of a speakeasy peephole in which the cutesy dialogue ("You just sit on your prat and keep your yap shut!") echoes the clunk of ice cubes in the cocktail shaker. Many of them (like "The Favor" or "The Kids") seem surprisingly overdramatic today, like portentous pastiches of Hemingway with a little Stork Club tinsel flung over the bare bones. But the old pro of "Pipe Night" and "Hellbox" strikes a perfect balance between the succinct and the superficial in stories such as "The

Skipper," "For Help and Pity," "All I've Tried to Be" and several other tales that brilliantly spotlight the jagged tips of matrimonial icebergs. The tension between insight and entertainment that O'Hara orchestrated like the slickest pulp writer comes back here with a curious sort of comfort, like slipping your dogs into Dad's old brogans and tearing off to a tail-gate party at the Yale game.

Good Samaritan and Other Stories

◆

The Bequest of John O'Hara: Exploration of a Hostile World

SHIRLEY ANN GRAU

When John O'Hara died, four years ago, he had published 17 novels and 11 volumes of short stories. He also left behind a considerable volume of finished but unpublished work, including 12 of these 14 short stories. All of them, however, were written during the 1960s, the last decade of O'Hara's life, so they are the product of a mature and possibly a weary writer. But no matter. There is no appreciable decline of powers. O'Hara remains, as always, O'Hara.

It's been almost 30 years since I read my first O'Hara. I found *Appointment in Samarra* in the high school library, read it, and was absolutely thunderstruck. I can still remember the empty feeling of amazed discovery with which I raced thru the pages. Here was a world I understood. It was more familiar than Faulkner's gothic South or Caldwell's comedic South. It was nearer my experience than the European scenes of Hemingway, with their emphasis on blood and courage. O'Hara seemed, somehow, so *real*. He was direct and honest in his treatment of disagreeable subjects. He was consistent and clear-eyed and very much his own man. And I did not like him at all. I disagreed with his basic values. I did not think his was a valid way to look at the world.

That was many years ago. In the meantime, I've read a great many more O'Hara books, but I've never really changed my evaluation. I can't like

Reprinted with permission of the author from *Chicago Tribune Book World*, 11 August 1974, 1.

O'Hara, can't agree with his point of view. But I can, and do, admire him tremendously.

He has fluency and great psychological insight—with his male characters his insights are simply breathtaking. He is incredibly adept at evoking the mood of a place, be it a town or a street or a single room. He lacks the subtle technique of a writer like, say, John Updike; he tends to overwrite, to use a club when a feather would suffice. His vision, his thinking, his feeling are quite limited, yet he has power. Because of this power he has had a prodigious effect on American writing.

Almost all the stories in *Good Samaritan* take place in the decades between World Wars. They carry with them, therefore, some of the nostalgia for the recent past, the same sort of interest that makes possible a revival of *The Great Gatsby*. In O'Hara's stories the elegant folk drive about in green locomobiles with "Westinghouse shock absorbers, twin spotlights bracketed to the windshield, and a double cowl in the tonneau." The less fortunate bounce about the wintry mountain roads this way: "The cars kept well in sight of each other, actually within the hearing range of each other's Klaxonettes." And as they skid and jolt about, they worry: "The side curtains were secure, we were not uncomfortable, but any minute we could expect the isinglass in the curtains to crack, and when that happened the wind and snow would rush in."

This is a world in which no proper gentleman appeared without a hat and no proper lady walked to her own backyard swimming pool without the protection of a robe. Young drunks popped Sen-sens into their mouths before going home to face their parents. And other young men drank lemon phosphates and queued up at the drugstore phone to call girls their parents wouldn't have approved of.

In a way, the background of an earlier time suits perfectly the leisurely narrative of most of the stories. They move slowly thru rambling conversations, stand perfectly still while characters explain themselves in page-long monologs. It's a technique seen more often in novels than in short stories. As a result these stories have a bear-like character—lumpy, shaggy, awkward, but compelling.

Most of these stories—certainly all of the really successful ones—explore a common O'Hara theme: For a man, sex and / or love is frightful trouble. A man is put to the ridiculousness of the pursuit—he must arrange dates, he must sneak into whorehouses, he must work late at the office, he must sidestep suspicious husbands. And even as he achieves his goal, he finds that it is worthless to him. Sex is unfulfilling. Love is totally uncertain. Happiness is something he can hardly remember and is not searching for anymore.

My favorite story is called "The Gentry." It's the first story in the book, and a fine introduction it is.

"The Gentry" springs from a blend of diverse influences, Ring Lardner and Sherwood Anderson, among others. The scene is O'Hara's typical small Midwest town, with its spiritual pettiness, its self-made obtuseness, its utter heartlessness. O'Hara is at his best here—controlled, firm; the echo of his mockery runs thru these pages. It is a frightful story, beautifully told.

Another extraordinary story is "A Man to Be Trusted." Here O'Hara slowly builds an elaborate mosaic of details into a fine climax. Briefly, it is the story of a young man and an older woman and the man's narrow escape from death.

There are terrible stories, too, and when O'Hara is bad, he is miserable. Take, for example, the story called "The Sun Room." A middle-aged couple from Vermont (he is a writer, she a teacher) come to visit a retired movie beauty, a woman of legendary amorousness and sexual dexterity. Years before the husband had been among her lovers. In the story the three of them sit about while the Beauty rambles on about her life and its excitement. She says things like: "I was practically a virgin, having had only one abortion." Perhaps that was shocking and daring 15 years ago, when the story was written, but today it's only silly.

The rest of the stories range somewhere between the high of "The Gentry" and the low of "The Sun Room." I remember in particular two quite successful ones: "George Munson," in which a policeman murders his nymphomaniacal sister-in-law because he himself desires her too much; and "Heather Hill," in which an English butler of only moderately cheating habits is ruined by his infatuation for an underaged hooker and an innocent man is killed by mistake.

As I read these stories, I kept thinking of George Meredith's line: "We are betrayed by what is false within." Basically O'Hara's characters do not struggle against outside forces—poverty, oppression, injustice. Those elements may be present, but they are not really important. O'Hara's characters collapse of their own weaknesses; they are nibbled to death by their own mistakes.

It is a grim world that John O'Hara has created. John Cheever, for example, writes about the same sort of people, lonely, spiritually empty, foolish and vicious by turns, locked into their own misery without the possibility of escape. But Cheever has sympathy, a great compassion for these poor lost souls, and he softens their nightmare world. O'Hara does not. In him there is no sympathy, no compassion, no love. There is only the defiantly courageous exploration of a hostile world.

Selected Letters of John O'Hara

♦

A Writer's Quest for Celebrity

WILLIAM KENNEDY

John O'Hara voted for Richard Nixon in 1960, which at first seemed to one reader to be hardcore proof that his previous seven years of sobriety, and three decades of success, had done him irreparable brain damage. But a reassessment of O'Hara's life, as seen through the words that gush all but visibly out of his mouth in this collection of wonderful letters, reveals him to be a figure permanently warped by the untimely and all-but-penurious death of his father. The family's subsequent insolvency frustrated John's social and educational ambitions, made him a bellicose, vainglorious scrambler after celebrity and other emptiness, an Irishman who would always view himself as superior to other Irishmen (including Nixon's 1960 opponent), and a compulsive writer of a high order who at times seemed to think that writing fast and fatly was as important as writing well.

Whatever his faults, O'Hara was a vital, witty maverick in 20th-century American literature, a man whose writing talent was obvious even when he was fired from the *New York Herald Tribune* in 1928 for being drunk—and city editor Stanley Walker cried at having to show him the door. O'Hara by then had already connected himself to *The New Yorker*, and became one of that magazine's most prolific contributors for the next four decades (except for the years 1949–60 when he sulked after feuding with the editors).

From *Washington Post Book World*, 20 August 1978, E1–E2. Copyright © 1978, The Washington Post. Reprinted with permission.

He is inseparable really from the history of *The New Yorker*, having almost singlehandedly set the style for its elliptical short stories of the early years. And yet we don't think of him as a permanent part of that New Yorker circle—Thurber, White, Gibbs, Benchley, Parker—even though he was; for he went on to write larger things: the novels and films and plays that made him internationally famous, a millionaire at his death, and appraised by some as the American Chekhov.

Reappraisal time is here for O'Hara, a new biography is under construction, and some critics are at work sifting the quick from the dead in his work. The odds offered from this corner are that his critical reputation will wing up from the grave now that he's not around to demand from the world what it always refuses to give to importuners.

O'Hara's own sifting of his work, as revealed in this collection of letters edited by Matthew J. Bruccoli, put his novel *From the Terrace* at the top of his preferred list. Everybody else's favorite, *Appointment in Samarra*, he placed in a favorite-but-flawed rank. He put himself on a level with Steinbeck, Hemingway and Faulkner in 1949 (giving Faulkner the edge) but few others have ever rated him so high.

O'Hara had to contend with negative visions of himself and his work all his life. One in particular rankled. Alfred Kazin called him "a social sorehead from the other side of the tracks" in 1962. O'Hara retorted publicly and also said in letters to friends that his lineage in America predated the American revolution, that his name in Ireland was one of a few that dated back to the 10th century and that his father had graduated from an Ivy League school (Penn) "when the Ivy League was known as the Big Four." He added: "I grow weary of the efforts of people like Kazin to squeeze all Irish-named people into a Studs Lonigan mold."

Instead of viewing assaults as irrelevant to the artist in him, O'Hara let them curdle his days. He wrote obsessively and vituperatively, and probably accurately, about many of the critics who punished him for his popularity and overlooked his achievements. He was vitriolic about the way they turned on Steinbeck after he won the Nobel Prize. O'Hara himself yearned desperately for the Nobel and wrote often and candidly of how many times he'd been passed over for it.

His social climbing never ended. He assuaged its fury with club memberships. Scott Fitzgerald put him up for The Brook but he was blackballed; and at the time of his death he was lobbying with insiders for membership in two English clubs, The Garrick and The Savile. His unrequited love for Yale (which he couldn't afford) was a lifelong cliché he couldn't abandon either. He preened when his daughter Wylie married a Yale man, and two years before his death in 1970 he thought of entering his newborn grandson into Yale's class of 1992, but decided this was impertinent.

O'Hara's refuge against isolation and rejection was his work, as he said over and over, which explains his compulsion but not his talent or imagination.

He wrote much that is belabored and overstuffed, but at his best there was no one who could equal him in putting the spoken language of so many varying Americans on the printed page.

In a letter to John Hersey, when Hersey's novel *White Lotus* was being panned, O'Hara explained his own record of literary Purple Hearts and pointed out to the freshly wounded Hersey that critics had destroyed James Gould Cozzens and Fitzgerald, had hurt many other writers, and that the only American writer who really escaped them was Faulkner.

"But he was made invulnerable by his genius," O'Hara wrote Hersey. "You cannot hurt a genius, even with a silver bullet."

O'Hara all but relished his own vulnerability: "To go through life as Faulkner [has], untouched, like Sunshine Biscuits, by human hands, is not my desire."

And he always touched back. He touched his enemies, his critics, he touched his editors, his publisher, he touched those who snubbed him and those he needed to snub in order to prove his own worth to his contentious and long-wounded self.

These letters form an epistolary novel which coalesces these and many other high and low truths of his life that O'Hara had put into the mouths of so many fictional people. The letters are wonderfully amusing and revealing, often shallow and oddly bumptious, deliciously vindictive, painfully wrong-headed and self-inflating, but thoroughly real and honest and intelligent in an anti-scholarly, wilfully bad-boyish way.

They are a record of a singular writer, a singular man, who tried to be aware of all his faults and almost made it. He wasn't Faulkner's equal in literature and he knew it. But he wrote better letters.

Collected Stories of John O'Hara

◆

John O'Hara at the Top of His Form

ROBERT TAYLOR

During his two decades in Princeton, N. J., John O'Hara was never once asked to read his work or talk to any of the students. His reputation had been cemented much earlier as a chronicler of surfaces, obsessed by the trivialities of brand names and the mating customs of the rich. "Hogan's knowledge of the Social Register was Koranic," S. J. Perelman wrote in a New Yorker spoof. "He could tell at a glance whether Joe Blow had prepped at Choate or St. Paul's, he was able to recite Laddie Sanford's every polo score and the name of every skipper in the Bermuda race since its inception, and he knew all the arcana of bobsledding, cotillions, and similar *goyim nachis*."

O'Hara came to accept such assessments, thinking himself a social historian faithful to realistic fiction as a vehicle for the experience of a white upper-middle-class early 20th-century American male (Eastern seaboard genus). Does he have anything to say now, however, this presumed laureate of materialism whose class distinctions appear footling in our decade of big-time greed? As Frank MacShane's splendid collection of 36 short stories demonstrates. O'Hara has more depth and variety than a majority of critics have ever suspected. He is another instance, like Mark Twain, of a demotic and hardly genteel author whose art challenges mandarin opinion. Furthermore, there is a great difference between what O'Hara assumed he was doing (preserving the history of his times) and what he actually was doing (presenting an idiosyncratic vision of

From the *Boston Sunday Globe*, 3 March 1985, A10–A11. Reprinted courtesy of the Boston Globe.

basic human drives). MacShane's epicurean choice reveals a need for the revision of a literary reputation: O'Hara is the writer of some of the indispensable short stories of the American language, and he is woefully misinterpreted.

The key to his work doesn't lie in his snobbism (he had a rebarbative personality, and his contemporaries usually reviewed him instead of his prose), but in his sensibilities as a lapsed Catholic. No one of O'Hara's talent, awareness and intellect, who has spent the formative years of his life among the rituals of the Catholic faith, abandons that faith easily, or if he does, it doesn't abandon him. O'Hara's passionate interest in country clubs, Brooks Brothers collars and Westinghouse shock absorbers can be read as the substitution of social ritual for liturgical ritual. Seldom in his short stories does he make overt reference to religion, unless you count the occasional priest who turns up, sometimes unflatteringly, but a lost faith is, nevertheless, an element absorbed into his art.

Like the fictions of Ernest Hemingway, many of O'Hara's stories concern characters coping with disorder in their lives through a kind of imposed order—attentiveness to precise detail. Instead of the rites of trout fishing, there are the rites of dandyism and status, but underneath, the same abyss stretches, the panic attendant on aging and losing control in a world without meaning. "For awhile he would just sit there and plan his own terror," ends "Over the River and Through the Woods." The sixty-ish grandfather of the story has just been called a dirty old man by one of his granddaughter's friends because he opened a door and found her nude. Through her callous and intemperate response, the girl prompts responses she could not possibly calculate, made all the more complex by his instinctive and guilty male reactions.

"In the Silence" confronts despair and nihilism directly. A newspaper reporter covering a story is put up for the night by a well-to-do couple; the husband has been traumatized by the war; the reporter is attracted by the wife, who overlooks his unstated but apprehended advances and gives the guest a present, a silver match box. "On one side was a picture of a pack of hounds baiting a bear. I think the other side was blank."

Characters major and minor, beset by nothingness, suffer a similar panic, notably an automobile salesman who, after his best sales day, goes home to his wife and sits in the dark with a 20-gauge shotgun in his lap. To be sure, the sickness unto death is merely an underlying factor: it is not O'Hara's central theme as a rule, for what he is really writing about is loneliness, human isolation and lack of connection in a world from which grace may have withdrawn. Men long-married or of considerable worldliness fall in love at first glance ("Our Friend the Sea," "The Pretty Daughters"); a married couple through their boozy infidelities tumble down the social ladder, yet find a certain sad acceptance in the promise of their son ("Imagine Kissing Pete"): a philandering husband returns to his wife on a winter night, and she realizes "more than to be free of her, he wished to be free of the other woman" ("Zero").

The stories get longer and better, on the whole, more complex and resonant, as O'Hara grows older, although "The Doctor's Son" (1935), with its autobiographical touches and its vivid picture of doctors practicing mass medicine among immigrants in the Pennsylvania anthracite country, belongs near the top. The range of O'Hara's characters and sympathies may surprise readers who consider him confined to a single class. A teeming human comedy populates his stories, proletarian female protagonists as well as male—hairdressers, bit-part actresses, telephone operators and the journalist of "Ninety Minutes Away," who wants to win acceptance in the male realm of the city room. (Newspaper writers and editors figure prominently, not the corporate types of present-day journalism but inhabitants of a seedy demi-monde, who live on due bills in hotels, skip town ahead of the law and drift from paper to paper). "Bread Alone" takes place at Yankee Stadium where the son of a black carwasher retrieves a DiMaggio home run and gives it to his father. "The Girl From California" is an ethnic comedy of manners in which a Hollywood director from Trenton brings home his moviestar wife to his bumptious Italian family, and mutual scorn, envy and celebrity-worship mingle.

Perhaps most surprising of all is O'Hara's contemporaneity. He does not, for instance, end his stories with a full stop, and this lack of closure makes the reader a participant, too. In his biography of O'Hara, MacShane points out that O'Hara's distaste for tightly plotted stories springs from his belief that life is more than a matter of cause and effect. "People die, love dies," he once said, "but life does not die, and as long as people live, stories must have life at the end." This was a disadvantage to him in writing novels, for he usually started off without knowing where he was going, and the inevitable result was a loose baggy monster indeed. But in the short story form, where his digressions are contained and the branching unexpected turns of the story reveal new dimensions of character, he was a master. O'Hara produced 11 volumes of short stories and three volumes of novellas in his lifetime, 400 works in all, and MacShane has rendered a signal service in selecting the best. Stories that have life at the end insinuate there is more than meets the eye, and, in a world bereft of grace, grace is still possible.

O'Hara's *Appointment in Samarra*: His First and Only Real Novel

JESSE BIER

It has been over a quarter of a century now since British reviewers like Peter Quennell enthusiastically received John O'Hara's *Appointment in Samarra*. It has taken the full measure of these twenty-seven years for Americans to catch up with our own. For the novel was greeted in the United States with varying degrees of reservation and regret, accorded a range of distressed reviews that went the distance from denunciation in *The Saturday Review of Literature* to mere though forceful disapproval in *The Nation*. In that initial chorus of complaint, voices like Henry Seidel Canby's, R. P. Blackmur's and John Peale Bishop's resonated about the vulgarity and pointlessness of the work. Only quite recently has the tenor of favorable criticism sounded clear, as in remarks by Norman Podhoretz and others who begin to grant, in that hyperconsciousness we have of our own epoch, the place of the novel as a modern classic, though they tend to do so by adversion to *Appointment in Samarra* while they review later O'Hara books. And so it is time, perhaps, to refocus on O'Hara's first novel all by itself.

In the period between the wars O'Hara's work is one of the few novels that rival Hemingway's *The Sun Also Rises*. At this critical distance from the Twenties and Thirties that point may be argued with relative safety. What makes the comparison less general and more useful is the further revelation, moreover, that as for Hemingway's novel so for O'Hara's: for both, World War I is an initial image and warfare a decisive background. All of which is to say that the Bagdad of O'Hara's epigraph and title from Maugham is the Western Front—the direct experience of which the hero has been spared; and the Samarra of the novel represents that quieter but equally deadly war of American social experience—to which, it turns out, Julian English is doomed primarily anyway. To make this case for O'Hara's book is also to comment on the extraordinary tightness of its naturalistic determinism. Indeed, it is the combination of subtlety and compactness, this latter stage of an almost

Jesse Bier, "O'Hara's *Appointment in Samarra*: His First and Only Real Novel," in *College English* 25 (November 1963): 135–41. Copyright 1963 by the National Council of Teachers of English. Reprinted with permission.

excruciating American economy of technical means, that marks off Hemingway and O'Hara and perhaps Fitzgerald at their best from their predecessors—and most of their successors—at *their* best.

But where Fitzgerald's *The Great Gatsby* is also a masterpiece of subtlety, we are on guard for it, so transparently allegorical as the book is, with what Lionel Trilling calls "ideographs" rather than characters. In the two best works of Hemingway and O'Hara, however, the subtlety is unexpected—and thereby more persuasive—because the action is so overt, the characterization so real, the style so natural and disarming that the allegory is quite rightly a substructure rather than a visible and distracting edifice. And so the comparison of O'Hara to Hemingway becomes more apt and exclusive the more we look at it, and it does so quite apart from what the two writers famously share as students in the upper and lower levels of the hardboiled school and quite apart from the sense of gratification O'Hara would feel at being placed, at least once, so near the prevailing genius of his times.

The Arab of Somerset Maugham's little parable flees Bagdad, where he has seen Death make a gesture at him; he flees hastily to Samarra, the city in which, indeed, Death claims him by appointment, having been merely surprised to see his victim previously at Bagdad. The Arab's situation is the same for O'Hara's protagonist, Julian English (who, we might add, continues to fascinate O'Hara himself, to judge by repetitive, even compulsive references to him in later works, like *From the Terrace* and the recent *Sermons and Soda Water*). In O'Hara's adaptation of the fable, Julian English had been too young for the Great War, getting close to his Bagdad only by virtue of his army training program at Lafayette College; O'Hara omits telling us if Death was surprised by the proximity. Probably not, for his appointments nowadays appear less skittish and personal than before—but if less exquisite, somehow more certain. In his story, O'Hara gives his hero a grandfather who has committed suicide himself and a father who is a fraudulent surgeon and a tyrannical, monstrous egotist. Placing a Cadillac agency in Julian's hands in the depression year of 1930, he mortgages his character to the up-and-coming Irishman, Reilly. In the locker room of the local country club drunken Julian English throws a drink in Reilly's face, the incident that begins both Julian's deterioration and downfall. Through worsening relations with his wife and a series of petulant reactions to accumulating circumstances, he experiences thorough alienation. When his last resource, his sexual prowess, ironically fails him—in particular, with a socialite reporter who calls at his home where he is alone—he commits suicide in his garage, characteristically rallying without effect at the very conclusion. A hereditary predilection, an overbearing family and social environment, and the baleful role of chance combine to annihilate him. But what is his significance that, with O'Hara, we are interested in, even fascinated by him?

It is Caroline English, closest of all characters to her husband, to whose consciousness O'Hara entrusts the thematic last words about Julian: "He was like someone who died in the war, some young officer in an overseas cap and a Sam Browne belt and one of those tunics that button up to the neck but you can't see the buttons, and an aviator's wings on the breast where the pocket ought to be, and polished high lace boots with a little mud on the soles, and a cigarette in one hand and his arm around an American in a French uniform. For her Julian had that gallantry." The image is unmistakable, and Julian had missed such a literal role only because he was too young, out of time. The figure is a controlling one, not merely a climactic simile; it is reinforced insistently by other pointed references to the war and to other military events. Only apparently obtrusive in technique, the "hand grenade" paragraph that begins the final chapter is inevitable in the context of the book; its implications are drawn out for us remorselessly as O'Hara emphasizes how much war is a prime symbol of chancy life in general. At almost regular intervals throughout his story, O'Hara refers to subsidiary characters, like Lute Fliegler, Julian's sales manager, who won the Croix de Guerre, or Froggy Ogden, ostensibly his best friend, who had lost an arm in combat, men who participated in the Great War. Similarly, there are pointed allusions to past military honors of Gibbesville families: Irma Fliegler's grandfather had received a Congressional Medal, an ancestor of Dr. English had fought in the Revolutionary War. The margin of Julian's past is filled with these cribbed notes of heroics, and the recent War in particular towers as a determining fact and casts its shadow as much over Gibbesville, Pa., as over Pamplona. But we come to see World War I itself, from Julian's point of view, as the glorious romantic doom he especially missed.

But if he has missed the glamour of an embattled Bagdad, he does not miss the doom of a more ambiguous Samarra—the other half of the image transferred from "Sheppy" and likewise reduced to a symbol of frequent violence, practically military in its significance. Because, for one thing, the trading center that was the legendary eastern Samarra is, in the American Gibbesville, a provincial business center permeated by racketeers. In this minor but indicative hub of American life, Julian sells fleet-wheeled Cadillacs as getaway cars to Ed Charney's gang, cops are bribed in organized fashion, "protection" is a systematic entry on one's expense account, and bootleggers are vital to a continued social life at the clubs. The malign threat of retaliatory murder for an affair Julian almost has with Charney's mistress is an oppressive potentiality. Julian's flirtations with revolvers have their own significance, too. Moreover, the hero senses that the only alternative to suicide or alcoholism for himself, as a response to the repression of life about him, is outlawry; as a matter of fact, it is his own act of trivial violence, throwing his drink at Reilly, that starts the action of the book. But more than all of these surface directions, it is O'Hara's steady picture of a fiercely competitive personal and business life that leads us more deeply into his view of the transposed, new Samarra. It is a view of an inimical and detonating American society with which, as a hostile environmental force, the hero is at subtle and continuous war.

The social stratification of the town makes for a club-minded, interlocking society, which perhaps no state in the union better exhibited than fraternity-dominated Pennsylvania. That state, either as some of us have known directly or as O'Hara has gone on to tell all the rest of us in his subsequent works, was also a model of deep social hypocrisy in those years, with its pretentions to Lutheran or any other respectability and conventionalism, its American Legion or Moose Hall alcoholism, its sexual amorality, and its sly gangsterism. What such a society does, at the most profound level, is to promote not merely deception but unreality. The closest people about us do not simply fail in loyalties, they fail in telling or even recognizing any truth.

" 'Caroline, dear!' said her mother. 'You ought not to say that till you're sure. That's a terrible thing to say.' 'Why is it? Why the hell is it? Who said so? Goddamn all of you! If he wanted to kill himself whose business is it but his own?' 'She's hysterical,' said her mother. 'Darling—' 'Ah, go away. You did it.' " In this total situation one of the final ironies for Julian is that Froggy's betrayal and one-armed punch at him is bound to be publicly misconstrued, so that "Aw," Julian simply complains in his penultimate death-agony, and he punches back furiously to foregone conclusions of general antagonism and ostracism. Julian English comes to see that the life around him is either sheer violence or sheer falsification, his society repressive, intimidating and finally prostituted—even the exclusive clubminded people are bought into by wealthy Reilly: the terms of life, such as they are, either given up or hopelessly confused. Such a view produces the only reaction it can in a character who is compelled by vitality into a violent, doomed revolt.

But crucial and even thematic as the environmental factor is in this book, it is only one of the three fateful forces of naturalistic determinism. The other two are not neglected, for O'Hara has Julian caught by circumstance and heredity as well.

When, at the last, Julian seeks to save himself by the only possible means for him of self-vindication, his sexual conquest, and fails with the visiting socialite reporter, he is truly finished. It is for this structural reason that O'Hara includes the controversial episode: Julian's irrepressive sexuality is a sign not of his vulgarity, but vitality, and when it is circumstantially thwarted in his supreme crisis—his wife having left him now—he has turned the last corner of the last street of his Samarra.

The role of chance or circumstance permeates the whole book, however, not just the last section. Julian and his friends are in Reilly's debt, especially difficult in 1930. There is an unbroken chain of events from the initial Reilly incident through Caroline's frustrated anger with Julian to Julian's attempted consolation with the gangster's mistress, producing Caroline's further anger, and so on to the end. That the *parvenu* Harry Reilly is a Catholic is purely accidental as far as Julian is concerned, though, of course, it is not to the local

Irish and Polish who are rising in the community. The succession of incidents
in the novel creates a veritable conspiracy of circumstance, even figured for us
at one point a trifle obviously: "Yes, there was one other good break this
morning; he had not been given a ticket for parking. At that moment a cross-
link in the tire chains broke." Even where a "link" snaps in the chain of events,
it does so to his disadvantage. When we add to these large and petty incidents
the simple biographical fact that Julian is not only too young to have been in
the Great War but is, in fact, younger than his wife or "out of time" with her,
his victimization by circumstance or chance is almost complete. What does
effectually close this second ring about him is the body of detail O'Hara
manages to give us about Julian's early upbringing and continuously hypocritical relations with his parents, with his "phony" surgeon of a father in particular.
The predetermining iron circle of a loveless existence—Julian basically unloved
by his parents, later rejected by his wife, denied by his friends, and pressured
by his community—is insupportable.

In the tradition, O'Hara treats the hereditary influence also. Through
social-financial indiscretion similar to his own, Julian's grandfather had committed suicide, as Julian ultimately does. There is, all told, a family incompe-
tence, for Julian's self-righteous father, almost melodramatically egocentric, is
a dismal if avid surgeon. But these details may be tricks. What is more to the
point, at a deeper level, is that Julian is predetermined to the trap of repression
and alienation by the very fact of temperament, his youthful vitality a curse
or final doom rather than a blessing. "But this time Caroline knew she would
not have come back this afternoon, and he had known it, and God help us all
but he was right. It was *time* for him to die." The inherited sex drive is
dominant in the book and notorious in O'Hara's work—his particular hallmark
in American realism. In this book, at least, it does not exist for its own sake.
Its bearing on the concluding incident with the socialite reporter I have spoken
of. What needs to be added is only to remark Julian's consistent motivations
of sexual jealousy, for he is after all in love with his wife, who is his last hope.
"So, Julian thought and thought about Caroline and Harry, and thought
against them, against their being drawn to each other sexually, which was the
big thing that mattered. And immediately began the worst fear he had ever
known." In this regard, all due credit must be granted O'Hara's careful though
light Freudian preparation for the marriage of Julian and Caroline: the primacy
of their childhood experiences together, and therefore the greater impact of
Caroline's ultimate rejection of her husband.

Julian English, then, by the traditional but unprogrammatic combination
of environmental, circumstantial, and hereditary factors, is fated to both
frustration and reckless explosion. He runs out his life—peevishly and fittingly
suffocated by carbon-monoxide—in the Great War of American living, fated
to a type of retarded adolescence and then death rather than to independent,
vital American manhood.

For with it all, the hero is a type of coward in his private war; however difficult the odds, he deserts. Thankfully, O'Hara does not portray Julian purely as a cut-and-dried victim of his society, but gives us a comprehensive picture of perennial boyishness—though Julian's society does not help him grow. Without this approach, indeed, the book would be disastrously doctrinaire and superficial. Ironically, what redeems Julian English for us as a character rather than a mere victim is his deepest weakness.

He is boyishly irresponsible, not only in action but in measuring consequences. He is irresponsible especially with Reilly's $10,000 loan, not husbanding it. He is child-like before marital upbraiding, the older Caroline a partial mother to him; he is often overborne by her high maternal manner and orderliness in general, impersonal as she is then. Boyishly, like many of Hemingway's fundamentally adolescent heroes, he desires a blindly loving woman. He has a child's impulse toward the older Irma Fliegler, wife of his employee now but former babysitting nurse. He retains, we can see closely, a boy's fear of his father yet. His very terms of thinking, against his Pennsylvania Dutch secretary and her milieu, are boylike: "Somehow her tone filled him with terror, the kind that he felt when he knew he was doing something bad." In a crisis, he reverts to boyhood memories almost automatically. Under moral pressure, he drives his car all over the highway, boyishly owning the road. Afflicted with the despair of life, his reaction can be tormentingly adolescent: "He put some cream in the coffee and lit a cigarette. 'I'd be all right if I could just stay here,' he thought. 'If I could just stay here the rest of my life.'" His alcoholism is clearly escapist, as is his increasing and compulsive desire for sleep. Once or twice he weeps immaturely in self-pity. Though he loves Caroline, we discover that he had previously loved a local Polish girl and was too cowardly to marry below his station. His whole life turns out to be a virtual career of ineffectuality, and this characterization of him O'Hara reinforces by having Julian fail to rally in his car, as he paradoxically wants to at the last minute, within the poisoned garage.

So that, in a real measure, Julian defeats himself. There is even a case for supposing that Reilly might have come to forgive him and that, in all, Julian overreads his total social rejection, as he does overindulge his jealousy for his faithful wife. A great deal comes from *within* the character, a quality which saves the work from the much published early charges of simple behaviorism.

Still, life in America between the hot wars and the cold wars scarcely insures the domestic tranquility of its people; instead, it does make it improbable, perhaps impossible, for Americans either to transcend or fulfill themselves, to grow. So that we are left, in a book characteristically replete with irony, with the erstwhile fiances of Julian and Caroline, Mary Manners and Ross Campbell, who meet later in New York. They each might have been better for Julian and Caroline, but they are good no longer; for O'Hara pretty forcefully—and maybe forcedly—implies that Mary is a callgirl and Campbell is working for Ed Charney's connections in New York. Therefore, these two are also no longer what they were or promised to be, having at last capitulated to their most mortal enemies respectively, and even entered into collaboration. And meanwhile over the whole story plays the ruling irony of the Christmas-time setting, of "goodwill to all men," save that there is no real armistice, seasonal or otherwise, in this subtle but internecine social war.

Only Lute Fliegler is, in our present critical terminology, a "norm": frank, simple, bantering, comfortably married, honest and, above all, undefeatist. "Aw, what the hell. We'll get by. Don't take it to heart too much . . . it'll work out one way or another. Shake?" Unpretentious, he is mature and he endures. But out of the gallery of characters in the book, he is the only favored one, an uncentral character who in his exceptionality is a foil for the rest of his society, not a hope.

What really hurts is that the humor in the book—for there is considerable humor—is not protective for a character like Julian. That counts heavily in an open-ended book and view, where comedy now intensifies rather than rescues or relieves the American tragedy. There are big and little jokes taking place in the novel, but there is nothing saving, cute even or finally hilarious in twentieth-century American experience: neither in the periodic Bagdads of world conflicts or the continuing Samarras of dead-level or eruptive American life in-between.

All that has been necessary is for American criticism to catch up with the book. And that is being done these recent years, as when Mr. Podhoretz refers to it in *Commentary* as a kind of "classic of our time."[1] Our remaining doubt has to do only with how fundamentally loaded the book is and that, too, the British reviewer had measured with uncanny accuracy. For Mr. Quennel had called attention in *The New Statesman and Nation* to the piled and disastrous conclusion O'Hara provided, and he had validated it. He could recognize at the time, though with the perspective of distance, that Americans were "a romantic and pessimistic race" actually, "not without a streak of the pre-war Russian" and with the same ticklish equilibrium; he thought O'Hara did full justice to "the romanticism and sentimentality of the American temperament" and found the whole charged story appropriately tragic and real.[2]

Indeed, O'Hara's insight into the doomed weakness and cheapness of a great part of the American experience may very well have frightened the earlier critics from getting O'Hara's deepest point; possibly harrowed, they had no alternative but to call the work vulgar and pointless. I risk condescension to think so, but I begin to believe that they could take the point of Hemingway's *The Sun Also Rises* because there were foreigners involved in *that* story and the setting was at least one long remove from native shores, not too close to bear.

And so O'Hara's book floats back into our ken, after a quarter of a century. Its tightness and economy, its precision of speech and characterization, its subtle thematic use of war, all place it with Hemingway's novel as exposés of a lost, expatriate generation abroad and of an unfound or skipped generation at home. In his first and only important work O'Hara seemed bent on examining that collaboration between predetermining forces and a virtual principle of weak American character which conspired against adulthood. This was the profundity toward which he was headed early—and from which, apparently, he saved himself later by writing his tawdry and mere romances of sexology. What is most telling of all in *Appointment in Samarra* is how convincing such a naturalistic determinist approach to American life continues to be. How much of that impact we may attribute to a static America or how much to O'Hara's first and only novel—he may not forgive us for calling it art—is a question.

Notes

1. Podhoretz, Norman, "On the Horizon: Gibbesville and The New Leeds," *Commentary*, 21 (March 1956), 269.
2. Quennell, Peter, "New Novels," *The New Statesman and Nation*, 8 (December 29, 1934), 972.

Appointment with the Dentist: O'Hara's Naturalistic Novel

Scott Donaldson

Appointment in Samarra, John O'Hara's first and best novel, achieved an immediate popular success in the depression year of 1934, but the critics were less enthusiastic in their response. R. P. Blackmur, for example, argued that the book's hero, Julian English, had no adequate justification for committing suicide; his death was morally pointless.[1] Henry Seidel Canby was disturbed by the "thoroughgoing vulgarity" of the novel; the characters had "no values" and writing about them, no matter how well, was "only craftsmanship."[2] Similarly, another reviewer concluded that the book amounted to a "a skillful bit of writing about perfectly worthless people."[3] Each of these readings suggests the frustrated moralist waiting in vain for useful generalizations about the shallowness of Gibbsville society; in vain, because O'Hara is too good a naturalist to let the didactic compromise the descriptive.

The reviews also reveal the kind of frustration suffered when reading mystery stories with loose ends. Where is the motive for this self-murder? Why does Julian English take his own life? This frustration, however, can be relieved. O'Hara supplies the answer through action and dialogue, not through intrusive commentary. Julian English's death is made inevitable by the kind of world he lives in *and* its psychological effect upon him. As O'Hara wrote of the novel, "what I really mean when I say it's true is that the psychological patterns were real."[4]

The title, of course, reinforces the idea of inevitability. According to the legend, a servant encounters the figure of Death in the marketplace at Bagdad, and flies in panic to Samarra. Death then meets the servant's master and explains how surprised he was to see the servant in Bagdad, since he had an appointment with him that evening in Samarra. The application of this legend to Gibbsville, Pennsylvania, O'Hara's home stamping grounds, begins on Christmas eve, 1930, when Julian English, 30, old-family, handsome, married to the beautiful Caroline, throws a drink in the face of Harry Reilly, an up-and-coming Irishman who has lent Julian $20,000 for his Cadillac agency.

Reprinted with permission from *Modern Fiction Studies* 14 (Winter 1968–69): 435–42. Copyright 1968 by Purdue Research Foundation, West Lafayette, Indiana 47907.

This seemingly trivial incident leads in the next two days to a chain reaction of socially unacceptable behavior, including an overt public attempt to seduce the mistress of the local bootlegger, a fight with another old-family type who's lost an arm in the war, and a private and unsuccessful crack at seducing the Gibbsville *Standard's* society columnist. Then, his marriage and business on the rocks, Julian gets roaring drunk, turns on his Cadillac's motor with the garage doors locked, and climbs inside to die. Throughout, O'Hara alternates straightforward development of the plot with flashbacks into the family history and youth not only of Julian English but of several others, including some minor characters. Blackmur objected to this "segmentary" attention to the background of such minor characters as Irma Fliegler and Al Grecco; although interesting in themselves, he maintained that "as agents of this novel they are incredibly wasteful and meretricious."[5]

These characters actually perform a critical function, however: they help to define the importance of social class in Gibbsville, an importance which is immediately and powerfully evoked in the first chapter of the book. *Appointment in Samarra* begins in the bedroom of Luther and Irma Fliegler, a middle-class couple (he works for Julian's auto company) who are admirably adjusted to each other, sexually. They are happier than any other married people in the novel, but there is a worm even in this apple, as we discover when O'Hara takes us inside the mind of Irma Fliegler. Irma is old family too, and pleased to be living on Lantenengo Street, where she knows she belongs, but not so pleased at having the Brombergs for neighbors, because the Brombergs definitely do not belong and might be followed by "a whole colony of Jews." The Flieglers do not yet belong to the Lantenengo Country Club, but may join next year, she reflects. Irma is proper, stuffy, and fond of euphemisms, the very model of an upwardly mobile middle class wife.[6]

The first chapter ends with the bootlegger's assistant, Al Grecco, driving into town with a carload of liquor for the party which Julian and Caroline English have scheduled for the day after Christmas. It is a working day for Al, who on remembering it is Christmas opens the windows of the car and hollers at the darkened homes of Lantenengo Street: "Merry Christmas, you stuck-up bastards! Merry Christmas from Al Grecco!" (20). Al Grecco, Italian-American, ex-fighter and ex-con, is making good money, but he's never going to make it to Lantenengo Street, much less to the Lantenengo Country Club, still less to the smoking room of the L. C. C., still less to the Gibbsville Club, and least of all to the board of the Gibbsville Assembly. Al considers himself superior to Jews, but his status is underlined when Mrs. Grady, Julian's cook, calls him a "dago wop" (146).

In the first chapter, then, O'Hara carefully constructs a ladder of social position in Gibbsville, and places Julian English at the top of the ladder. English is introduced, in the middle section of the chapter, as he is partying in the smoking room of the country club among some twenty others who are the spenders, drinkers, and socially secure. His social position seems unassailable, but one of the things O'Hara is saying in this book is that such a position, however solid it may seem, is necessarily precarious and depends on adherence to certain unwritten but nonetheless inviolable rules of behavior. Julian has done nothing in particular to deserve his status; it is the joint product of his and his wife's family background. As a consequence, he is constantly trying to prove himself, to deserve the social superiority conferred upon him. He sets out to prove his worth in those activities where he excels: as a drinker, as a clubman, and above all as a lover. Ironically, these attempts to prove his superiority lead to his social downfall—for Julian, a fate worse than death.

Julian throws the drink at Harry Reilly partly because he is drunk, but still more because Harry Reilly is the kind of story-telling Irishman who signals the end of a story by slapping his knee and roaring at his own punch line. Reilly's presence in the inner circle of the smoking room crowd, though not yet of the Gibbsville Assembly, represents a kind of challenge to Julian's pre-eminent social position. "Reilly had gone pretty far in his social climbing" (12), Julian reflects before the incident; afterwards, when Caroline and others chide him for his action, he feels that most of them "would agree that Reilly was a terrible person, a climber, a nouveau riche in Gibbsville where fifty thousand dollars was a sizable fortune" (71). Still later, beginning to understand his motivation for throwing the drink, Julian recalls that it was Harry's ubiquity, his constant presence in those situations reserved for the best of Gibbsville society, that annoyed him: "You went to the Gibbsville Club for lunch; Harry was there. You went to the country club to play squash on Whit Hofman's private court, and Harry was around. You went to the Saturday night drinking parties, and there was Harry! inescapable, everywhere. Carter Davis was there, too, and so was Whit; so was Froggy Ogden. But they were different. The bad new never had worn off Harry Reilly" (148). What right had Harry Reilly, "bad new" and Irish to boot, to associate with the good old families?

Even more than Irma Fliegler, who longs for the day she will join the country club, and Al Grecco, who takes the outcast's revenge by accumulating money, Julian English's actions are dictated by his social position—and the way he feels about it. *Appointment in Samarra* is a naturalistic novel in several ways. There is the lavish attention to surface details, the breaking of the Howellsian taboo against sex, and the physical violence associated with naturalism. Most conspicuously of all, because it is spelled out in the epigraph and title, there is the theme of determinism. Heredity is hinted at as a possible explanation for Julian's suicide; his grandfather, after embezzling some money, had taken his own life, and Julian's father, a basically incompetent and over-enthusiastic surgeon, privately attributes his son's demise to the bad seed having skipped a generation. But if hereditary influences have in fact contributed to Julian's tragic end, O'Hara implicitly argues, these influences have stemmed from the stern and unloving figure of Dr. Billy English, not from grandfather. In any case, it is not heredity but the social environment—the "rigidity of social class lines," as one critic puts it—which acts as the most powerful deterministic agent.[7] It is difficult to climb up the status ladder (although Harry Reilly is making the climb, and so, less sensationally, are the Flieglers); one must climb carefully, one rung at a time. Having reached the top rung, it is still more difficult to maintain one's position, especially since others are jostling the ladder. When you lose your place, you are liable to slip all the way to the bottom.

Julian English is terribly jealous of his place on the ladder, willing to share it with only a few others, and eager to demonstrate his right to pre-eminence. In short, he is a howling snob. His very name underlines his status. The surname is English, WASP. The middle name is McHenry, and he likes his monograms to read J. McH. E., a fact that only Caroline knows. The elegant given name contracts, in the speech of his wife and close friends, to "Ju," and he is most uncomfortable when someone who does not know him really well, such as the dentist Ted Newton, uses this nickname (13). The reason is transparently clear; Jews are barred from the higher status levels of Gibbsville, just as they are barred from membership at the Lantenengo Country Club. Julian functions as a self-appointed gatekeeper for all his clubs; whenever he is challenged, he responds by bringing up the question of membership. Bobby Herrmann undertakes the job of kidding Julian about the drink-throwing episode, and Julian retaliates weakly with the membership gambit: "Who is this man? Did he come here with a member?" (61). Later, when he is brutally criticized at the Gibbsville Club by Froggy Ogden, who has the distinction of having fought and lost an arm in the war, Julian tries to avoid fisticuffs until a Polish lawyer intervenes on Froggy's behalf. Once again, Julian's immediate response is to ask whether the lawyer is "by any chance a member of this club" (153). The question is only seemingly irrelevant; if lawyers named Luck, or "Lukashinsky, if I know anything," are allowed to join the Gibbsville Club, Julian's pride in the exclusivity of his status is wounded. He'd be a hard man on the membership committee.

Similarly, Julian English behaves very badly indeed at the first hint of any presumption on the part of the hired help. He is a regular guy to the gangster Ed Charney, who regards "the English" as "copacetic" (16). Ed is a source of liquor supply, and a Cadillac customer as well. But Al Grecco, who works for Ed, is another matter, as Julian drunkenly makes clear: "Just call me Mr. English, Al. You call me Mr. English and I'll call you Al. The hell with this formality. We've known each other all our lives" (113). The next morning, hung over, he argues with Mrs. Grady, the cook, because he is annoyed by her contemptuous manner: "There it was again: servants, cops, waiters in restaurants, ushers in theaters—he could hate them more than persons who threatened him with real harm. He hated himself for his outbursts against them, but why in the name of God, when they had so little to do, couldn't they do it right and move on out of his life?" (128).

Such attitudes reveal a deep-seated, basic insecurity; so do Julian's dealings with Lute Fliegler and Mary Klein, his best salesman and secretary at the Gibbsville-Cadillac Motor Car Company. Lute quite cogently and dispassionately spells out for his boss the probable consequences of the drink-throwing incident (they'll lose a sale or two they can ill afford to lose to the Buick dealer), and Julian listens without rancor. Although a Pennsylvania Dutchman, Lute Fliegler is, for Julian, "one of the swellest guys that ever lived." He has a theory to explain that anomaly, however; maybe "Lute's mother had had a quick one with an Irishman or a Scotsman." Mary Klein is Pennsylvania Dutch too, plain, solid, respectable, Lutheran middle class Pennsylvania Dutch. Though she is Julian's employee, she also plays another role by giving her boss the kind of approval he requires. Thus Julian comes to the office with his hangover and jots down some figures on a pad, looking very busy and hoping "he was making a good impression on Mary Klein" (141).

The pattern that emerges is that of a desperately insecure man, trying to live up to a social position he knows he has not earned. Julian can stand only so much rejection by others, since he knows such rejection will mean loss of his social status. One way he has always been able to satisfy the idea of himself as a superior person (an idea which society imposes on him and he unquestioningly accepts) is through the conquest of women. Even as a young boy he had been able to "get away with murder" where women were concerned. Irma Fliegler, who taught him in Sunday School, never reported him when he sneaked out to go to the ball game instead. Irma, he realizes, would make the ideal confidant as his troubles multiply; Julian wishes he could tell her all, but she is also the wife of one of his employees and he "must not forget that" (131). Mary Manners, a beautiful Polish girl, fell in love with Julian and did whatever he asked her to do. Snobbishly, the one thing he could not ask her to do was to marry him. There were others, too; Julian had either had an affair, or been on the brink of an affair, with almost every female member of the country club crowd. In most of these relationships, Julian placed himself in the role of the bad boy who misbehaves *in order to* be forgiven. (In boyhood, he had stolen a flashlight at the dime store: his father, sensitive to family history, concluded that Julian was a thief and never forgave him.) Thus when Caroline goes to bed with him on Christmas afternoon, the act represents for Julian a form of forgiveness for throwing the drink at Harry Reilly. When, later that night, she declines to meet him at the car for another sexual engagement, Julian immaturely decides to be as bad as possible: it is then that he gets roaring drunk and takes Ed Charney's mistress out to the car in her stead.

When Caroline breaks their midnight date in the car, Julian's uneasy accommodation to Gibbsville society starts to come apart at the seams. Harry Reilly won't talk to him or accept his apology. Froggy Ogden reveals that he had never liked him, partly because of his success with the Polish girl and with Caroline. The news takes him back to childhood, to horrible Saturday mornings at the dentist's, when the rest of the kids were playing but he had to face something painful (152). Still greater pain lies in store when he returns from the fight at the Gibbsville Club and discovers that Caroline will no longer take his side without question. Julian does not tell her the details of his get-together with "Captain Ogden, the war hero," but he does make an appeal: "This is a pretty good time for you to stick by me. . . . Blind, without knowing, you could stick by me. That's what you'd do if you were a real wife, but, what the hell" (165).

The final blow comes when the society columnist, Alice Cartwright, refuses his attentions. Julian attempts to seduce her in his own home, when she comes calling to check on the guest list for the party Caroline has called off. Miss Cartwright, who is no beauty and no virgin, admits to a yen for Julian, but turns him down because he's "married to a swell girl." He foresees one rejection after another—"all the pretty girls in Gibbsville, trying to make him believe they all loved Caroline." He also envisions his own precipitous plunge down the status ladder in attempts to assert the sexual superiority that is slipping away with his youth:

> Thirty years old. "She's only twenty, and he's thirty. She's only twenty-two, and he's thirty." She's only eighteen, and he's thirty and been married once, you know. You wouldn't call him young. He's at least thirty. No, let's not have him. He's one of the older guys. Wish Julian English would act his age. He's always cutting in. His own crowd won't have him. I should think he'd resign from the club. Listen, if you don't tell him you want him to stop dancing with you, then I will. No thanks, Julian, I'd rather walk. No thanks, Mr. English, I haven't much farther to go. Listen, English, I want you to get this straight. Julian, I've been a friend of your family's for a good many years. Julian, I wish you wouldn't call me so much. My father gets furious. You better leave me out at the corner, becuss if my old man. Listen, you, leave my sister alone. Oh, hello, sweetie, you want to wait for Ann she's busy now be down a little while. (177–178)

Only after he traces out this depressing future does Julian decide to get really drunk for the last time and to take his life. His cigarette burns the phonograph and he considers a lie (Julian has always lied, fixed tickets, sought the easy way out) to explain the burn before realizing, for the first time, that "it would not make any difference." The burn will not matter when he is dead (179).

Why does Julian English kill himself? After the fight at the Gibbsville Club, he drove out of town to escape, but "something . . . pulled him back. You did not really get away from whatever it was he was going back to, and whatever it was, he had to face it" (156). The something which pulls him back to disaster is not an incomprehensible and foreordained fate. Julian is controlled by the interaction between society and himself. Society has given him a certain elevated stature. He wants to live up to this position, which has been imposed upon him by the accident of birth. But he also feels guilty because he has done nothing to earn his place on the status ladder, and insecure because others are climbing up to threaten his position. Rudeness to the lower classes serves to reinforce his pride of place, and sexual prowess provides him with a pleasing sense of control over others, but he still remains insecure. When the servants start talking back and when his sexual powers begin to flag, he realizes that society has decided against him. Julian's tragedy is that he accepts society's judgment as both inevitable and final. Society's standards are his own; rejected by others, he rejects his own existence rather than take the slide down the status ladder. Caroline, who had always loved him but comes to understand him only in death, concludes that "God help us all but he was right. It was *time* for him to die" (188). All that remained for him was one horrible endless Saturday morning in the dentist's chair.

Notes

1. R. P. Blackmur, "A Morality of Pointlessness," *Nation*, CXXXIX (August 22, 1934), 220.

2. Henry Seidel Canby, "Mr. O'Hara and the Vulgar School," *Saturday Review of Literature*, XI (August 18, 1934), 55.

3. Herschel Brickell, New York *Post* (August 18, 1934), 34.

4. John O'Hara, *Appointment in Samarra* (New York, 1953), foreword.

5. Blackmur, 220.

6. John O'Hara, *Appointment in Samarra* (New York, 1945), pp. 6–8. Subsequent page references within the text are to this edition.

7. Russell Carson, *The Fiction of John O'Hara* (Pittsburgh, 1961), p. 3.

Naturalism Revisited: The Case of John O'Hara

CHARLES W. BASSETT

Death, in April, 1970, seems to have slowed the appearance of the fiction of John O'Hara only slightly. Readers worldwide, accustomed to the annual O'Hara book, have been obliged by Random House, long O'Hara's publisher, with three posthumous works: *The Ewings* (1972), a novel; *The Time Element and Other Stories* (1973) and *Good Samaritan and Other Stories* (1974), collections of short fiction. O'Hara's editor, Albert Erskine, estimates that the author wrote a short story every month for the last ten years of his life; still another volume of stories is forthcoming.[1]

Moreover, interest in O'Hara the man and writer has spawned two biographies since 1970: the first, *O'Hara*, by Finis Farr, got a lukewarm reception in 1973; the definitive biography, *The O'Hara Concern*, by Professor Matthew Bruccoli, is due in October, 1975, too late to be considered here. Bruccoli, however, has lauded O'Hara's work in the past, and it is known that *The O'Hara Concern* makes the case for ranking John O'Hara among the major writers of American fiction.

Bruccoli's enthusiasm notwithstanding, reactions to O'Hara's posthumous fiction vary little from the general critical consensus of the '50's and '60's.[2] The preponderance of reviews (O'Hara once put it at 90%) had always featured phrases like these: "the limitations of phony naturalism . . . I stopped reading naturalism some years ago . . . no depths, no subtleties . . . he mistakes facts for truth, statistics for reality." This litany is continued by Anatole Broyard, a *New York Times* reviewer, in a recent appraisal of *The Time Element and Other Stories*: "O'Hara's people . . . don't have emotions; they have some sort of Pavlovian reflexes invented by the author."[3]

This annual set-to between critics and audience, traditional since the appearance of *A Rage to Live* (1949), became in time a kind of ritual: critics deplored and readers bought O'Hara's books religiously. In point of fact, everyone knew that O'Hara's work would not change, that his audience would continue to read him respectfully, and that the critics—aesthetic sensibilities assuaged—had done nothing to disturb a relationship that was one of the most profitable and enduring in recent American literary history.

Reprinted with permission from *Colby Library Quarterly*, 11 (December 1975): 198–218.

For John O'Hara was an enormously popular writer, perhaps the most popular *serious* writer of his time. Even O'Hara's most virulent critics (Gore Vidal, John W. Aldridge) refused to rank him with Spillane and Fleming; no one called him a hack, ever. Readers loved his stubborn sensibility, his plain style, his scorn for fictive actions consciously mirroring archetypal patterns. Indeed, the fiction of John O'Hara stands as probably the most obvious contradiction to those critical analyses which declare old fashioned and psychologically unacceptable the methods and insights of literary naturalism.

And it is true that even O'Hara himself seemed to have become an Establishment. During the ten years before his death, he became a vocal exponent of political, social and literary conservatism. In the '60's, his newspaper columns, "My Turn" (later collected in a book with the same title), anathematized radical long-hairs and boosted de Gaulle, Goldwater, and the Policeman's Benevolent Association. By then, his fiction had made him an authentic millionaire, wealthier after each sale to Hollywood or to the paperback reprinters. Living regally with his third wife (a Whitney cousin) at "Linebrook" in Princeton or on the beach at Quogue, O'Hara had no time for "fads."

"When you pass sixty," he told his last interviewer in 1969, "you just naturally become conservative. It's a lot easier to be conservative . . . You can't concern yourself with all the problems of the world. My concern right now is right here, writing."[4] As a young man, O'Hara had considered his writing a "form of protest" and himself "in rebellion." But his most rigorous battles had occurred when censors attempted to ban his or others' books for frank depictions of human sexuality. Comparing himself to Dreiser, he asserted: "At least *some* of the liberties that younger writers enjoy today were paid for by me, in vilification of my work and personal character."[5]

At the same time, O'Hara scorned young writers, who "haven't learned their business" and "lack intimate knowledge of people." His juniors took the easy way, he told the *New York Times*, "without putting in an apprenticeship of observation and diverse writing. . . ."[6] O'Hara had earned his own way (no "God damn foundations" had supported him while he wrote) by battering away at his craft until the public was forced to pay attention. Self-discipline and dedication had won him his place in the world.

It was not easy becoming an author of stature, a dream that O'Hara had pursued unswervingly for years. He felt that his talent was "God-given" and that he owed devotion to it. "The way I feel about writing, which is practically a religious feeling, would not permit me to 'dash off' a story."[7] As early as age 20, he had told readers of his hometown newspaper that he intended to write The Great American Novel.[8]

Irving Howe once pointed out the contradiction between the religiously dedicated author and the relentless low-brow whose literary opinions were those of an authentic redskin. O'Hara's aesthetic judgments added little to his stature as a thinker. Samples: "For stubborn cases of insomnia, following days when rain has kept me off the golf course, almost any volume of verse will do the trick."[9] On Shakespeare: "So I didn't like *Twelfth Night*. So more than that I am always bored by Shakespeare's plays. What is more, I don't even admit that they're good to read (that is, all the way through)."[10] On love: "I don't take love or oxygen for granted, but I'll bet you that if I'd praised love publicly more than I have, people would not think that all I approve of is fucking. . . . Statements on Love and Man, delivered in tones and terms that perish the thought of fucking and pederasty, automatically put the speaker among the majority of gentlemen who attended the Last Supper. . . ."[11]

Despite these literary gaucheries, Howe concludes that "in his own stolid way [O'Hara] seems driven to the consecration to art we associate with a Flaubert or a James . . . diagramming all the hidden channels of our social arrangements."[12] On a less grandiose scale, O'Hara defended himself this way: "Being a cheap, ordinary guy, I have an instinct for the ordinary guy's taste."[13]

As an Ordinary Guy, O'Hara knew that his readers would not be impressed by spurious high culture. Neither great novelists of the past nor touted contemporary experimentalists impressed him much. "I should admit," O'Hara once told an audience at the Library of Congress, "or confess, or simply state that there is probably no one in this room who is more than thirty years old, who has not read more novels than I have."[14] Determinedly his own man, he claimed: "For more than two years I have not read any current fiction . . . because I have been at work on my own novel. The reason is not only that I have wanted to avoid being influenced, however slightly or subtly, but because I am an extremely slow reader of fiction. . . ."[15] The theme became obsessive: "I'm not some hairy philosopher. I'm just an ordinary guy who happens to write well."[16]

On the other hand, Ordinary Guys rarely publish thirteen novels, five novellas, fourteen collections of stories, six plays, and two books of essays. Ordinary Guys do not ordinarily work for *Time*, write football for *The New Yorker*, do a column for *Newsweek* and *Newsday*, or contribute pieces to such disparate journals as *The New Republic* and *Ringling Bros. & Barnum & Bailey Circus Magazine & Program*. Never has a truly Ordinary Guy been awarded the Medal of Merit for the Novel by the American Academy of Arts and Letters.

O'Hara disaffiliated himself from the rest of the Ordinary Guys by styling himself a "pro," a lonely and embattled toiler whose life was his craft. "If you're a pro you keep going; if you're not a pro, you get the hell out." A pro is sustained by "sensitivity, alertness, active intelligence, and work."[17] The Puritan ethic burned in the lapsed Roman Catholic from Pottsville, Pa.: in 1956, O'Hara claimed, "I'm probably the hardest working author in the U.S."[18] Twelve years and ten books later, he wrote his daughter: "It is pretty hard for most authors not to be jealous of me, because I make it look easy and they know it is not."[19]

It most assuredly was *not* easy, particularly for O'Hara whose last twenty years were dedicated to writing as few other men's lives were. With Trollopian regularity, he would closet himself in his Princeton study, following his old working habits by writing every night from midnight until dawn. Much has been made of O'Hara's refusal to re-write his fiction, his "page-proof prose," but a marvelous memory, a tape-recorder-like ear, and a highly developed narrative sense allowed him to get it right the first time.

Literary critics were consequently baffled by John O'Hara. Confronted with a writer whose sincere dedication to his art they had to honor, they had also to contend with a rather mean-spirited and highly competitive anachronism. O'Hara knew that he was out of date; he said as much in his Medal of Merit for the Novel acceptance speech: "in the context of present-day writing I am regarded as obsolescent, and rightly so."[20] Reviewers ultimately came to look upon O'Hara as they might a skilled producer of buggy whips. They admired the independent doggedness but sneered at the product as passé. Why, in the name of Pynchon, did all those middlebrows continue to read O'Hara?

A partial answer was O'Hara's style, called by John Cheever "a splendid baritone voice—a persuasive and perfectly pitched organ."[21] That style—flat, prosaic, exact, authoritative, knowing—was an achievement wrought from scrupulous attention to traditional language and a desire to make that language embody a reality that is irrefrangibly physical. No solipsistic wordplay or interposition of internal values for O'Hara. Let John Barth use a rhetorically complex style calling attention to itself as the principal meaning of his work; O'Hara's words stood for *things*—precise, familiar, "ordinary" things.

John O'Hara's attention to things—particularly to things historical, verifiable, statistical, and factual—struck a chord for millions. Numbed by the chaotic eschatology of a Burroughs or a Hawkes, O'Hara's readers found in his work a serious commitment to the details of familiar reality. And O'Hara knew how comforting this could be: "a big block of type which contains a lot of detail is restful. The reader . . . sees a lot of nouns and relaxes, but he remembers."[22]

Yet O'Hara's ubiquitous catalogues of details—to his critics "purposeless and insignificant"—have a reality of their own. More than a novelist's trick, O'Hara's catalogues pile brand name on statistic, clinical description on calendar date, in an attempt to reveal hitherto concealed interrelationships and their socio-psychological consequences. Irving Howe sees them as attempts to "discover the secret of all that moves us and emerge . . . into the blazing light of meaning."[23]

The fictional world of John O'Hara, jammed with details demonstrably similar to those in the "real" world where his readers must spend the major portions of their lives, turns out to be dominated by failure and misery. Nevertheless, the *post hoc* explicability of the relationships between men and things in O'Hara's fiction, tragic though it often proves even to the most alert, wary character, affords some pleasure to the reader. Before reading O'Hara, readers could only wonder at the confusing dissociation of men from their history so often the subject of other contemporary American novelists. Perhaps no other American writer of this generation was so committed to the implications of the social fact as John O'Hara.

O'Hara's commitment arises from two sources: his experiences as a journalist and his engagement with historical method (emphasizing causal relations between concrete facts).

October 1924 marked John O'Hara's first reporter's job; only several months later did he get $6 a week on the Pottsville *Journal*. But O'Hara early on learned to treasure accuracy and thoroughness. Getting "the facts" became his quintessential mission, the more the better. Elderly *Journal* staffers recall O'Hara as something less than a dedicated researcher (he was unhappy at home, drank excessively, and loved a young woman he could not marry), but O'Hara's later short stories celebrate the indefatigable "digger," an ever-curious reporter who keeps after a story through musty courthouse records and clandestine meetings with unsavory sources.

Such a journalist was a pro, a man who met a writer's responsibilities. "It's been about thirty years that I've been a pro," O'Hara told his readers in 1954, "and in that time, I have not missed a single deadline."[24] Writing under pressure seemed beneficial to him: "The newspaper influence is a good one for a writer. It teaches economy of words. It makes you write faster. When you're on re-write as I was, you can't fool around at half-past nine trying to write beautiful lacy prose."[25]

As a re-write man for newspapers like the *New York Herald Tribune*, O'Hara learned to organize and reshape the farrago of data fed him by colleagues. Comely rhetoric had to give way to clear, readable prose, the style subordinate to the facts themselves. Literal precision and concrete diction became O'Hara's watchwords: "Prose writing in 1949 I don't think should be anything but accurate. I keep away from figures of speech."[26] His prejudices marked his fiction, both in style and substance, as this passage from *Butterfield 8* indicates:

> There was a time in a man's life when he has a secret so dirty he will never get rid of it. (Shakespeare knew this and tried to say it, but he said it as badly as anyone ever said it. "All the perfumes of Arabia" makes you think of all the perfumes of Arabia and nothing more. It is the trouble with all metaphors where human behavior is concerned. People are not ships, chessmen, flowers, racehorses, oil paintings, bottles of champagne, excrement, musical instruments, or anything else but people. Metaphors are all right to give you an idea.)[27]

True to his theory, O'Hara rarely used metaphors in his own fiction, difficult as it was not to. "It's almost impossible," he once said, "in ordinary speech to avoid metaphor and simile. They're so convenient. You have to care a helluva lot about the written word to avoid putting them down. Before I use a word, an ordinary word, I look it up in the dictionary."[28] While some critics objected to the poverty of imagination this theory demonstrates, others called him "the master of a frugal, penetrating style." Most importantly, however, O'Hara's disavowal of figurative language represents his belief that words *are* things, to be used objectively in the service of reality. One does not need metaphors "to give you an idea" if reality itself is palpable in those thing-words.

Also attributable to O'Hara's journalistic experience is the tone that vitiates the vaunted objectivity of his style. The accuracy of O'Hara's language cannot mask an underlying irony so often attributed to the cynical reporter. O'Hara suspected that people did not want the whole truth about a "story," and social pressure often forced even the best of reporters to equivocate. But the reporter knew, even if he could not tell, the truth. Therefore, O'Hara's reportorial tone is often ironically superior; he is an omniscient observer whose objectivity demarcates the distance between himself and the consistent venality and dishonesty of his sources.

Distance is necessary for another reason as well. When "the story" is tragic, a reporter's ego defenses demand non-involvement. To empathize would be to fail, and that way lies despair and pessimism. Knowing the inevitability of disaster, the reporter has a duty to report it but not to be caught in the conflagration. Several of O'Hara's more trenchant critics have pointed out that the tense objectivity of his tone inadequately conceals his real feeling for the pathetic victims of his fiction.[29] Yet that feeling ought never to be obvious, most of all to the one who feels it. Held in check, sympathy could allow O'Hara this boast: "I'd say I wrote the story of my times better than anyone else."[30]

For O'Hara it was a short jump from journalist to social historian. Perhaps the clearest (and most often quoted) statement of O'Hara's feelings about his mission as historian is his Foreword to *Sermons and Soda Water* (1960):

> I want to get it all down on paper while I can. I am now fifty-five years old and I have lived with as well as in the Twentieth Century from its earliest days. The United States in this Century is what I know, and it is my business to write about it to the best of my ability, with the sometimes special knowledge that I have. The Twenties, the Thirties, and the Forties are already history, but I cannot be content to leave their story in the hands of the historians and the editors of picture books. I want to record the way people talked and thought and felt, and to do it with complete honesty and variety.[31]

With a credo like this, it is little wonder that O'Hara began *Ten North Frederick* (1955) with this Foreword:

> This, of course, is a work of fiction, but I have also taken liberties with those facts which sometimes help to give truth to fiction. To name one: the office of Lieutenant Governor was created by the 1873 Constitution, so it would have

been impossible for Joe Chapin's grandfather to have been Lieutenant Governor at the time I state. There are one or two other deliberate errors of that kind, but I hope they will be pardoned by the alert attorneys who are sure to spot them. If this were straight history, and not fiction, I would not ask to be pardoned.[32]

Obvious, then, is the fact that O'Hara considered social history an integral part of his function as a novelist.[33] "Those facts which sometimes help to give truth to fiction" held, for O'Hara, an almost mystical power. His library crammed with reference books and almanacs, the recorded minutiae of history, O'Hara searched for the ineluctably accurate long after most imaginative writers gave up and trusted to the reader's indulgence.

John O'Hara's overwhelming fictive preoccupation was "rightness." Praising the fiction of A. Conan Doyle for its realism he wrote: "It is literature of a high order. The sights, sounds, smells, social customs, conversation—all so right and good that you don't have to read anything else to get the feeling of a period."[34] Scorning abstract "messages" in fiction, he praised Booth Tarkington's Penrod stories and Sherwood Anderson's *Winesburg, Ohio*: "Their message—which will be news to a lot of people is: That's how it was."[35]

As literal precision was important to style, absolute accuracy was the keystone of realism. Errors in fact were not simply sloppy, they were illusion-shattering lies: ". . . I am extremely critical, and I have never been able to get beyond the first page of one of the most famous novels of our time because the author has made a 'weather' mistake (something about snow on the ground) that proves to me that he isn't a good writer."[36]

Combining remorseless research for the factual with the historian's desire to render "the way it was" meaningful, O'Hara seems to be defining his work as the best possible picture of the social construction of reality specific to America in the second, third, and fourth decades of this century. His given social world is highlighted by the tensions and terrors attending the process of socialization by which American society confers identity on its members and struggles to maintain some semblance of social continuity. O'Hara's work, from his early *New Yorker* short stories in the late '20's through the posthumous fiction, is all of a piece: as a social historian, critics like Malcolm Cowley assert, O'Hara is "less interested in making each book a unified and balanced work of art in itself" than in "flow."[37] Aware of the formal demands of art, O'Hara nonetheless subordinated them to the demands of history—recording and analyzing the past. Some, like Matthew Bruccoli, thought this successful: "There is no working writer who matches O'Hara's importance as a social historian."[38]

Whether or not historians class O'Hara as a social historian is immaterial here. For our purposes, it is enough that John O'Hara saw himself as a historian; the form and content of his fiction, the very nature of his fictive world, is greatly influenced by his perception of his function. O'Hara's work, then, is best read *in toto* with the reader aware of the sense of historical inevitability that characterizes his fiction.

A perhaps more telling criticism of O'Hara's range as a social historian has been leveled at his concentration on the American rich or near-rich. *Ad hominem* denigrators explain this penchant by styling O'Hara as an incurable snob and social climber, cherishing grudges begotten of his social ostracism as the oldest of eight children in an Irish Catholic family in Protestant, Anglophile Pottsville, Pa.[39] Amateur psychologizing aside, it is true that O'Hara liked to call himself "a student of the manners and the customs of the rich."[40]

O'Hara tried to disarm critics who objected to his fascination with the wealthy by reversing the coin: Americans traditionally have been ambivalent about money, and those who found fault with *his* obsession should examine their own. Further, O'Hara was not the first to realize that Americans seem insatiably curious about the rich. Beyond this banality, however, O'Hara had several reasons for writing about money:

(1) the conflict between the secure, inherited-money rich and the ascendant *nouveau riches* provided O'Hara rich material for the dramatization of the destructive effects of socialization on the individual. Security in a society without hereditary class distinctions is tenuous, so the American rich fight even harder to preserve their ascendancy in the face of pressure from below. No one—save fools and mystics—is unscathed in this struggle, and nowhere but among the rich is the battle so pitched, so subtle, so lethal. O'Hara also believed that in a country where most means best, money conferred identity, security, even personality on its possessors. More graphically than its poor, America's rich are its representative figures, captives in the plush dungeons of their own money.

(2) As a result of their guilt about being wealthy, many Americans rationalize by justifying the money in terms of customs, rules, rites, and other arcana of exclusivity in order to generate the conclusion that wealth is somehow indicative of social worth. Still, as prisoners of an inflexible social rubric, the rich experience conflict when beset by their instinctual human natures, particularly their sexual drives. John Cheever summed up the resulting rift this way: "This then was O'Hara's vision of things, the premise of money, generated by a ceremonial society and an improvisational erotic life."[41] O'Hara's rich, convinced of their superiority, assert themselves sexually with freedom and impunity, but their creator knows that they will eventually be crushed beneath the strictures of their own self-generated conventionalism.

As a social historian, therefore, O'Hara could control his research by specializing in a certain socio-economic class, while at the same time he could achieve a novelist's range by implying the symbolic representativeness of his wealthy Americans. O'Hara's rich lived everywhere (Park Avenue, Beverly Hills, Palm Springs, Hobe Sound, Southampton, Philadelphia's Main Line, Texas), but despite seeming differences, O'Hara cursed them all with a strong deterministic fate, the sure defeat that awaits their misguided attempts to redefine themselves. Of anyone, the rich should know that only manners are truly definitive, but the monied are no smarter than the impoverished. Unlike F. Scott Fitzgerald's Tom and Daisy Buchanan, O'Hara's rich cannot "retreat back into their money or their vast carelessness or whatever it was that kept them together, and let other people clean up the mess they had made. . . ."[42] The envious will always spy the mistake, the violation of the sanctity of class solidarity.

For that reason, punishment is inevitable because O'Hara knew that society enjoys nothing more than a righteously indignant slash at a miscreant. Bloody and bowed, the rebel understands too late that even in bed he is not in control of his own destiny. Because *every* act has social consequences, society's ubiquitous voyeurs will sniff out the slightest deviance and harshly condemn the deviant.

Even when society momentarily withholds its censure, an O'Hara character might still be a victim of hereditary weakness. Often walking exacerbations of the sins of their fathers, an O'Hara protagonist—even the most glamorous, vital one—must contend with the character disorders humming down the genetic chain.

Finally, to compound the agonies of O'Hara's doomed heroes, he made them all universally unlucky. In *Ten North Frederick*, an O'Hara character completes his formula for success in life this way: "Seventh, figuratively speaking, carry a rabbit's foot." Crucial to anyone, luck is absolutely beyond human control, and O'Hara's men find that to carry a rabbit's foot is to die of tularemia. Still another character, this one in *Ourselves to Know* (1960), accurately divides O'Hara's world: "He was one of the good people in the world. You must know that there are some people who are lucky. In the same way, some people are good. And some are unlucky, and some are bad."[43] Good and bad may in part be matters of free moral choice, but luck never is. Some men's fates are determined by whim.

Small wonder, then, that O'Hara's work was considered troglodytic; his ideas and techniques put him firmly among the practitioners of literary naturalism. Like the tradition from which he rose, he depended to a major extent on an accurate and literal observation of reality; he purported to present human experience honestly and convincingly; and his best work reflected a deterministic view of events—scientific in its preciseness—that was represented in the operation of biological and social forces.[44] Strongly pessimistic about loss of the human freedom he depicts, O'Hara never completely accepts the view of a universe wholly amoral and predatory. Yet only the author's tight-lipped superiority of tone stands between the reader and the everpresent disasters of the fiction. And O'Hara's enormous popular success at home and abroad—in the face of mostly negative reviews—is clear evidence that contemporary naturalism bores only the critics.

Yet most of those who loathed his naturalism admit that *Appointment in Samarra*[45]—O'Hara's first novel—raises documentation / verisimilitude / determinism to the level of solid imaginative art. This novel, full of the deadly effects of social snobbery and impulsive sexual appetite, is set in the small Pennsylvania city of Gibbsville, a street-by-street recreation of O'Hara's native Pottsville. *Appointment in Samarra* was an immediate popular success when it appeared in August, 1934, and over the years has worn best of all O'Hara's novels.

The fatally deterministic atmosphere of the book commences with O'Hara's epigraph, repeating the legend of the man who seeks to avoid Death in Bagdad by escaping to Samarra, only to find that Death in fact expected to meet him there. Influenced by this clue, critics have stressed unnecessarily the force of Fate in *Appointment in Samarra*, asserting that Julian English, the protagonist, is caught in the jaws of cosmic irony. O'Hara's conception of his hero, however, admits determinism while maintaining the potential exercise of free will (and escape) throughout the novel. Never unaware that Julian English might, by using common sense, slip away from the forces of heredity, environment, and bad luck that dog his every act in Gibbsville, O'Hara still concentrates on the unavoidable captivity of a character whose self-identity is completely formed by the opinions of his society. Moreover, in a society both morbidly insecure and still hypersensitive about its class structure, Julian— Gibbsville's own—is inevitably a victim of the vindictiveness with which he so closely identifies.

John O'Hara sets up Julian's predicament in Chapter I. Structurally, the chapter is in three parts, the introduction of Julian English sandwiched between scenes of the Lute Flieglers (Gibbsville's solid, pedestrian, "safely" aspiring middle class) and Al Grecco (an ex-con and petty gangster from the lower class). Each of these classes poses no immediate threat to Julian, even though we see the latent envy and possible violence that characterize the class consciousness of each group. Irma Fliegler is a flaming anti-Semite, and Al's feelings for his economic betters are expressed in his holiday greeting: "Merry Christmas, you stuckup bastards." Still, tradition, fear, and torpor are able to keep class lines intact in Gibbsville until a real victim appears.

Julian's own scene in Chapter I is set in the smoking room of the Lantenengo Country Club, exclusive province of the "secure" rich in Gibbsville, and it is here that Julian begins his rapid and terrifying decline by throwing a highball in the face of the enemy: Harry Reilly, a "witty Irishman . . . [who] had gone pretty far in his social climbing" (p. 15). This drunken, silly, fatal gesture is based in part on Julian's jealousy of Reilly's attentions to Caroline English, his pretty and conventional wife, but it is also Julian's violent attempt to show everyone that *he* can repel a maladroit outsider and get away with it.

Nevertheless, the times are not right for such snobbish gestures, particularly for Julian McHenry English. His name a symbol of his WASP status in Gibbsville, Julian has had to borrow $20,000 from Irish Catholic Harry Reilly who ". . . now practically owned the Gibbsville Cadillac Motor Car Company, of which Julian was president" (p. 15). With his usual patrician financial abandon, Julian has borrowed $10,000 more than necessary, blowing the extra money on an impractical concrete driveway, *two* motorcycles, and $1766.45 worth of trees. "Julian knew to the penny what they cost, but he was still not sure of the name of them" (p. 216). No economy measures for Julian English, especially when dealing with the despised Reilly: "he figured he might as well get a good hunk while he was at it" (p. 215).

Analysts of *Appointment in Samarra* have pretty much ignored the Depression as a force in the novel, even though the action takes place on 24–25–26 December 1930. And O'Hara is not primarily concerned with capitalism's failures. Yet the gathering storm of economic disaster hangs over Gibbsville, a coal-mining community. "The anthracite industry was just about licked" (p. 64), and even though the inherited-money rich and the professional men in Gibbsville still had money, many were spending principal. "Mr. Hoover was an engineer, and in a mining country engineers are respected. Gibbsville men and women who were in the market trusted that cold fat pinched face as they had trusted the cold thin pinched face of Mr. Coolidge, and in 1930 the good day's work of October 29, 1929, continued to be known as a strong technical reaction" (pp. 64–65).

However, O'Hara's novel makes it clear that English might have been able to pass off his tactlessly violent insult to Reilly as a gesture of warped *noblesse* or Ivy League horseplay had he thrown the drink in 1925. Then the rich bought his Cadillacs or lent him money. The Black Thursdays and Tragic Tuesdays of 1929, on the other hand, are forcing lords of the Country Club smoking room to take money wherever they can find it, and many have borrowed from Harry Reilly. Accordingly, Julian and his cohorts must pay sullen attention to the Harry Reillys, to Harry's clannish Irish Catholic friends, to "all the Christiana Street kind of people who he knew secretly hated him . . ." (p. 219). In the 1920's, Julian's Lantenengo Street paralleled Christiana Street; in 1930, Julian finds that the streets cross.

The stringency of the incipient Depression is likewise reflected in the hangover motif that runs through *Appointment in Samarra*. The frothy champagne of the Twenties has begotten the dull headache of the Thirties, despite Julian's frantic attempts to maintain the old gaiety, the heedless party, the adolescent rituals. In fact, the Reilly loan is symbolic of English's pursuit of a buoyant dream now turned nightmare. The dumb dismay that gripped many Americans during the early Depression is mirrored in English's halting realization that the party is over at last: "Julian, lost in the coonskins, felt the tremendous excitement, the great thrilling lump in the chest and abdomen that comes before the administering of an unknown, well-deserved punishment. He knew he was in for it" (p. 182).

Gone are the days when charm, attractive looks, inherited social position, and carelessness could allow Julian a reflection like this: ". . . servants, cops, waiters in restaurants, ushers in theatres—he could hate them more than persons who threatened him with real harm. He hated himself for his outbursts against them, but why in the name of God, when they had so little to do, couldn't they do it right and move out of his life" (p. 198). After the Reilly incident, Julian is in financial jeopardy, marital difficulty, and social insecurity. He has begun to understand the jealousy and outrage of one of those hated cops who stopped him for speeding: " 'You'd think you owned the road,' the patrolman had said; and Julian could not answer that that was exactly what he had been thinking" (p. 214).

The cops and servants and secretaries used to be good for laughs, but the very impermanence and insecurity of class lines based on money in a Depression—indeed, the insecurity of any position in a venal and materialistic society in which prestige can be conferred for owning a Cadillac and taken away for failing to replace divots on the golf course—drives Julian into wild emotional gyrations.

Insecurity in any event has been his lot from the beginning. Julian's grandfather an embezzler and a suicide, his father a righteous hypocrite, his mother a faceless weakling, English himself seems heir to hereditary character weaknesses. As the son of Dr. English, physician to the "good" families in town, Julian can inherit a place in the upper stratum of Gibbsville society, but his family has neither the money nor the real social confidence to make him feel at home there. Therefore, Julian rebels. As a boy, he steals, runs away, courts disaster, and of course is punished.

However, Julian loves to be punished. His very insecurity leads him to seek chastisement, in effect proving to himself that others care enough about him—as one of their own—to want to "correct" him. Throwing the drink in a creditor's eye, trying to seduce a gangster's mistress, punching a one-armed war veteran at the Gibbsville Club, and reviling his wife are Julian's naughty pranks, but Gibbsville, always alert for a victim, will have no more of them.

Though English only too late comes to know it, O'Hara's persistent references make the reader aware that a war is raging in Gibbsville, a violent and deadly war. Julian had sat out World War I at Lafayette in the S. A. T. C.; he has never really left Gibbsville. At the same time, others were wounded in France (Lute Fliegler's scarred back, Froggy Ogden's missing arm). These men have returned, proud of their survival, yet they have been made aware that violence is man's fate. They know—as Julian does not—that beneath the surface of society's reactions to apparently inconsequential breaches of etiquette hides revenge and envy and mayhem. " 'The war's over,' " Julian tells the angry Ogden at the Gibbsville Club. The reply—" 'Yeah, that's what you think" (p. 236)—underscores the permanence of the latent violence informing all social relations in *Appointment in Samarra*.

Julian eventually does realize that he cannot escape Gibbsville, for Gibbsville is everywhere. The Cadillacs that he drives and sells—symbols of assertiveness, mobility, freedom—are on a circular track. Pressed on all sides, Julian does run, but "you did not really get away from what he was going back to, and whatever it was, he had to face it" (p. 242). So he aborts his flight and returns to the no man's land that Gibbsville has now become for him. Like a child, he reasons, "He was too tall to run away. He would be spotted" (p. 243).

And Julian has managed to close all the doors in Gibbsville. He has estranged his wife, Caroline, who, even though she has compounded his immaturity by using her sexual favors like a carrot and stick, has been a strong stabilizing force in his life. He has outraged his morally punctillious father. He has made enemies of Lantenengo County's mobsters, war veterans, Irish Catholics, clubmen, and sober citizens. He even fails, in a last desperate maneuver designed to shore up his masculine sexual self-esteem, to seduce a gauche society reporter from the Gibbsville *Standard*. Finally, in an alcoholic haze, English can recall only "a slang axiom that never had any meaning in college days: 'Don't buck the system; you're liable to gum up the works' " (p. 276). His world in shards about him, he decides to punish himself: aptly ironic, his suicide weapon is the carbon monoxide from his own Cadillac in his own garage.

But O'Hara does not end the novel with Julian's suicide. Comparing the death to the explosion of a grenade, O'Hara charts the sorrow and face-saving and revenge and self-pity that Julian's suicide means for Gibbsville. The war continues in the violent little city, even though Caroline English mourns her dead husband as "some young officer in an overseas cap and a Sam Browne belt" (p. 293). Julian was "like someone who had died in the war," for, she concludes, "it was *time* for him to die" (p. 294).

O'Hara buttresses his study of the neurotic, doomed hero with endless documentary detail: menus for the 2.50 dinner at the Country Club (filet mignon); Reo Speedwagons, Condax cigarettes, Delta Kappa Epsilon, " 'Is it a real Foujita or a copy?' " All of these *things*—the badges of status in Gibbsville—have enormous power and relevance for an understanding of Julian's world. O'Hara's ear for dialogue—acknowledged by all critics as flawless—produces an endless and ungrammatical verisimilitude, the accurately reproduced accents marking the speakers as members of a specific social class. And despite O'Hara's objective tone, board-fence irony intrudes often enough to demonstrate the author's opinion of the hypocrites and fools of *Appointment in Samarra*.

Best of all, O'Hara manages to make most readers care a great deal about Julian English. Perhaps, as Edmund Wilson once wrote, O'Hara never knew what a heel Julian was. But heel or tragic victim, Julian English is more than a sociological case study; he has the attributes of a fully rounded character. For years the people of Pottsville, Pa., Gibbsville's prototype, have been trying to identify the model on whom Julian was based. John O'Hara, defending his artistic realization, claimed that they never would: "They try to pinpoint the figures, but unsuccessfully, because the characters have two patterns. One is superficial—clothes, schools, social positions, jobs. The other is psychological. Julian English of 'Appointment in Samarra' was superficially two or three fellows. On the psychological side, he happened to be a guy I knew living on the wrong side of the tracks."[46] O'Hara's novel demonstrates how well he integrated the "superficial" with the "psychological," for Julian's shallow self-pity and lack of moral resource is directly determined by his society's obsessive concern for the superficial. No one knows the name of a tree in Gibbsville; no one admires a Lantenengo County hill unless it contains coal; no one can laugh until he has had three whiskeys. Julian English—Gibbsville's finest—seems real enough.

O'Hara produced several brilliant short stories and at least two first-rate novels after *Appointment in Samarra*. The irony of determinism and fatalism marks them all, but nowhere else in the O'Hara canon are his naturalistic values and techniques translated into more noteworthy imaginative expression.

The French naturalist Emile Zola once wrote: "I take my documents where I find them, and I think I make them mine."[47] A century later, O'Hara told an interviewer: "Within my limitations and within my prejudices, I wrote down what I saw and heard and felt. I tried to keep it mine, and when I was most successful, it was mine."[48] *Appointment in Samarra* had John O'Hara's stamp of success.

Notes

1. Foreword to *Good Samaritan and Other Stories*, p. ix.

2. Bruccoli's thesis in *The O'Hara Concern* justifies O'Hara's life-long paranoia: the "critical-academic axis" or Literary Establishment conspired consistently to underrate O'Hara's fiction. O'Hara himself had made the same argument many times, most cogently to John Hutchens in a letter cited by Farr, *O'Hara* (Boston, 1973), p. 254: "Perhaps that's one reason I don't get Their approval: I do go back to work, which is a sign that They have been unable to knock me out as They did Fitzgerald. . . ."

3. *New York Times*, 18 December 1972, p. 37.

4. Quoted in Don A. Schanche, "John O'Hara Is Alive and Well in the First Half of the Twentieth Century," *Esquire*, Aug. 1969, p. 142.

5. Acceptance speech, presentation ceremonies of the Award of Merit Medal for the Novel, joint meeting of the Amer. Acad. of Arts and Letters and the Nat. Inst. of Arts and Letters, 20 May 1964. Reprinted in Farr, pp. 277–78.

6. Quoted in Alden Whitman, "O'Hara, in Rare Interview, Calls Literary Landscape Fairly Bleak," *New York Times*, 13 Nov. 1967, p. 45. Ironically, Bruccoli's scholarly biography of the self-made O'Hara was aided by a Fellowship from the John Simon Guggenheim Memorial Foundation.

7. Foreword to *Assembly* (New York, 1961), p. x.

8.   "A Cub Tells His Story." *Pottsville Journal*, 2 May 1925. In O'Hara file, Pottsville (Pa.) Public Library. Reprinted with a Preface by Bruccoli (Iowa City, 1975).

9.   *Sweet and Sour* (New York, 1954), p. 131.

10.   "Entertainment Week," *Newsweek*, 2 Dec. 1940, p. 46.

11.   Letter to Charles Poore, quoted in *Catalogue of Charles Hamilton Auction*, No. 56, 9 Mar. 1972, p. 45.

12.   Review of *Lovey Childs: A Philadelphian's Story*, by John O'Hara, *Harper's*, Feb. 1970, p. 114.

13.   "Entertainment Week," *Newsweek*, 13 Jan. 1941, p. 52.

14.   "Remarks on the Novel," in *Three Views of the Novel*, Irving Stone, John O'Hara, and MacKinley Kantor (Library of Congress, 1957), p. 18.

15.   "The Novels Novelists Read or 'Taking in the Washing,'" *New York Times Book Review*, 3 Aug. 1949, p. 3.

16.   Quoted in Schanche, p. 142.

17.   *Sweet and Sour*, pp. 160, 118.

18.   "Appointment with O'Hara," *Collier's*, 22 June 1956, p. 6.

19.   Quoted in Farr, p. 266.

20.   Farr, p. 278.

21.   Review of *The Ewings*, by John O'Hara, *Esquire*, May 1972, p. 14.

22.   Quoted in Farr, p. 274.

23.   Howe, p. 114.

24.   *Sweet and Sour*, p. 111.

25.   Quoted in Harvey Breit, *The Writer Observed* (New York: World, 1956), p. 82.

26.   Quoted in Breit, p. 82.

27.   (New York, 1935), p. 298.

28.   Quoted in Schanche. p. 86.

29.   See, e. g., Edmund Wilson, "The Boys in the Back Room," in *A Literary Chronicle: 1920–1950* (New York: Anchor, 1956), p. 222; but see Alfred Kazin, *On Native Grounds* (1942; rpt. New York: Anchor, 1956), p. 304. Kazin denigrates O'Hara tone as "excessively knowing," a defect of "metropolitan journalism."

30.   Quoted in obituary story syndicated by United Press International on 12 April 1970.

31.   (New York, 1960), p. x.

32.   (New York, 1955), n.p.

33.   O'Hara told the Historical Society of Pennsylvania (28 Jan. 1963) that he was particularly interested in the interplay of history with fiction. A record of his remarks is in the Univ. of Pennsylvania Library, but O'Hara barred direct quotation of his statements.

34.   "Appointment with O'Hara," *Collier's*, 1 Apr. 1955, p. 8.

35.   "Appointment with O'Hara," *Collier's*, 25 June 1954, p. 6.

36.   "The Novels Novelists Read . . . ," p. 3.

37.   Review of *O'Hara*, by Finis Farr, *New York Times Book Review*, 18 Mar. 1973, p. 4. In a review of *The Horse Knows the Way*, George P. Elliott had presaged Cowley this way: "Each story is a segment of [O'Hara's] world, not a little work of art to itself." *Harper's*, Apr. 1965, p. 112.

38.   "Focus on *Appointment in Samarra*," in *Tough Guy Writers of the 1930's*, ed. David Madden (Southern Illinois University Press, 1968), p. 129.

39.   See William V. Shannon, *The American Irish* (New York, 1963), pp. 244–49.

40.   "Appointment with O'Hara," *Collier's*, 13 Apr. 1956, p. 6.

41.   Cheever, p. 14.

42.   *The Great Gatsby* (1925; rpt. New York, 1953), pp. 180–81.

43.   (New York, 1960), p. 407.

44.   Characteristics of naturalism used by Haskell M. Block, *Naturalistic Tryptych: The*

Fictive and the Real in Zola, Mann, and Dreiser (New York, 1970), p. 78. See also V. L. Parrington, *Main Currents of American Thought* (1930; rpt. New York, 1958), III, 323–27.

45.   (New York, 1934). Subsequent page references are to this edition.

46.   Quoted in Lewis Nichols, "Talk with John O'Hara," *New York Times Book Review*, 27 Nov. 1955, p. 16.

47.   Quoted in Block, p. 91.

48.   Quoted in Schanche, p. 142.

Caste and Class War: The Society of John O'Hara's *A Rage To Live*

John L. Cobbs

As diverse critics from Harry Levin[1] to Georg Lukacs[2] have noted, the central concern of the modern novel of realism seems to be the delineation of a particular society at a particular time in a particular place. In American literature we find Edith Wharton's aristocratic New York at the turn of the century, Sinclair Lewis's middle class small town after the First World War, and John Steinbeck's picture of proletarian California in the Twenties and Thirties. There are dozens, perhaps hundreds, of other exhaustively defined fictional societies. No American writer, however, is more thorough in his treatment of a particular society than is John O'Hara in his portrait of eastern Pennsylvania in the first half of the twentieth century.

It was a society that O'Hara saw as his own literary province, a world that he claimed to know better than any other writer, and with a "special knowledge."[3] Through seven novels and a multitude of novellas and short stories, O'Hara presented with scrupulous detail the society of what Sheldon Grebstein calls "The O'Hara Country,"[4] that slice of southeastern Pennsylvania which O'Hara chose to define, and which for him represented American society as a whole, and upper middle class society in particular.[5]

Each of O'Hara's Pennsylvania novels presents a portrait of a town or small city in the O'Hara country. The Gibbsville of *Appointment in Samarra* and *Ten North Frederick*, the Swedish Haven of *Ourselves to Know* and *The Lockwood Concern*, the Port Johnson of *From the Terrace*, and the Spring Valley of *Elizabeth Appleton* are all examined thoroughly, and the reader gets the look and feel of the society of each town. But none of them are as absolutely presented as is Fort Penn in *A Rage to Live*. Both the physical size of the novel[6] and the completeness of its accent upon society as opposed to individual character mark *A Rage to Live* as the most total portrait of a community in the O'Hara canon. To understand the social mechanics of Fort Penn is to understand the society of O'Hara's most important fiction.

If there is a single dominant theme in *A Rage to Live*, it is that of social hierarchy. O'Hara's world in this novel, far more than in *Appointment in*

Reprinted with permission of the author from *John O'Hara Journal* 2, no. 1 (Winter 1979–80): 24–34.

Samarra, for example, or *Ourselves to Know*, is one in which characters are not individual people interacting with each other as free agents with discreet personalities; they are caught irrevocably at various levels of a class structure. Caste is everything in Fort Penn, and there is literally no aspect of this novel that is not determined or affected by the author's premise that this is a world in which social class is all-important. Brock Caldwell is an unmitigated "son-of-a-bitch," but it matters more that he is a Caldwell. In the long run, he and the humane Edgar Martindale are more alike, both being born and bred gentlemen, than are Brock and Roger Bannon, Grace's vicious "lace-curtain" Irish lover. When push comes to shove, Grace and Brock, with the help of the other "respectable" forces of the town, combine to destroy Bannon. The structuring of Fort Penn society is rigidly inflexible, and every character in the novel fits into a niche, neatly classified socially and frozen within an elaborate structure of stratification.

At the very top of the social pyramid are the Caldwells, the apotheosis of whom is Grace, heir to the family throne that her older brother Brock abdicates to live a life of sloth and royal ease. Although O'Hara deals repeatedly (some critics believe obsessively) with the rich and powerful, there is really not another parallel in his fiction to the Caldwells. They are "the Stuyvesant Fishes or Astors, the Fort Penn 'creme de la creme.'"[7] Yet they are more, for within the world of Fort Penn they have no real equals. Immediately about them cluster the rest of the Fort Penn aristocracy—rich Anglo-Saxons of blue blood with an occasional token Catholic.[8] The Schoffstals, the Martindales, the O'Connells, and a dozen or so other families are of the Caldwell's "set," and yet all acknowledge that the Caldwells are a little bit better, their position a trifle securer. One thinks of Boston, where "the Cabots speak only to Lowells, and the Lowells speak only to God"; O'Hara tells us that Emily Caldwell thought herself "on very good terms with God." Hearing that Will Caldwell has mentioned his family's custom of gathering at every turn-of-the-century, Edgar Martindale, himself one of the elect, says: " 'Can you beat it? Will Caldwell's family have a tradition that they all get together every new century! People like you and me are satisfied to get together every Thanksgiving, but not Will Caldwell. Every *century*, that's the way the traditions run in the Caldwell family. Jesus H. Christ!' " (p. 67)[9]

As always in O'Hara, the Tate / Caldwell social position is far more than a matter of quaint tradition and brittle old letters spotted with tears. Position in Fort Penn means money and power, the second being more important than the first, but following from it automatically. So organic is the relationship in *A Rage to Live* between social position, money, and power, that it seems almost impossible to dissociate the three elements or to tell which arises from which. At one point in the book a narrative surrogate for the author says that, "as nearly as [I] can tell, Caldwell money came from the land, but very far back" (p. 142), and of course the stress is on the age of the money in addition to the size of the fortune. The point is that money, power, and position all exist as a priori conditions for the action of the novel. This is no social *bildungsroman* like *The Red and the Black* or a study of shifting social fortunes like *The Financier, The Rise of Silas Lapham*, or *The House of Mirth*. Those are novels of progress into or out of society, and fittingly each fixes on a single character whose locus vis-a-vis the society is a constant point of reference. The Caldwells are not merely *at* the tip of the social pyramid, subject to decline and fall, they *are* the tip, and for purposes of the novel their position is frozen. As such, they present O'Hara's richest and most complete picture of upper class society. Sheldon Grebstein was close to the mark when he wrote: "Perhaps the most remarkable aspect of this large created world, twenty years in the life of an American city, is O'Hara's depiction of the money, power, and privilege of the highest aristocracy. In contrast to the merely well-to-do characters portrayed in *Appointment in Samarra*, the millionaires of *A Rage to Live* are virtually above punishment from the social consequences of their actions."[10]

Although the most obvious division in *A Rage to Live* is between the social and economic "haves" and the "have nots," the novel presents an hierarchical structure which is stratified rather than polarized. The society of the city is an infinitely subtle, honeycombed labyrinth, and each character's rank depends upon distinctions of background, breeding, and behavior. It is better in Fort Penn to be Polish than Negro, Italian than Polish, Irish than Italian, and Pennsylvania Dutch than Irish, although this distinction does not always hold. Jessie Jay, a German-American, speaks of a scandal involving "'the Italian doctor and the white—I mean, American woman'" (p. 110), although the Italian like herself is a second-generation American. Roger Bannon's father makes his political career by stirring up the Italian laborers against "'them Dutch bastards'" (p. 118), who are only one step higher on the social scale, and who Bannon points out are legally represented by Desmond O'Connell, "'an Irishman, not one of their own thick-headed kind'" (p. 118).

Racial background, in fact, is not the only basis after money for social distinction, but it is far and away the most important one, and like the law and the prophets, all others hang upon it. In *Appointment in Samarra* the one unpardonable crime was to bring a Jew to the country club; in *A Rage to Live* race remains the foundation of social organization, and other distinctions are derivative. Religion, for example, is directly hinged to ethnic origin: Irish are Catholics, Pennsylvania Dutch are Lutherans, and Anglo-Saxons are congregationalists or Episcopalians if they are anything.[11] The Caldwells, however, are nothing; characteristically, they donate an organ to an Episcopal church so that Grace, who shows not a particle of religious feeling throughout the novel, can be married in a "family" chapel.

As was the case in *Samarra's* Gibbsville, there are two ethnic groups in Fort Penn whose social standing is less absolutely definable than the rest. These are the Irish and the Pennsylvania Dutch. Evidently, to be of either ancestry is not entirely to bear the mark of Cain in the high society of the O'Hara country. Ties of family and friendship, accompanied always by money legitimized through years of local residence, lift people like Desmond O'Connell and Sidney Tate's friend Paul Reichelderfer almost to the top ranks. Interestingly, the protagonists of two later novels, Robert Millhouser of *Ourselves to Know* and George Lockwood of *The Lockwood Concern* are both "a bit Dutchy" and still become the local aristocracy in Swedish Haven. But Swedish Haven is not Fort Penn, where the true heights are almost entirely a WASP preserve.

Even within racial classes in Fort Penn, of course, there are distinctions and classifications. This is particularly true among the Anglo-Saxons. There is an enormous distance between the Caldwells and the dross of the Anglo-Saxon community, most of whom are distinguished as dross by having to work for a living.[12] Even Jack Hollister, Grace Tate's second lover, although both he and his father are college men and his family has been established in Fort Penn for generations, is well down the social ladder. This is evidenced by his marriage to the daughter of a railroad worker and his serious consideration of a second marriage to an Irish girl who works on the make-up desk of the newspaper he edits.[13]

The book is full of examples of stratification among the ruling classes. A typical account is that of the pecking order at the barber shop in the Schoffstal House: "It was patronized regularly by all members of the Fort Penn Club, by the men on the Club waiting-list, by members of the Fort Penn Athletic Club, by men who could have joined the Fort Penn Club, by men who could have joined the Athletic Club, by senators and assemblymen who had served more than one or two terms, and by total strangers. The patrons were served in that order and in that order they were treated, from deference down to common politeness" (p. 157).

The Schoffstals themselves are another fine example of O'Hara's presentation of hierarchy even within an extended family group at the highest level. There are more than two pages delineating the strata of Fort Penn's "second family" (pp. 56–58), and the picture is almost a prototype for the society as a whole: ". . . a man's standing in his township or borough sometimes was determined by the closeness or remoteness of his kinship with the Fort Penn Schoffstals, and particularly the Isaac Schoffstals, who were the parents of Connie and Ham. . . . In Fort Penn alone there was a Schoffstal at every little step, all the way up" (p. 57).

What is true at the top is true at all other levels, and the other ethnic groups are similarly stratified. There is no contempt more scathing than that of the Irish social climber in *A Rage to Live*, who terms lesser Irishmen "Micks," and the distinction between "decent colored people" (p. 49) and "Niggers" is one drawn by black and white alike.[14]

But the social rigidity is not total. Characters rise above their original station, as does Pennsylvania Dutch peasant George Walthour, who convinces the establishment to let him be mayor.[15] They also fall, like Roger Bannon, whose viciousness and debauchery manage to negate the efforts of his social-climbing forebears. There is even some real social interpenetration between the classes. Father Brophy, of the non-aristocratic Irish, becomes a friend of Will Caldwell, and he is entertained for dinner in the inner sanctum of the Caldwell home. There is also a kind of limited democracy among the young, such as exists among the members of Julian English's boyhood gang in *Appointment in Samarra*. Brock Caldwell and Duncan Partridge are close friends as boys with Charlie Jay, who is from the wrong side of the tracks, but who becomes, with the perverse help of Brock, the agent of Grace's sexual initiation.

These isolated examples of apparent egalitarianism are anomalous and deceptive. For the main the feeling between classes is hostile and ugly.[16] Roger Bannon's father's bigotry lays the groundwork for Roger's desire to "get" Grace, physically and emotionally. Edgar Martindale predicts that when the affair with Hollister becomes public, " 'the people of Fort Penn will rub Grace's nose in it' " (p. 547), because of their resentment of her position. It doesn't take much pressure for the standards of propriety to slip away at all class levels and reveal the anger beneath: when a young Irish lawyer panics at exposure to polio in Grace's house, Charles Partridge snaps, " 'You'll go back to the pick and shovel like your father,' " and slaps his face (p. 336). O'Hara himself said that central to *A Rage to Live* was, "the idea that any social situation is likely to blow up in one's face."[17] The source of much of this volatility is the uncompromising antipathy of class against class.

Latent class hatred simmers throughout the novel, but frequently it manifests itself in real violence. The raw, the brutal, and the primitive in man is never far from the surface in O'Hara, and the human capacity for spontaneous overflow of savage emotion in violence is as evident in *A Rage to Live* as in any of the other Pennsylvania novels. Roger Bannon is the most violent character. When he is first rebuffed by Grace, his reaction is a desire to beat up men in the Fort Penn Club (p. 192). Later, when the still unreachable Grace tells him, " 'It'd take a lifetime to explain the difference between you and the men in the Fort Penn Club' " (p. 194), his outrage leads him to beat a transient prostitute nearly to death, unleashing his brutality on a creature even lower on the social ladder than himself. Fittingly, Bannon dies as he has lived, driven by Brock to what amounts to suicide in a flaming car wreck. Brock says of his death, " 'He killed himself. We're all living in the jungle, Grace. He was just a—a kind of hyena that went after a lion [the Caldwells], and that's the same as killing yourself' " (p. 499).

Other elements of the Fort Penn social jungle show their teeth repeatedly. At the time of the announcement of Grace's engagement, labor rowdies throw bricks through the window of the Caldwell house (p. 128); Amy Hollister vents her rage by attacking Grace with a gun; and Charlie Jay, who eventually succeeds Walthour as mayor, works out his frustrations by acting weak and effeminate in bars and then beating the laborers who taunt him. As E. M. Forster points out about the death of Leonard Bass in *Howard's End*, so does

O'Hara assert that the class war is one in which real blood is often shed, and there is sometimes literal death.

As Brock's comment about the hyena and the lion indicates, the establishment has nearly all the power and nearly always wins. There is little, within limits, that the Caldwell clique cannot do. It is in the power of Grace and the Caldwells to "make" Miss Holbrook's School for Girls (p. 66), just as it is within Grace's power to have one of her daughter's teachers there fired when Grace is displeased over a minor matter. Betty Martindale's decision to stop any talk about Grace's affair with Bannon was "a useful warning to Grace's friends, who had only to think twice to conjure up a situation in which the Caldwell-Tate-Schoffstal-Bordener-Partridge-et. al. alliance could do them harm, socially, financially, politically, or all three" (p. 394).

If there is an incident in *A Rage to Live* that is representative of the social war on all fronts, it is the Baum Case (pp. 105–115). When Grace is nineteen, a German-American, Baum, kills his wife and her Italian-American lover; O'Hara lovingly details the circumstances and the wounds. The Italian colony of Fort Penn is aroused and screams for revenge. Although the German community backs Baum, it does so with reservations, since "he had also shot his own wife, who was not Italian at all but good, German stock, for which reason there was some reaction against Baum among his own people" (p. 106). Baum cannot afford a good lawyer, and his relative, Jessie Jay, who is a poor cousin of Emily Caldwell, begs Emily for help: "'. . . you have power,'" she says, "'and I want to borrow some without any hope of ever paying it back'" (p. 110). When Emily refuses, Mrs. Jay accuses her of killing Baum by not helping him, and the conversation becomes very ugly indeed. But Mrs. Jay is armed with the knowledge that her son Charlie has been sleeping with Grace, and she uses it to try to blackmail Emily, who says: "'But do you think you can blackmail us with it? Do you think you can do anything at *all* with it?'

'Yes,' said Jessie, whispering. 'I just did, Emily. I did do something with it. I couldn't blackmail you with the story, but I hurt you, didn't I? That's all I wanted to do. . . .'

'It's true, Jessie. It's true. But I'm still me, and you're still you. I imagine that hurts you almost as much'" (p. 113).

Emily decides to save Baum out of *noblesse oblige*, the last, most subtle, and in some ways the cruelest weapon of the aristocracy. She convinces her husband that because Jessie's son is a friend of Brock's, the Jays have an obscure claim to be what Will Caldwell facetiously but accurately calls, "'members of our clahss.'" Will agrees to get Desmond O'Connell to defend Baum, saying, "'if we belong to a clahss, or a class, it's not worth much if we don't come to the rescue when one of us gets in trouble'" (p. 115). Baum is spared.

The Baum case shows a good many of the elements of the O'Hara social scene in *A Rage to Live*—the visceral class polarity and the strength of class loyalty, the desire to inflict pain across class lines, physical violence, sex, and the power of the establishment. In short, we see the law of the jungle.

It is a law that informs the social picture of each of O'Hara's novels. But nowhere is it as thoroughly drawn as it is in *A Rage to Live*. Because of the size of the novel, its uncompromising accent on society rather than individual character, and the consummate realist talent which the novelist brings to bear on his creation of Fort Penn, *A Rage to Live* stands as the apotheosis of O'Hara's vision of society. Considering the magnitude of O'Hara's ability to observe the social scene, it is no small creation.

Notes

1. "Society as Its Own Historian," *Contexts of Criticism* (New York: Atheneum, 1957), pp. 171–189.

2. "Critical Realism and Socialist Realism," *Realism in Our Time* (1956; rpt. Harper Torchbooks: New York, 1964), pp. 93–135. Lukacs writes, of course, in ideological terms, and he tends to deal with realism primarily in terms of what he calls "Socialist Realism." Still, he presents a thorough discussion of realist fiction and its creation of particular societies.

3. *Sermons and Soda-Water* (New York: Random House, 1960), p. x. This foreword to *Sermons and Soda-Water* has been frequently cited by O'Hara critics as a succinct summary of the novelist's attitude toward himself as a social historian: "I want to get it all down on paper while I can. . . . The United States in this century is what I know, and it is my business to write about it to the best of my ability, and with the sometimes special knowledge I have. The Twenties, the Thirties, and the Forties are already history, but I cannot be content to leave their story in the hands of the historians and the editors of picture books. I want to record the way people talked and thought and felt, and to do it with complete honesty and variety."

4. *John O'Hara* (New York: Twayne, 1966), p. 33.

5. As O'Hara's works exhibit, there is no real American aristocracy, and O'Hara is hardly likely to waste his reporting on Baby Jane Holzer and Stash Radziwill. There was a decayed aristocracy of sorts in New York around the turn of the century, but O'Hara has left the recording of it to Mrs. Wharton, who was much better equipped to deal with the subject, having her own "special knowledge."

6. *From the Terrace* at nearly nine hundred pages and more than half a million words is a larger book than *A Rage to Live*. It is set, however, in a number of places, notably New York and Washington, and its accent is far more on individual character than on society.

7. John O'Hara, *A Rage to Live* (New York: Random House, 1949), p. 69. All subsequent page references within the text are to this edition.

8. O'Hara always includes a Catholic family or two in his portraits of upper class society, but despite the novelist's own Catholic background, there is not a single Catholic character central to any of his Pennsylvania novels.

9. This is a fine example of O'Hara's folding the sublime and the ridiculous into a single passage. The Christ allusion, particularly with the emotion that Edgar puts behind it, strengthens the aura of sanctity about the Caldwells. But it is introduced unpretentiously; not symbolically, but realistically through an entirely believable oath. This is much like the irony of a cop's remark about the Caldwells later in *A Rage to Live*— " 'These bastards know how to live' " (p. 584)—or Al Greco's famous salutation to the rich in *Appointment in Samarra*—" 'Merry Christmas, you stuck up bastards!' " O'Hara's dialogue is always completely realistic, and yet it is full of allusion and reference that often lends it a meaning beyond the pure functional.

10. Grebstein, *John O'Hara*, p. 46.

11.   It is strange, dealing with eastern Pennsylvania extensively, that O'Hara gives such short shrift to the Quakers. In all his novels there is not a single Quaker character of any importance. Perhaps this is because the principles of Quakerism are so totally at odds with the standards of O'Hara's nasty social world that such a character would have been unbelievable. Could O'Hara have created an unfriendly Friend?

12.   Work, in the O'Hara country, is generally considered degrading at the highest social level, at least in Grace Tate's day. The three "possible" jobs for a man of good family, besides managing the family business, were law, medicine, and farming (at the "squire" level, as is the case with Sidney Tate). Alfred Kazin is hardly correct when he claims that "O'Hara's world is one of total ambitiousness . . ." in *Bright Book of Life: American Novelists and Storytellers from Hemingway to Mailer* (Boston: Little, Brown, 1973), p. 108. The upper class characters in *A Rage to Live* have nothing to be ambitious for.

13.   Anyone who has ever worked for a newspaper knows that the make-up desk is the lowest level of employment. Only the advertising staff is more contemptible. It is the home of cast-offs and trainees.

14.   As in his other Pennsylvania fiction, O'Hara does not spend much space in *A Rage to Live* delineating the depth of anti-Negro sentiment in eastern Pennsylvania, only because it is a commonplace in his fiction. Similarly, Tarkington in *Seventeen* is not making a social comment when he has Jane say of the handyman Genesis, " 'He's a colored man; he brings in the coal,' " in the same tone that Penrod says, " 'Here's my dog, Duke.' " It is simply assumed in the O'Hara country that Negroes are a lower order of creature. There is one incident in *A Rage to Live* that demonstrates the extent of prejudice: Charlie Jay and Duncan Partridge are enraged when Brock Caldwell, as a joke, tells them that he has discovered that they have a trace of Negro blood.

15.   Walthour's rise from humble Pennsylvania Dutch origins to become the mayor of Fort Penn reminds us of the similar character "Wie Geht's" Yates who becomes mayor of Gibbsville in *Ten North Frederick*.

16.   James W. Tuttleton in a short but thorough discussion of O'Hara as a novelist of manners claims that all O'Hara's Pennsylvania fiction is informed by a consciousness of "spurious democracy:" "But his Lantenengo County [Pennsylvania] novels are informed by one overriding idea: America is a 'spurious democracy' marked by the intense hatred of its rival social classes . . . for all our egalitarian claims, ours is essentially a society of antagonistic classes defined by money, family, occupation, region, religion, education, and ethnic background." James W. Tuttleton, *The Novel of Manners in America* (1972; New York: Norton Library, 1974), p. 193.

17.   Letter to Frank Norris, July 22, 1949. Quoted in Matthew J. Bruccoli, *The O'Hara Concern* (New York: Random House, 1975), p. 196.

"All that you need to know": John O'Hara's Achievement in the Novella

NANCY WALKER

Ten years after his death, John O'Hara is regarded by those who reflect on his canon as a master of the novel and short story forms. His twelve novels[1] are characterized by the dense detail and historical sweep of what we have come to call the "traditional" novel, and his short stories are similarly "classic" in form: brief, pointed revelations of character, circumstance, or mood crystalized in significant action. Less often recognized are O'Hara's achievements in yet another form, the novella or novelette. Between *Sermons and Soda-Water* in 1960 and *A Few Trips and Some Poetry* in 1969 O'Hara wrote ten pieces which belong to this genre, more than almost any other modern author except Henry James, and he seems in this last decade of his career to have found the proper form in which to develop characters fully and singlemindedly, without the complexity of focus common to the novel.

Throughout his career, O'Hara alternated between writing short stories and novels. The novels were large projects, requiring research and great absorption; the short stories were often, especially later in his career, bread-and-butter pieces, written for magazines (chiefly *The New Yorker* and *The Saturday Evening Post*) in order to buy time for the novels. As he grew older and less certain of having time to complete the novels he envisioned, he at least twice declared a moratorium on short story writing so that he could concentrate on his longer works. In 1955 he wrote: "I don't think I'll write any more short stories. In very recent years I have been made sharply aware of the passage of time and the preciousness of it, and there are so many big things I want to do. But during the Thirties and the Forties these stories were part of me as I was part of those nights and days, when time was cheap and everlasting and one could say it all in two thousand words."[2] And in 1964, this somewhat more tentative statement: "For a while, at least, this [*The Horse Knows the Way*] will be my last book of short stories."[3]

O'Hara never did entirely quit writing short stories, however, and 139 of his short pieces were published during the 1960's.[4] But beginning with *Sermons and Soda-Water*, he experimented with a form—the novella—which

Reprinted with permission of the author from *John O'Hara Journal* 4, no. 1 (Spring / Summer 1981): 61–80.

allowed him to record those people and events which crowded his memory and imagination without having to spend the time on research and writing which the novels required. In the foreword to *Sermons and Soda-Water*, after having credited Edith Wharton, Thomas Mann, Ernest Hemingway and others for using the novella form before him, O'Hara says: "The Twenties, the Thirties, and the Forties are already history, but I cannot be content to leave their story in the hands of the historians and the editors of picture books. I want to record the way people talked and thought and felt, and to do it with complete honesty and variety. I have done that in these three novellas, within, of course, the limits of my own observation. I have written these novellas from memory, with a minimum of research, which is one reason why the novella is the right form."[5] Without defining the novella form except by reference to the practice of other authors, O'Hara suggests here that the form, for him, is a convenient mode for presenting social history. The familiar narrator-observer Jim Malloy is present in each of the three novellas, functioning as the central consciousness for the reminiscences.

With the exception of *The Horse Knows the Way*, each collection of O'Hara stories published during the 1960's contains one or more long stories or novellas, ranging from 8500 to 47,000 words.[6] Some of these, like "Mrs. Stratton of Oak Knoll" and "Claude Emerson, Reporter," are extended character sketches; others, such as "The Bucket of Blood," are primarily portraits of places rather than people. All are considerably longer and include far more character development and sense of place and time than does the typical O'Hara short story.

In 1968 O'Hara announced that he was working on a new form, the novelette, which he described as "a full unit of about 30,000 to 38,000 words. Without becoming a novel it tells all that you need to know about certain people in certain circumstances so that those people become figures in the reader's personal library."[7] The example of this form to which O'Hara evidently refers is *A Few Trips and Some Poetry*, which appeared in the collection *And Other Stories* (1969). Though O'Hara's remarks on the novelette are more specific than those on the novella in that he stipulates the length of the former, he does not really help us to distinguish between the two forms. In fact, *A Few Trips and Some Poetry* contains about 47,000 words, whereas the stories in *Sermons and Soda-Water* are more nearly in the range O'Hara designated for the novelette. And surely Charlotte Sears and Bobbie McCrea are as much "figures in the reader's personal library" as is Isabel Barley. Despite Schanche's[8] and Bruccoli's[9] attempts to distinguish between the two forms on the basis of tightness of plot structure, it seems that O'Hara was merely using a longer version of the novella form he had developed in *Sermons and Soda-Water*.

The terms "novella" and "novelette" are frequently used interchangeably today, and although O'Hara used them to refer to what he intended as two different forms of fiction, the differences between the two terms are actually as slight as the differences between *The Girl on the Baggage Truck* (in *Sermons and Soda-Water*) and *A Few Trips and Some Poetry*. "Novelette" has been used rather indiscriminately by editors and anthologizers to refer to works which fall somewhere between the short story and the novel in length—usually 20,000 to 50,000 words. The *OED* defines it as "a story of moderate length having the characteristics of a novel," and at the turn of the century Brander Matthews gave it permanent diminutive status by defining it as "a slight Novel, or a Novel cut down."[10]

The term "novelette" is merely the diminutive of "novel," and has no further intrinsic meaning; and the form to which it is now properly attached is the same as what Henry James called the "nouvelle" and other authors have called the "novella." "Novella" has been gaining prominence as a term recently,[11] though historically it refers to an Italian form which is not followed by modern authors.[12]

Whatever terminology is used, the important point is that O'Hara used a form (or two forms with slight differences) which he knew to be different from the novel and the short story, and in which he attempted to accomplish something different from the deft glimpses of the short stories or the dense social texture of the novels. In the foreword to *Sermons and Soda-Water* he speaks of needing to capture a time period as only he can do it, and in his statement about *A Few Trips and Some Poetry* he emphasizes character. Both remarks are suggestive. The novellas of John O'Hara's last decade are works in which one or two fully-developed characters pass through a particular span of historical reality, and change and grow with that time. The story develops no subsidiary interests—i.e., no "subplots"—but remains focused on a single relationship, conflict, or interest over a period of time, as though it were one thread from a novel. Other characters are used as catalysts, sources of information, or reference points, but seldom become real people as they would in an O'Hara novel, with their own histories and ambitions.

In addition to the ten novellas of this period in O'Hara's career, there are eight stories[13] which are considerably longer than the 3000-to 5000-word O'Hara short story of this period, and before exploring the novellas, it is useful to consider the difference between them and these long stories. Length alone is not the distinguishing factor. "Ninety Minutes Away," for example, is more than 5000 words longer than the novella *A Case History*,[14] but in terms of what it accomplishes, it is a short story. Though Harvey Hunt comes close to being a fully-developed character, the story deals with only a fragment of his life, and O'Hara is more concerned with sketching the moral climate of Philadelphia during Prohibition than with developing a conflict to its logical outcome. The unusual length of the story is largely a result of his presenting—in the form of dialogue or authorial comment—the backgrounds of the three characters who come from different social origins to the same moment in history. The end of the story, rather than demonstrating any real resolution of character or conflict, merely shows Hunt at a somewhat different stage of his life than when the story began a year earlier.

This story, like several other long stories in this group, seems to be a sketch for a novel. The lives of the characters, here presented as "confessions" to the Malloy-like Hunt, could, if presented in detail and followed to a conclusion, have formed the nucleus of a novel. Much the same is true of the somewhat shorter "Yucca Knolls." The first quarter of the story summarizes the lives of Cissie Brandon, Pop Jameson, Sid Raleigh, and Earl Fenway Evans, four Hollywood personalities whose fortunes and careers have brought them together despite vast differences in temperament and talent. The actual conflict in the story is between Cissie and Earl, but it develops toward the end of the story and is not resolved so much as ended by the suggestion that Earl will be arrested for his crimes. "Yucca Knolls" could have been expanded into a novel similar in theme to *The Big Laugh*, but here O'Hara was content to provide a great deal of biographical detail, much of which is incidental to the short story which finally emerges.

Another example of a short story which is given length by the use of much background information is "The Engineer." The impact of the story depends upon the abrupt revelation of Chester Weeks' homosexuality rather than upon the reader's knowledge of Weeks as an individual, and the long, gradual introduction of Weeks to the town of Gibbsville serves to tell the reader more about the politics of the "Company" and the town than about Chester Weeks. And as in "Ninety Minutes Away" the ending is the abrupt conclusion of the short story. Just as the reader begins to expect to know the characters as something other than stereotypes, the story ends.

A variation on this structural pattern of the long story may be seen in "The Bucket of Blood." Rather than presenting the life story of Jay Detweiler in summary form at the beginning of the story, O'Hara uses this section to give the history of the bar which Detweiler eventually owns, and a flashback near the end of the story provides Detweiler's history. The remainder of the story has more to do with the methods of graft during Prohibition than with any conflict or development involving Detweiler, and his rise to a form of respectability seems merely the vehicle for a story of place and time. Here, too, the ending is abrupt; the relationship between Detweiler and Jenny has not been the major concern of the story, so the final scene between them provides little resolution for the story as a whole.

This structural pattern of a long build-up to a sudden ending is quite different from that of the O'Hara novella or novelette. In the latter he achieves a depth of character development not possible in the short story by employing a structure which consists of episodes in the character's life over a long period of time, interspersed with passages of summary. The novella form thus allowed him to accomplish what could not be accomplished in either novel or short story: a detailed portrait—"all that you need to know"—of a single character, relationship or conflict over a considerable period of time. The long stories are mood pieces or sketches which often seem incomplete despite their length, but the novellas are fully-realized units which convey a sense of completion almost like that of the novel.

Most of the O'Hara novellas occupy the familiar settings of Gibbsville, Philadelphia, and New York, and characters and places which are part of the usual O'Hara landscape make their appearances here. The most familiar character is Jim Malloy, who is the narrator in each of the three novellas in *Sermons and Soda-Water*. Malloy's reminiscences form the core of each of the three stories, and his role as narrator provides a restricted point of view which sharpens the focus of the story being told. In *The Girl on the Baggage Truck* the story is that of Charlotte Sears, a Hollywood actress whom Malloy comes to know in his capacity as press agent for the studio; Junior and Polly Williamson are minor characters in this novella, but become more fully developed in the third novella, *We're Friends Again*. In *Imagine Kissing Pete*, Malloy tells the story of Bobbie Hammersmith and Pete McCrea; the story is set almost entirely in "the Region," and aside from Malloy, characters from the other two novellas do not appear.

Each of the three novellas is a self-contained unit, a separate story told from the perspective of Malloy, who is primarily an observer rather than a participant in the action of the story. Because Malloy's knowledge of the people he tells us about is the partial knowledge of the limited human being rather than the omniscience of the author-creator, we do not follow the detailed, day-by-day activities of the characters as we would in a novel. Instead, O'Hara presents a series of episodes consisting of Malloy's sporadic contacts with them, with long gaps of time in between. This device allows O'Hara to cover long periods of time in each novella without becoming involved in the development of minor characters who would detract from the force of the single story line.

O'Hara points up this device by having Malloy comment on it in several instances. In *Imagine Kissing Pete*, Malloy says:

> Such additions I made to my friends' dossiers as I heard about them from time to time; by letters from them, conversations with my mother, an occasional newspaper clipping. I received these facts with joy for the happy news, sorrow for the sad, and immediately went about my business, which was far removed from any business of theirs. I seldom went back to Gibbsville during the Thirties—mine and the century's—and when I did I stayed only long enough to stand at a grave, to toast a bride, to spend a few minutes beside a sickbed. In my brief encounters with my old friends I got no information about Bobbie and Pete McCrea, and only after I returned to New York or California would I remember that I had intended to inquire about them.[15]

The casual tone of this structural comment is belied by the careful structuring of the novellas to allow alternation between scenes of dramatic intensity and periods during which Malloy knows little about the characters' lives, and which therefore pass in quick summary. The role of the writer in creating patterns out of the apparent chaos of life is stated in another of Malloy's comments, this time in *We're Friends Again*: "The way things tie up, one with another, is likely to go unnoticed unless a lawyer or a writer calls our attention to it. And sometimes both the writer and the lawyer have some difficulty in holding things together. But if they are men of purpose they can manage, and fortunately for writers they are not governed by rules of evidence or the whims of the court" (pp. 64–65).

Malloy "holds things together" in these novellas by imposing the logic of his own perspective upon the lives of his friends, and he does this without becoming a fully-developed character in his own right. We know of the major events of Malloy's life, but usually in the barest of summaries: ". . . during those ten days I met a fine girl, and in December of that year we were married and we stayed married for sixteen years, until she died," (p. 64). His involvement with the other characters is sufficient to establish his credibility as a friend in whom they confide their stories, but most of the time he remains in the position of detached narrator.

The Girl on the Baggage Truck deals with the relationship between Charlotte Sears and Thomas Hunterden, although Hunterden remains a somewhat mysterious character and only Charlotte is developed in any depth. Most of the action takes place within a week in 1930, but a remark early in the story indicates that Malloy is remembering these events thirty years later, and toward the end of the novella Malloy returns to the present to account for the intervening years until Charlotte Sears' death. This final section of the story includes several brief conversations between Charlotte and Malloy while she is in the hospital and one later episode when he visits her in California. Our sense of having read about a complete life is heightened by O'Hara's use of the thirty-year flashback; the very length of time adds dimension to the story of the actress even though many of the details of her life are unavailable to Malloy and therefore to us.

O'Hara uses similar devices in *Imagine Kissing Pete*, which is also the story of a single relationship. Here, too, Malloy is the source of all information, and the story covers the same length of time. The episodes, however, are more evenly spaced, with gaps of a few years in between. A more significant difference is that Malloy disappears as the ostensible narrator for the last third of the novella. It becomes apparent at the end that he has been the source of information throughout, but his effacement as a first-person narrator for part of the story foreshadows the fact that in later novellas O'Hara would abandon, temporarily, the use of a narrator. *Imagine Kissing Pete* traces the relationship between Bobbie and Pete over a period of thirty years, and as in *The Girl on the Baggage Truck*, the story ends with a sense of resolution and completion. O'Hara tells this story in chronological order, and again allows Malloy to be overt about the process of telling a story. Just before his disappearance from the story for example, Malloy says: "As we again take up [Bobbie's] story I promise the reader a happy ending, if only because I want it that way. It happens also to be the true ending . . ." (p. 73). The final section of the story eventually proves to be composed of information Malloy has gathered from a conversation with Bobbie during a visit to Fair Grounds, and then Malloy reappears to take the story to its conclusion in 1960.

In *We're Friends Again*, the third novella in *Sermons and Soda-Water*, O'Hara uses a simple flashback structure. The first scene involves Charley Ellis' announcement to Jim of the death of his wife, Nancy, which triggers Malloy's reminiscences of the Ellises as he has known them through the years since 1937. This novella is somewhat more diffuse than the other two: O'Hara departs from the story of Charley Ellis to develop other characters who are significant in his life, and Malloy becomes more involved in the action than in the two previous stories. This novella and *The Girl on the Baggage Truck* are to some extent companion pieces, in that characters introduced in one are developed in the other, particularly Junior and Polly Williamson, whose marital problems are mentioned in *The Girl on the Baggage Truck* but become part of the fabric of *We're Friends Again*.

As evocations of a period of time in American culture, these three novellas succeed admirably. In addition to creating memorable characters, O'Hara has provided vivid scenes of the decades he mentions in his foreword by having his characters move through them as they develop. In *The Girl on the Baggage Truck* he evokes images of the astounding wealth and publicity attendant upon the early years of the Hollywood "star" system, and provides glimpses of Prohibition night life and the pre-suburban Long Island estate. In *We're Friends Again* Roosevelt's New Deal and World War II place the story in a particular social framework. Part of the story takes place in Washington during the war, and Malloy and Nancy Ellis have a running argument about Roosevelt. The characters in *Imagine Kissing Pete* are less involved in national or world affairs, but through the McCreas O'Hara chronicles changes in the Pennsylvania coal country during these same years. Instead of long passages of historical background, O'Hara uses the everyday experiences of his characters to present social and political reality.

The rest of O'Hara's novellas follow patterns similar to those established in *Sermons and Soda-Water*. All cover long periods of time and all are basically character studies—"figures in the reader's personal library"—which go far beyond the limits of the short story but which are much more restricted in scope than the novel. In his next two novellas, *A Case History* (*Assembly*, 1961) and *Pat Collins* (*Cape Cod Lighter*, 1962), O'Hara abandoned the narrator and relied upon careful plot structure to keep the focus on the single story line. Both novellas begin with their respective characters at or beyond middle age, in fairly stable—if not entirely comfortable—circumstances, and then return to the young manhood of the characters to trace the events which have brought them to this point.

Both novellas are set in Gibbsville. *A Case History* is, as its name doubly implies, the history of a man in the medical profession, Buz Drummond, whose outward respectability is a mask for his rather disordered emotional life. Throughout the story O'Hara shifts the point of view from that of the omniscient author to that of Drummond himself to that of his wife, Sadie, his mistress, Minnie, and even that of Mike Slattery, a local politician who maintains what he calls a "dirty file" on Drummond to be used if he ever seeks political office. This multiple view eventually reveals Drummond to be, in keeping with the flatness of the title, a fairly average individual with no more than an average number of skeletons in his closet, outwardly successful and respected, inwardly somewhat unfulfilled. The use of the multiple perspective is a reminder of the public nature of a private life in a small town.

O'Hara divides *A Case History* into six numbered sections, each representing a different period in the life of Buz Drummond, and each consisting of one major scene plus attendant summary. Gaps in time are not explained, as they are by narrator Malloy in *Sermons and Soda-Water*; each section is a discrete unit, conveying by mention of a change in circumstance—"since his marriage"—or a date—"the year was 1939"—that time has passed. The technique is similar to flipping through the pages in a photograph album and recognizing by the style of dress or the growth of a child that time has passed between one page and the next. The first section, which is by far the longest, begins with Buz Drummond in his sixties, semi-retired, and then returns to the beginning of his career in Gibbsville, his affair with a nurse, and then his careful search for the proper wife. The second section consists primarily of a discussion between Mike Slattery and his wife about Drummond's new stature in the community and Slattery's file of Drummond's private sins.

Section 3 is told from the point of view of Drummond's wife, Sadie, and takes place in the third year of their marriage, when she is beginning to feel neglected and useless. The continuing affair between Drummond and Minnie Stokes occupies the fourth section. Section 5 consists of two scenes, one between Drummond and Sadie as her drinking continues to be a problem, and one between Drummond and Minnie, who is now married. Section 6 brings us to the present again, featuring a conversation between Drummond and Arthur McHenry in which Drummond reminisces about his life in the medical profession. The first and last sections thus provide accounts of the "public" Dr. Drummond, respected medical practitioner who took good care of an alcoholic wife, and the middle sections provide glimpses of the "private" Drummond, whose life is not as shocking as Slattery's "dirty file" would make it sound, but which has been hidden beneath a careful public exterior.

O'Hara is not as concerned here as he was in *Sermons and Soda-Water* with presenting a social history of the times he was writing about. It is possible that having presented much of that history through the characters and events in those three novellas, he was content to concentrate on character development. And in fact, except for the two Hollywood novellas, *Natica Jackson* and *James Francis and the Star* (*Waiting for Winter*, 1966), he used the novella form almost entirely as a vehicle for lengthy development of character, as is indicated by the fact that half of the titles are characters' names. However, even in these novellas O'Hara provides a rich sense of time and place by means of references to social or political circumstances. In *A Case History*, for example, when Peg Slattery asks her husband to get her a beer, he responds: "All right. But it's illegal. Ten years ago it wasn't illegal. Ten years from now it won't be. But now it is. That's law for you" (p. 407). And at the beginning of section 5 O'Hara notes that: "It was the day after Thanksgiving and the year was 1939, in which there were two Thanksgiving Days: the officially proclaimed, or FDR holiday, and the second a week later on the traditional fourth Thursday" (p. 416).

In the spring of 1962 O'Hara apparently had plans to repeat the format of *Sermons and Soda-Water*, for he announced that his fall publication that year would be a volume of four novellas about Gibbsville, with the tentative title *Third Class City*. The four pieces he intended for this volume may be the four long pieces in *The Cape Cod Lighter*, which was the Thanksgiving volume that year. Of the four, three are extended short stories—"The Engineer," "The Bucket of Blood," and "Claude Emerson, Reporter"—and one, *Pat Collins*, has the depth and full character development of the novella form. *Pat Collins*, like *A Case History*, is a life story, beginning in 1923 and covering about forty years of Collins' life. Also like *A Case History*, it has a circular structure, beginning in the present and immediately going back to trace the major events of Collins' life before ending again in the present.

O'Hara here uses a device for character development which he would use several other times in the novella: the second character who serves as a dramatic foil to point up characteristics of the first. Here the foil is Whit Hofman, a man different in background, social status, and temperament from Pat Collins, but with whom he forms a close friendship which is destroyed by Hofman's affair with Pat's wife, Madge. The story begins with both men—"Now they are both getting close to seventy, and when they see each other on the street Whit Hofman and Pat Collins bid each other the time of day and pass on without stopping for conversation" (p. 254)—and ends with them: " 'Hello, Pat.' 'Hyuh, Whit.' Never more than that, but never less" (p. 326). Between these two apparently contiguous passages, O'Hara explains the relationship between the two men by telling the story of Pat Collins' rise and fall in Gibbsville society.

As a man of modest means and aspirations, Pat Collins is counterpointed to the wealthy, privileged Whit Hofman in a series of episodes which begin in the mid-1920's. O'Hara uses neither a narrator nor numbered sections to signal changes in time, but instead weaves this information smoothly into the fabric of the narrative, as in the following passages: "Immediately after Christmas the Hofmans went to Florida. They returned for two weeks in late March, closed their house, and took off on a trip around the world. Consequently, the Collinses did not see the Hofmans for nearly a year" (p. 274).

"For nearly three years these men [in Dick Boylan's speakeasy] sustained Pat Collins in his need for companionship, increasingly so as he came to know their problems" (p. 313). However, the use of the second character—in this case Whit Hofman—serves much the same purpose as does a narrator in that the narrative is restricted to only those occasions when the two men's lives impinge on one another, just as Jim Malloy can only convey to us what he actually knows of Charlotte Sears or Bobbie McCrea. The former technique has the advantage of being much less obvious, but the result is very similar: we are told only the most crucial episodes in a character's life, the ones which advance the single conflict of the story.

This single conflict is the frustration of Pat Collins' desire to live an ordinary successful life. His friendship with Whit Hofman raises Pat's social status to a level which Pat could not have attained on his own, and at the same time carries the seeds of his destruction in the form of Whit's eventual relationship with Madge. Whit, protected by wealth and power, can afford to be careless in his private life; Madge cannot, and her confession of the affair to Pat signals the end of his relationship with Whit and his status as a hardworking pillar of the community. Most of the episodes in the novella concern the few years of their close friendship and the affair which ends it. After Pat begins neglecting his work and spending his evenings at Dick Boylan's, most of the story is told in summary, except for a flashback to Madge's actual confession and the final scene in which George Shuttleworth stakes Pat to a new start. The conversation which ends the story has apparently been taking place, unchanged, for many years since these crucial episodes in his life.

There is little overt social commentary of an historical nature in *Pat Collins*. O'Hara restricts himself telling the story of a life, and there are few references—occasional dates, makes of cars, and mention of the founding of the country club—to fix the story in time. The story of the cuckolded husband is timeless, and the interesting part of this one is the Everyman quality of Pat Collins for whom O'Hara enlists our sympathy.

O'Hara's next two collections, *The Hat on the Bed* (1963) and *The Horse Knows the Way* (1964), contains no novellas, though the former includes two long stories, "Ninety Minutes Away" and "Yucca Knolls." But the 1966 collection, *Waiting for Winter*, contains four novellas of roughly the same length as the *Sermons and Soda-Water* pieces. Two of these, *The Skeletons* and *Andrea*, are set primarily in "The Region," and two—*James Francis and the Star* and *Natica Jackson*—have Hollywood settings. Taken together, the four novellas in *Waiting for Winter* demonstrate most of the techniques and concerns of the O'Hara novella.

The Skeletons has a structural pattern quite similar to that of *Pat Collins*. O'Hara begins with a present circumstance—a relationship—and then begins tracing the origin of that relationship. George Roach is used to counterpoint his brother Norman in much the same way as Whit Hofman counterpoints

Pat Collins, and the relationship between the two serves to illuminate the character of Norman Roach, who is the main character. Like Whit Hofman, George Roach gradually disappears from the story, having served his purpose as a foil for Norman. The brief opening paragraph establishes a contrast between the two brothers, both living on inherited money but dealing with enforced leisure in quite different ways, and then O'Hara takes the story back to 1931, when Norman gave up his club membership, and then further back to briefly summarize the two men's histories before taking up their stories after the Second World War. Here, as in other novellas, O'Hara makes use of the quick summary and suggestive fragment of dialogue to cover great amounts of time with economy of words.

The major part of the story concentrates on Norman Roach and his family, all of whom are the "skeletons" of the story. In contrast to George, who has had a happy marriage and now has a satisfying relationship with another woman, and who maintains his respectability by adhering to a schedule of social engagements, Norman, with a dull marriage and two unlovely daughters, has become a figure of ridicule in Gibbsville because of his aimless wandering around town. As the story proceeds with a series of episodes detailing the various shames of Norman Roach's family, George Roach becomes a background figure of apparent social success against which we measure Norman's failure to derive anything meaningful from his life. What emerges is a portrait of dullness and ineffectuality which has its effect on Norman's daughters, one of whom becomes a lesbian while the other marries hastily out of boredom.

O'Hara alternates passages of summary with conversations between the two brothers or members of the Norman Roach household, and the passage of time is indicated briefly in references to birthdays or years. He interweaves past and present throughout a basically chronological narrative structure by making reminiscence part of the emphasis in conversation, as in the chance meeting between George and Norman on George's fifty-ninth birthday. In addition to showing the continuing tension between the two brothers, this conversation also involves George's dead wife, Elsie, Norman's military service, and the brothers' comparative physical conditions. In addition to providing information to the reader about the two characters, this conversation also points up their avoidance of one another in its inclusion of topics which closer friends would have long since exhausted. After this point in the novella, George Roach does not appear again as a character, and O'Hara concentrates on Norman's family as a reflection of his character and habits. The ending is close in time to the beginning, and although O'Hara does not tie the two together so obviously as he does in *Pat Collins*, there is implicit linkage in Bertie Roach's reply to her husband's question about what their daughter does with her time: "You're a fine one to ask," (p. 400).

Aside from an oblique reference to the Depression as Norman's reason for dropping his club membership, and brief references to both World Wars, there is little social history here of the sort O'Hara detailed in *Sermons and Soda-Water*. As in *A Case History* and *Pat Collins*, the emphasis is on probing below the surface of a character's life and exposing the private reasons for the public image, in far greater detail than would have been possible in the short story.

In contrast to the sense of completion and resolution in most of O'Hara's novellas—the reader's perception of having seen a life to its logical end and having a thorough knowledge of a character—the novella *Andrea* suffers from a hasty and contrived ending. Andrea's sudden suicide, despite the problems she has recently been forced to confront, does not grow logically out of the character as we have come to know her, nor does anything in the scene which precedes it seem adequate to trigger such complete desperation. The ending is the sort we might expect in a short story, in which there may be motivations which are only hinted, and in which an action may be substituted for an explanation of behavior. The use of a narrator—the first since *Sermons and Soda-Water*—contributes to the unreality of the ending in that it places us at such a distance from Andrea that we cannot comprehend her state of mind at this point. Although he has known her for years, Philip is not close to Andrea emotionally, and does not have the insight of Jim Malloy, so he is as astonished by her action as is the reader.

Although it is the weakest of O'Hara's novellas, *Andrea* is interesting for its view of Gibbsville from the outside—a perspective which O'Hara had on his native Pottsville for much of his life—and for its close focus on the circumstances of the continuing affair, a frequent occurrence in O'Hara's fiction. The narrator, known only as Philip, has moved away from Gibbsville when he first meets Andrea at a Gibbsville dance. He is in law school, ten years older than the sixteen-year-old Andrea, and will not return to Gibbsville to practice. Thereafter he returns only in his capacity as an increasingly successful Philadelphia attorney, and he knows about Andrea's Gibbsville experiences only from her own accounts. Thus, instead of going inside the private lives of Gibbsville residents, as we do in *A Case History, Pat Collins*, and *The Skeletons*, we have only an outline of Andrea's family story, culminating in a ruined business and an alcoholic mother. What is of concern to O'Hara is the relationship between Philip and Andrea, and he takes pains to exclude almost all other parts of their lives from the story.

Until the ending, the story line is clean and chronological, consisting of those episodes which detail the infrequent meetings of the lovers and with the barest summary of the intervening periods of time. The voice of the narrator is reminiscent of Jim Malloy as he accounts for the passage of time: "She had a way of turning up just as I was beginning to convince myself that I ought to put an end to my bachelorhood. Two or three times as much as a year would pass without my hearing from her except for a message scribbled on a Christmas card" (p. 36). Andrea's problems with men are a frequent topic of conversation during their meetings, and gradually Philip becomes the only stable point in her life. The final episode follows a period of separation after an argument, and serves a reconciliation, which, given the relationship the two have had, is not at all surprising. But the gratuitous fall from the hotel window seems an illogical ending to what has been to this point a well-developed story. Andrea is, apart from this, an interesting example of the insecure, dissatisfied woman whom O'Hara portrayed so often, and we come to know her well enough here to feel some sympathy for her.

O'Hara's two Hollywood novellas, in contrast, are among his most successful. As he suggested in the foreword to *Sermons and Soda-Water*, the novella form was well-suited to his sort of social history, allowing the development of place and time which would be impossible in the short story, and yet restricting the focus of the story to a few characters and a single conflict. Both *James Francis and the Star* and *Natica Jackson* convey the texture of the early film industry while presenting some memorable characters. The number of minor characters is larger than in some of the other novellas, because part of O'Hara's intention is to portray a variety of Hollywood types, just as he presents characters like Charley Ellis and Junior Williamson in *The Girl on the Baggage Truck* to lend authenticity to the period. But the novellas center on the characters named in the titles, and the other characters furnish the background of their stories.

In *James Francis and the Star* O'Hara uses the structural pattern which had worked so well in *A Case History, Pat Collins*, and *The Skeletons*—most of the story is a long chronological flashback which explains the situation described at the beginning—and, as in the latter two of these novellas, he uses a second character—here, the "star"—as a foil for the major one. By chronicling the changing relationship between James Francis Hatter, a Hollywood script writer, and Rod Fulton, an actor, O'Hara provides a full portrait of James Francis as well as giving a picture of the rise and fall of fortunes in the film industry. James Francis has given Rod Fulton his start in Hollywood, but at the beginning of the story Fulton has become a success and James Francis is being left out of his life. What follows is an episodic account of more than twenty years of their friendship. Although the point of view is not consistently that of James Francis Hatter, his is the dominant consciousness in the novella, and he therefore enlists our sympathy. Rod Fulton is seen from this perspective as a somewhat selfish man, easily swayed by the most persuasive and influential person, and James Francis, by contrast, seems the more admirable person even when he is having an affair with Fulton's first wife. O'Hara's message seems to be that success is a corrupting force, and that the sort of power which accrues to the Hollywood "star" is destructive to friendship. Even this message is not unmixed, however; Fulton's party on the occasion of James Francis' fiftieth birthday indicates that he is entitled to some of the admiration James Francis has for him.

The Hollywood which O'Hara presents here is a gossipy small town not much different than Gibbsville, in which the studio replaces the coal company as the all-powerful force. Details of the business of films and the politics of the industry are logical parts of the action in the novella rather than separate explanatory passages, so the focus remains on the characters as individuals. A minor character whom Rod Fulton romances as part of the publicity for a film is described as a "New York actress," a term which O'Hara briefly defines as "a stage actress who had not acquired a motion picture reputation," (p. 225). O'Hara indicates the time period of the story not only by references to World War II as an interruption of Rod Fulton's career but also by mention of actual Hollywood figures. And James Francis is disturbed to learn that Fulton has gone hunting with Ernest Hemingway without telling him, calling Hemingway, "the only guy I wanted to meet," (p. 220).

The passage of time is handled here in the ways which had by now become standard in the O'Hara novella. The following transition is typical: "He had seen very little of Rod Fulton during his marriage to Melina. . . . But he came as soon as he was asked," (p. 216). The longest gap of time in the novella occurs after James Francis has shot the tennis player in Palm Springs, and when the rift in his friendship with the star is most serious. At this point O'Hara pauses for a page-long summary of the intervening years, which ends with the passage quoted above and begins, "It was often said in later years that Rod Fulton, whether you liked him or not, had stood by James Francis Hatter when Jimmy got into that jam in Palm Springs," (p. 215). The ending of the novella is linked to the beginning by the mention of Fulton washing James Francis' car, a reference to the beginning of their relationship and evidence of their reconciliation.

Hollywood as an entity is even more apparent in *Natica Jackson*. O'Hara here tells the story of the rise of a young actress to star status, and the tragic effect of her attempt to have a life beyond the studio. Thus the studio, or her contact with it in the form of her agent, Morris King, becomes a major factor in the story. Appropriately, Hal Graham, the "outsider" with whom she has an affair, remains a rather undeveloped character, while Morris and his wife Ernestine are drawn in considerable detail, and provide the world of contracts and power plays within which Natica has chosen to live. O'Hara makes many references to the daily business of making films, as in the following passage: "Acting was the last thing you did after everything else was ready, and you did that for two minutes at a time. Then they glued those two minuteses together until they had eighty minutes that made sense—and then they put you in another picture" (p. 266). But this is far from gratuitous detail; Natica is new to Hollywood, and this is one of her attempts to explain the business to herself, to understand why "she was . . . the only Santa Ana girl who had been kissed by Robert Taylor," (p. 266). Because the story is told primarily from Natica's point of view, her conversations with Morrie King about contract negotiations also function as part of her attempt to comprehend her new world.

Although *Natica Jackson* covers several years of the actress' life, its time span is shorter than that of the typical O'Hara novella, and with the exception of several brief flashbacks it is told in chronological order. Natica's encounter with Hal Graham early in the story is followed by a section in which O'Hara deals with Natica's rise to prominence in films, and then the story builds to its critical point with a switch to the Graham household and Beryl Graham's suspicions of her husband. The final scene between Natica and the Kings demonstrates her final acceptance of the ways of the Hollywood world: "I have complete confidence in Morris," (p. 318).

When John O'Hara wrote what was to be his last published novella, *A Few Trips and Some Poetry* (*And Other Stories*, 1969), he was careful to call it a "novelette" rather than a "novella," but in this work he turned again to the structure and even some of the characters of the 1960 *Sermons and Soda-Water*, which he had been equally careful to call "novellas." To further complicate the matter, the jacket blurb for *And Other Stories* calls it "a novel of medium length," but it is strikingly similar to the 1960 novellas, including the use of Jim Malloy as narrator. There is even an oblique reference to a couple who could be the McCreas of *Imagine Kissing Pete*.[16] *A Few Trips* is one of the most successful of O'Hara's novellas, and although it is the longest of his efforts in this form, it follows the pattern which O'Hara had established for his work in the genre: a study of one or two characters as they develop over a long period of time, a clean story line unadorned with sub-plots and digressions.

Insofar as *A Few Trips* is the story of an affair, it has elements in common with *Andrea*. In both works the major character is an attractive woman who is married more than once but who has a continuing relationship with the narrator which represents a kind of stability in her otherwise chaotic life. Andrea and Philip call their relationship *société anonyme*; Isabel Barley, in *A Few Trips*, refers to Jim Malloy as her "permanent, sporadic lover." But *A Few Trips* is a much better novella, and Isabel Barley is a more complex character than Andrea Cooper. The fact that Isabel becomes a lesbian is in keeping with O'Hara's increasing use of homosexual characters in his later fiction, and is consistent with what we know of her early history.

A Few Trips is divided into nine sections by the narrator's announcements of time having passed. The first eight sections are episodes in the relationship between Jim and Isabel, and cover, chronologically, about twenty years with gaps of several months or years between episodes. The final scene takes place thirty years afterward, and constitutes a sort of coda, much like the final scene of *The Girl on the Baggage Truck*. The narrator is here, as in *Imagine Kissing Pete*, the one who has left "the Region" and who has only intermittent contact with the subject of his story. As Malloy states after the first section of the story: "Here, with an almost brutal lack of consideration for the line of my story, certain events of my life took place: I left town and got a job in New York. New interests, new friends, new loves separated me from the immediate past, and I was not making enough money to afford frequent homecomings" (p. 64). This passage shows the same consciousness of being a storyteller that

Malloy exhibits in *Sermons and Soda-Water*, though Malloy is much more involved in the action of the story in *A Few Trips*, as he explains in this passage about two-thirds of the way through the story:

> These reflections on my intellectual processes are set down in this chronicle because I have made myself a character in them. Isabel had married a young business man, who was killed; she had married an older man who was a cripple; she had had half a dozen affairs with other men and at least one girl, and unless I was very much mistaken, she was now about to satisfy her curiosity about Horse McGrath; and her one constant if sporadic lover was I. Of course the probability did not escape me that she retained me as lover because of the sporadic nature of our affair, which gave the relationship the nature of several affairs. We had come from adolescence all the way into our thirties, with time lapses that had had significant effects upon each of us. Whatever it was that made us return to each other regardless of the distractions of others in between, the continuing relationship was unique to her and to me. The physical pleasures we shared were surely stimulated by our separations, but not only by the separations. Always some of the old Isabel was gone and aging had created something new, and for her this must also have been true of me. And yet we had, as it were, a joint personal history, exclusive of all others, which minimized the strangeness whenever we were reunited. I was a character in these chronicles because of my relative importance to Isabel, the heroine. (pp. 133–34)

The "joint personal history, exclusive of all others," is a clue to the nature of the novella form as O'Hara used it, and is the key element separating this form from his novels. In writing a novella he concentrated on a single character or relationship, introducing other characters or incidents only for the purpose of illuminating or making plausible an action or a character trait. Of several examples in *A Few Trips*, two will suffice to make this point. Samuel Turner, though an ever-present figure in the story, is not fully developed as a character. He exists in the story for two purposes: to bring Jim and Isabel together at the beginning and to place Isabel in Turnersville through her marriage to him. He is a functional character rather than a central focus of the reader's attention. Horse McGrath serves much the same purpose; the fact that Jim "rescues" Isabel from McGrath tells us something important about their relationship, and afterward McGrath disappears from the story.

If there is a common theme in O'Hara's ten novellas, it is the curious nature of human relationships, whether based on hate, as in *The Skeletons*, friendship, as in *James Francis and the Star*, or love, as in *A Few Trips and Some Poetry*. Although he explored this theme in novels and short stories as well, the novella afforded him the opportunity to concentrate on a single story without the diffusion created by the novel's mass of historical detail and multiple character development. To accomplish this blend of depth of treatment and clarity of development, he employed certain structural patterns and devices which would allow for the passage of time and the omission of explanatory material not directly related to the action of the story. One of these devices is the narrator, which he used in half of these works, the observer with a limited exposure to events and people. The structure of all the novellas is episodic, whether the episodes are introduced by section numbers, a narrator, or the omniscient author. Instead of following the daily lives of his characters, O'Hara presents them only at points which bear upon the conflict or relationship he is developing. One manner of ordering these episodes which he found particularly useful in providing limits for his story was a circular structure: the novella begins with the concluding circumstance, and the events leading to it are recounted in a long flashback consisting of a series of more or less chronological episodes.

Whatever the technique, O'Hara's novellas share a tone of reflection appropriate for an author in the last decade of a long career. Though they contain varying amounts of what might be called social history, all ten novellas evoke a sense of reminiscence and even nostalgia. That this sense is stronger when O'Hara uses Jim Malloy as a narrator who can say, "That was thirty years ago . . ." is not surprising, but even when no narrator is present as the obvious reflective consciousness, it is clear that O'Hara is drawing upon memories of people and times which were very much a part of his life and career. The ambition he expressed in the foreword to *Sermons and Soda-Water*— "to get it all down on paper while I can"—seems to have been the motivation for the subsequent novellas as well, and one result is our awareness of a mature author contemplating the nature of loyalty and love and many other ways in which people relate to one another. O'Hara is not unique among modern authors in his use of the novella form. Others as disparate as Lawrence, Porter, and Faulkner have found it appropriate to certain circumstances. But few modern authors have devoted so much attention to its possibilities, or, indeed, have achieved so much in its use.

Notes

1. I omit here *The Farmers Hotel*, originally a play and later a short novel, and *A Family Party*, a long monologue which cannot be classified in the usual categories of fiction.

2. Quoted by Albert Erskine in the Foreword to *Good Samaritan and Other Stories* (New York: Random House, 1974), p. vii. This statement was originally written for the introduction to the Modern Library *Selected Stories*, published in 1956, but was never published.

3. Foreword to *The Horse Knows the Way* (New York: Random House, 1964), p. v.

4. Matthew J. Bruccoli, *The O'Hara Concern* (New York: Random House, 1975), p. 281.

5. (New York: Random House, 1960), n.p.

6. In the spring of 1962 O'Hara stated that he would publish a volume of four novellas about Gibbsville, called *Third Class City*, linked by location as the *Sermons and Soda-Water* stories had been linked by the character of Jim Malloy and dealing with different social classes. No book with that title or format appeared, but *The Cape Cod Lighter*, which was published in the

fall of 1962, contains three long stories and a novella which may have been those intended for the separate volume. (*The O'Hara Concern*, p. 292.)

7.   Don A. Schanche, "John O'Hara is Alive and Well in the First Half of the Twentiety Century," *Esquire* (August 1969), p. 49.

8.   Schanche, p. 49.

9.   *The O'Hara Concern*, p. 264.

10.   *The Philosophy of the Short Story* (New York: Longman's 1901), p. 26.

11.   See especially Marlene Springer, *Forms of the Modern Novella* (Chicago: University of Chicago Press, 1975).

12.   The term "short novel" is also sometimes used interchangeably with these two, and is perhaps the most confusing of all, especially in the mid-twentieth century when many novels do not approach the length of O'Hara's typical ones. *The Big Laugh* is a novel, though a short one for O'Hara: *The Farmers Hotel* is an even shorter one, but both are novels nonetheless.

13.   This number includes "The Doctor's Son" (*The Doctor's Son and Other Stories*, 1935). Published twenty-five years before *Sermons and Soda-Water*, it marks O'Hara's earliest published attempt at an intermediate form.

14.   For the reader's convenience, I will use quotation marks with the titles of short stories and italics in the titles of novellas, even though most of the latter were not published as separate volumes.

15.   *Sermons and Soda-Water*, p. 54. All quotations from O'Hara's works are taken from the first Random House editions, and are hereafter documented by page numbers in the text.

16.   "Another girl in our crowd married a boy in our crowd and they lived in a poor section of town and stayed away from their old friends for obvious reasons" (p. 97).

The Suburban Vision in John O'Hara's Short Stories

KATHRYN RILEY

Critics of John O'Hara traditionally have classified the settings of his works according to three social and geographical divisions. New York, Hollywood, and the small Pennsylvania city of Gibbsville, modeled after his home town of Pottsville.[1] While most of O'Hara's fiction does indeed fall into these divisions, critics have overlooked a series of stories from his later collections that cannot be placed in the New York / Hollywood / Gibbsville categories. Where O'Hara had tended to write, in earlier stories, about characters in relatively specialized and removed worlds—Hollywood actors and actresses, smalltime hoods moving in their own moral framework, aristocrats imprisoned in the protected shell of the past—the stories discussed here, those set in post–World War II suburbs, reflect O'Hara's movement beyond the concerns associated with the major settings of his earlier fiction.

All of O'Hara's suburban stories deal, to some extent, with the tension between day-to-day "normality" and the intrusion of emotions and events that conflict with the *status quo*. The setting of these stories reinforces that conflict for O'Hara's depiction of suburbia ties in with his protagonists' attempt to maintain a façade that belies a deeper unrest. Within this general area of concern, the stories fall into several groupings that show O'Hara gradually adapting his earlier approaches to more modern material and themes. Additionally, they reveal his ability to universalize the suburban experience without falling into the easy trap of stereotyping it.

Most of O'Hara's suburban fiction appeared in the 1960's, for several probable reasons. In addition to the fact that the suburbs were themselves coming into prominence during the decades following World War II, O'Hara had moved to a suburban residence near Princeton in 1957. Also, according to his preface to *Assembly* (1961), he had written almost no short fiction between 1949, when he broke with *The New Yorker* over Brendan Gill's negative review of *A Rage to Live*, and 1961. Returning to the short story after this hiatus, O'Hara approached the form with new vigor.[2]

Reprinted from *Critique: Studies in Modern Fiction* 25 (Winter 1984): 101–13. Reprinted with permission of the Helen Dwight Reid Educational Foundation. Published by Heldref Publications, 4000 Albemarle St., N. W., Washington, D.C. 20016. Copyright © 1984.

This new period, in turn, brought with it several shifts in the author's approach to the short story. Changes in both technique and, to a greater extent, tone between O'Hara's earlier and later work have been noted. The later stories gain in length and complexity while still retaining the economy that characterizes O'Hara's short fiction. Overshadowing the irony and satire of his earlier work is a more compassionate tone, one that remains realistic rather than sentimental but that reflects O'Hara's greater empathy with the mature characters who populate his later work.[3]

The first group of stories to be discussed recalls O'Hara's earlier, more naturalistic work and reflects fairly strongly the popular image of suburbia at the time he was writing, in the early 1960's.[4] In "The Twinkle in His Eye," "Justice," "The Jet Set," and "The Madeline Wherry Case,"[5] O'Hara brings to the suburban setting his career-long concern with secrets that build up over time toward irreversible, and often fatal, emotional and physical violence. The length and complexity of these pieces also lend them a "case history" flavor, as does the omniscient narrative point of view that probes the characters' intricate psychological motivations. These stories reflect a writer in transition, taking a traditional approach to contemporary material.

The melodramatic quality of these stories about suburban violence also derives from their overwhelming atmosphere of seemingly preordained corruption. O'Hara gives credence to the power of social codes, both internally and externally imposed, yet invests the neatly structured suburban world with an undercurrent of more turbulent, less easily codified passions. In "Justice," for example, the protagonist Norman Daniels is exiled by the community after his lover is murdered by her jealous husband. The complex issue of Daniels' guilt is sustained by the first-person narrative viewpoint. He tries to explain and justify his role in the scandal, and it quickly becomes clear that Daniels "doth protest too much": he both deceives himself about the extent of his involvement and fails to convince the reader of his moral superiority. Having confused *de jure* innocence with *de facto* innocence and unable to comprehend why his public image cannot exculpate him, he sinks into moral limbo.

In a similar act of self-deception, Gordon Whittier, of "The Twinkle in His Eye" harbors a passionate hatred of his wife, a hatred founded on small incidents that, unknown to her, have built up his resentment over the years. His hatred comes into conflict, however, with his equal passion for maintaining a respectable façade. Hence, he remains imprisoned in a state of permanent mediocrity, unable to act upon the emotions that obsess him. Characters like Daniels and Whittier, who rationalize their own weaknesses by pleading the need to protect a public image, quickly reveal themselves as hypocrites—not only in our eyes but in the eyes of their communities as well.

"The Jet Set" and "The Madeline Wherry Case" also use violent death to dramatize the question of moral responsibility. In the first story, a man's knowledge of a dark secret in a woman's past eventually drives her to suicide. Lawrence Graybill's culpability, O'Hara suggests, is shared by the community at large; these suburbanites, banded together by their "passion for competitiveness," choose toughness over compassion. The story points toward one inescapable clause in the moral contract, that of accepting responsibility for one's actions and of refraining from the disabuse of powers over others.

The question of victimization by the community also arises in the second story, which recounts the events that drive an adultress, Madeline Wherry, to murder her husband. By tracing Madeline's actions before the murder, O'Hara builds up the contrast between her vital relationship with her lover and her stifling marriage to a husband who has himself been unfaithful. Here again the protagonist is caught between two worlds, that of an external social code and a more powerful one of private emotions. As in the other stories of destruction, O'Hara hints at no reprieve for Madeline Wherry: just as surely as she will be punished for her crime of passion, her life with Bud Wherry would have constituted a more subtle but equally dehumanizing punishment. While Lawrence Graybill and Madeline Wherry arrive at greater self-knowledge than do Whittier and Daniels, they attain it too late to act positively on it.

This first group of stories, then, contains O'Hara's most disparaging view of suburban life, one in which emotional and physical violence are as much a part of the landscape as are the country club and the commuter train. In one sense, he seems merely to filter stereotypes of suburban corruption through the lens of melodrama. Despite their violent and somewhat sensationalist nature, however, these stories do not limit themselves entirely to expose tactics or a fatalistic condemnation of suburban life. Although both adultery and violent death are consummate within the pages of "Justice," "The Jet Set," and "The Madeline Wherry Case," O'Hara handles the baser details of such acts off-stage, so to speak, leading us to look for the story's focus beyond the obvious sources of drama in its plot.

If we follow this lead, we discover a more complex vision than might be immediately apparent. In several cases, it is not the victim of the violence who gains our interest but, instead, a protagonist who has had a relationship with that victim. O'Hara draws a direct correlation between the protagonist's self-knowledge and his freedom to act, and this theme is intimately related to the suburban setting. In all of the stories, we encounter characters whose self-knowledge has been clouded and distorted by their acquiescence to the suburban social structure.

O'Hara's point is that while suburbia may seem to be the villain in these stories, this is not entirely so. The suburbs in these stories, like their inhabitants, exhibit varying degrees of morality. The protagonists within them all fail to meet the same challenge: that of recognizing the point where the community can no longer define their moral code and where they must begin defining it themselves. Norman Daniels and Gordon Whittier never achieve the ability to control their own actions; Lawrence Graybill and Madeline Wherry achieve it, but too late.

A pattern that recurs in a second group of suburban stories involves a more subtle kind of disruption, an outsider's intrusion into a protagonist's calm existence. The conflict in this set of stories, like that in the first, lies in the disparity between acceptable morality and behavior and violations of that code. While in the stories just discussed this conflict manifests itself in irreversible consequences, in this second group of tales O'Hara remains more ambivalent about the possibility of balancing the *status quo* and the inner life. The protagonists of these stories begin with the assumption that, by obeying outward signs of social and moral propriety, they are operating under a self-sustaining philosophy of life. An interruption of the external routine, however, forces the central character to the point of greater self-awareness.

The intrusion of such an outsider forms the basis for "Saturday Lunch," in which two suburban housewives suddenly realize that they have both been sexually propositioned by the same man, a seemingly harmless real-estate man named Duncan Ebberly. As the disrupter of their world, Ebberly embodies the ugliness that lies just beneath the calm surface of suburban existence. Carol Ferguson and Alice Reeves' encounters with him open their eyes to that sordid dimension of life which their society denies simply by ignoring its existence.

Although much of this narrative recounts the incident during which Ebberly approaches Carol, the real revelation O'Hara is aiming for has more to do with Carol and Alice's relationships with their husbands. Even more disturbing than Ebberly's advances is the distance between Jud Ferguson and Joe Reeves' images of their wives and the private ordeal that these women have sustained. O'Hara implies that even apparently "normal" suburbanites have secrets that are belied by the appearances they maintain, just as Ebberly appears to be no more than a harmless, stammering, middle-aged bachelor. The author makes this point subtly, through interchanges such as this one between Jud and Joe, remarking on their wives' sensitivity to the weather:

" 'Is anybody cold here?' said Carol Ferguson. 'Jud, will you go back and see if that kitchen door blew open?' 'I wasn't going to say anything,' said Alice Reeves. 'But I think there must be a door open somewhere.' 'So delicate,' said her husband. 'Christ, aren't they?' said Jud Ferguson" (295–96). Both husbands display a protective, slightly patronizing attitude toward their spouses, absurd in light of what the reader has learned about the women. In surburbia, the same reliance on appearances that allows Ebberly to prey on women also prevents his victims from retaliating.

A similar lack of communication—a problem that lies at the heart of many marriages in O'Hara's suburbs—is revealed in "The Clear Track." Although composed of eight pages of almost straight dialogue, this story really concerns the Loxley's inability to talk to one another about the problems at the crux of their marriage. Their respective affairs with others are discussed only by accident, in the course of conversations about other things, and neither partner has the courage or the energy to follow through on them. As a result, each gives the other the "clear track" to pursue infidelity, even though both immediately realize that it is not the direction they want to take.

O'Hara's method in this story reinforces his message: by focusing on "the numerous small transactions that are the formalities of a marriage during trying times" (13), he shows the Loxleys relegating their marital problems to the same level of small talk with which they discuss interior decorators and other instances of "how things will look." By the end of the story the reader feels the same sense of frustration that informs the couple's relationship, for the barrier of triviality surrounding their marriage prevents either confrontation or resolution. Just as the dialogue in "Saturday Lunch" and "The Clear Track" leaves the most important things unsaid, so their characters' hesitancy to ruffle the smooth surface of their existence prevents them from getting to deeper issues.

Chance encounters with outsiders also figure in "The Time Element" and "Sunday Morning." The irony of the first story derives from the reversal in the circumstances of Rob Wilson and Kit Dunbar, two former lovers who meet after nearly a decade. Their conversation reveals, subtly, that her life has steadily improved in an almost inverse pattern to his inward demise. Despite their superficial similarities—both have several children and are in the same social class (Wilson has learned about Kit's life in Chicago because his wife "gets the Junior League magazine")—telling changes have upset the balance of power between them. Kit, Wilson notices immediately, is more beautiful at thirty-five than when he jilted and deceived her nine years before; she vetoes sitting in a bar because, she says, "I don't want a drink and I'd rather you didn't too"; she has given up smoking ("I suppose I ought to," he replies) and is clearly in control of the interview: "I can ask questions, and you can't. I didn't ask to see you, you know" (125–26). Although their conversation is short and mainly factual, it is filled with the undertones of Kit's disgust toward Wilson and her anxiousness to end the meeting.

By the end of their interview, Wilson understands the nature of the "simple mysterious thing," the indefinable malaise that has been bothering him: reminded of how he betrayed Kit, he realizes how his dishonesty has affected his own marriage. The narrator suggests that Wilson's former self-deceit will be replaced not by optimism but by the middle ground of realism: "He would be late for dinner, but not very late" (128). O'Hara's understated handling of the story's end, like that of "Saturday Lunch" and "The Clear Track," complements his subject: the sense of a confining existence that, by relying more on form than on content, leaves its inhabitants in a paralyzed, static state that must be resisted.

Similarly, "Sunday Morning" takes its protagonist to the point of revelation but leaves her just short of transcending her ennui. The action consists of Marge Fairbanks' brief trip into town for the Sunday papers. Within this apparently simple story, O'Hara relates a series of small events from Marge's point of view, leaving the reader with a full sense not only of her daily life but also of her frustration with it. Her "independence" is measured by small acts of defiance and attempts to break out of the routine existence she has fallen into.

Her sojourn into town exposes her, and the reader, to small reminders of the pettiness and hypocrisy of her fellow suburbanites: she sees, on their way to Mass, a couple who were too drunk to drive the night before; she is greeted rudely by the drugstore proprietor; most disturbingly, a neighbor sounds her out on the possibility of having an affair. Her exchange with Ralph Shipstead reveals her own ambivalent feelings and the fortuitous set of values by which she lives. She brushes him off abruptly; but then, driving home, her thoughts go back to their meeting. She finds him a "loathesome man"— ostentatious, unrespectable, overconfident—but still, "he wanted her, and it excited her to think that in her present frame of mind he could almost have her. Almost" (354).

Marge's conflicting emotions range from sarcastic thoughts about her neighbors ("Would anyone be interested to learn that Nannie Martin was thinking of changing to Presbyterian? Would the *Herald Tribune* send a reporter to interview Dixie Green if they knew that Dixie had once had a date with a gentleman who now sat in the White House?") to a dread, all the more disturbing for its vagueness, of returning home to her mundane family life. Her exact problem lies in the mediocrity of her situation, for she is defined only by her position as a wife, a mother, a potential partner in adultery: "But what was *she*, Marge Fairbanks? A secure wife, yes and a conscientious mother, yes. But what else? But she, she, she? What was she, apart from husband and children, apart from Ralph Shipstead's mechanical lechery for her? And worst of all, what did she want, what could she be, other than what she had and what she was? Was this all? Was it worth it?" (355).

Marge Fairbanks' malaise, then, is brought on not by the presence of any definable qualities in her life but rather by the absence of those qualities. From an outsider's perspective, she really has nothing to complain about: her life, like her husband's lovemaking, is "usually all right." The seriousness of her situation is not revealed until the end of the story, when the car, out of gas, stalls on the road to her home, and she sits there in reverie: "The drizzle on the windshield reminded her of tears, and she waited for the thought to bring the tears, but they did not come. She was not even that unhappy . . . "She put the keys in her pocket and got out of the car, and as she began the homeward walk she kicked the front tire. It hurt her toe, and now she could cry, a little" (355–56). This final scene, which shows her need for an external reason to cry and to release her emotions, suggests that she is just beginning to attain a tentative self-knowledge. Although able to ask herself some crucial questions, she remains nonetheless unable to answer them because the apparently "all right" nature of her suburban life prevents her from seeing beyond its, and her own, surface.

Although less overtly dramatic than the tales of physical violence discussed above, this second group of stories nevertheless contains disturbing elements. Their lack of catharsis and their overwhelming tone of anticlimax and stasis are in their own way as pessimistic as the destructive outcome of a story like "The Madeline Wherry Case." In these stories we are more likely to perceive the suburbs as a place of potential psychological entrapment; for while the characters in the first group do achieve a kind of dismal escape through adultery and violence, characters like the Loxleys and Marge Fairbanks may be doomed to repeat the present.

A final group of stories offers O'Hara's strongest suggestion of an alternative to the violence seen in the first group of stories and the ennui portrayed in the second. O'Hara never goes so far as to suggest that life in the suburbs can be idyllic; his characters all, invariably, face threats to that illusion. What he offers as a means of coping, in its place, are a willingness to compromise and, more important, a sense of compassion. In keeping with the technique used in the second set of stories, O'Hara uses the pattern of an epiphany effected by an outsider or an unexpected incident. The characters in this final group of stories, however, unlike those in the first two, seem able to incorporate their new knowledge into their suburban existence.

Several of these stories revolve around domestic scenes including not only a husband and wife but also their children. O'Hara thereby suggests that encounters between parents and children are one way of investing values and ideals with new vitality. In "The Father," "The Lesson," "Appearances," and "Family Evening," O'Hara examines the difficulties and rewards of achieving understanding through such encounters. For example, Miles Berry in "The Father" undergoes a change when his sister sends him an old photograph of his wife, a newspaper clipping that shows Vilma as a young, single woman of seventeen at a Frank Sinatra concert in 1945. His shock of recognition at this evidence of her once-vital spirit comes amidst the banality of their current life, placing the present in sharp relief against the past. The photo is a reminder of Vilma's and, by extension, his own lost youth and romanticism.

Fortunately, the contrast is strong enough to show Berry how precious that romanticism is, and he is able to translate his awareness into a new sensitivity toward his daughter, Ava. The final implication is that Berry will alter his habit of taking his wife and daughter's emotions, as well as his own, for granted, and of subordinating the sentimental to the pragmatic (O'Hara— not accidentally, it would seem—assigns Berry the occupation of a mechanic). The structure of this story reinforces its theme, the ability of small, seemingly unassociated incidents to evoke strong memories and emotions and to provide everyday reminders of age and mortality. Consistent with O'Hara's overall treatment of suburbia, the protagonist's revelation comes in an almost accidental way. Its effect is no less profound, however, for its understated quality.

In a similar way, the daughter in "The Lesson" must bridge the gap of years and emotions between her divorced parents. Having grown up with her mother, the daughter learns from her father that, prior to the divorce, both parents had been involved in a series of affairs. Unexpectedly, this insight gives both father and daughter new knowledge and respect for one another. Mimi, now married and about to have her own child, must reassess her mother's version of her father—"She's made you sound like such an awful son of a bitch that you couldn't possibly live up to it" (206). But she has also built up an image of him, through pictures, as a football hero in his college days. She learns from their meeting that neither of these black-and-white extremes is accurate.

The father, in turn, is equally surprised by his daughter's mature ability to accept the past without condemning him. While Mimi's insight is accompanied by a slight edge of cynicism, she gains in perception what she loses in idealism. Like Miles Berry, both Mimi and her father must acknowledge shortcomings in their own assumptions before they can connect with other people. Again, the changes in them are more subtle, internal ones, unlikely to change the outward patterns of their lives but certain to transform their private visions.

"Appearances" reverses the roles of parent and child somewhat: in this story the daughter's affair has broken up her marriage. By building the story's structure around three separate conversations—between father and mother, father and daughter, and mother and daughter—O'Hara delineates the different degrees of communication among these three family members. Once more, he focuses on the need to temper an adherence to the *status quo* with an acceptance of weaknesses in oneself and others, and again he reinforces that theme through a series of understated events that culminate in a subtle but transforming revelation.

The three conversations in "Appearances" lend several levels of meaning to the title. Following a talk with his daughter Amy, Howard Ambrie believes he has had a breakthrough in communication with her, though actually he has barely scratched the surface of the truth concerning her marriage and divorce. Amy appears to have been "a hell of a nice girl," but the history of her marriage indicates otherwise. Only the mother, Lois, who regards her daughter first as a woman and only then as her child, is able to act as Amy's *confidante*. Like Mimi in "The Lesson," Lois Ambrie transcends the expected behavior associated with her family role and, hence, brings honesty and compassion to her dealings with Amy.

The potential for maturity in a parent-child relationship also forms the subject of "Family Evening." Like "Appearances," this story comments on the bond between mother and daughter; like "The Father," it suggests the positive power of the past. Bob Martin, the guest whom Norman and Libby James invite to dinner, belongs to what their daughter Rosie jokingly refers to as the "B. D.'s"—Better Deads—a categorical term for anyone over thirty. As the evening evolves, it gradually becomes clear that Martin was once Libby's old flame. The subtle humor derives from Rosie's viewpoint as the youthful chaperone of the group and her clear disapproval of her mother's sudden gaiety.

After dinner, alone with Rosie for a few minutes in her room, Libby wants to suggest that they all "step out." During a poignant moment, Libby studies herself in the mirror and asks her daughter how she "really" looks: " 'You look fine,' said Rosie. 'No, I don't,' said her mother. She turned away from the mirror. 'Do me a favor, Rosie. You suggest it.' 'Me! . . . All right, if you stop feeling sorry for yourself all of a sudden. You and the rest of the B. D.'s.' Her mother smiled. 'Dear Rosie. It hurt, but it worked.' She got up and followed Rosie down the hall, humming 'Do It Again,' a danceable number of 1922" (133).

The reversal of roles here, with Rosie assuming the task of being the "sensible" member of the group, demands that she suspend her youthful disapproval of her mother's frivolity. In addition, she foregoes an after-dinner outing with her own friends in order to give her mother a chance to "step out." By doing so, she earns her mother's gratitude and willingness to confide in her as well as a new degree of maturity.

Two final stories in this third group show how compromise tempered with compassion can rescue individuals from seemingly hopeless situations. In both stories, O'Hara returns to the paradox explored in "The Twinkle in His Eye" and "The Time Element": that of a materially successful man who nevertheless feels despair. Unlike the more fatalistically inclined characters in those stories, though, the protagonists of "How Can I Tell You?" and "The Pig" are saved by their ability to connect with other human beings.

In "How Can I Tell You?" O'Hara recounts a day in the life of Mark McGranville and creates a disturbing portrait of alienation and confusion. Each event that should, theoretically, raise McGranville's spirits—a highly profitable afternoon in his job as a car salesman, a leisurely drink after work— leaves him not merely depressed but in an even worse state, that of an undefinable neutrality and emptiness.

When, in their bedroom, his wife Jean tentatively asks him what's wrong, he replies, "How the hell can I tell you when I don't know myself?" (121). After she falls asleep, and after he himself has slept for an hour, he quietly slips back out to the living room and tries to analyze his feelings: "He was thirty years old, a good father, a good husband . . . His sister had a good job, and his mother was taken care of. On the sales blackboard at the garage his name was always first or second, in two years had not been down to third. Nevertheless he went to the hall closet and got out his 20-gauge and broke it open and inserted a shell." As he sits in semi-darkness smoking a cigarette he hears his wife: "Her voice came softly. 'Mark,' she said. He looked at the carpet. 'What?' he said. 'Don't. Please?' 'I won't,' he said" (122).

These final lines, while hardly optimistic, suggest an affirmative vision. O'Hara emphasizes Jean's intuitive quality as Mark watches her sleeping, "making the musical notes of her regular breathing, but the slight frown revealing that her mind was at work . . . in ways that would always be kept secret from him, possibly even from herself" (122). In contrast, Mark's own sleep is so "busy, busy, busy" with mental activity that he does not even realize he has been asleep until he looks at the clock.

By juxtaposing their two ways of sleeping, O'Hara underscores the contrast between their reactions to Mark's despair. Each of their reactions is, in its own way, extreme. Mark's of course, because of the irreversibility of the act that he contemplates; Jean's because of its understated quality. Yet the gentleness of her request is precisely what reveals her understanding of her husband. While not the "logical" approach to the situation, Jean's is, intuitively, the right complement to Mark's failure to find rational sources for his ennui. It also allows him to change the course of his actions while saving face: his wife, by recognizing her husband's isolation and expressing her need for him, provides him with the crucial human connection that breaks through his emotional barrier.

Lawrence Chandler, the protagonist of "The Pig," also contemplates suicide, but for a reason more definable than Mark McGranville's: Chandler has just learned that he has terminal cancer. On the way home that evening on the commuter train, he confides in his friend and business associate, Mike Post. Chandler's alternative plan to committing suicide is to postpone telling his wife, Ruth, of his impending death. He fears that Ruth, because of the lingering nature of his disease, will eventually wish that he would stop "hanging on." Post understands but tries to persuade him otherwise.

To make his point, Post relates a parable about Pig Pignelli, a soldier who served under him in World War II. "Before we were shipped overseas he was hopeless. Always out of uniform, buttons undone, hat on crooked, dirty equipment," he tells Chandler. "But once we got overseas . . . he became the most reliable soldier I had" (316). The Pig volunteered for what was essentially a suicide mission, an act that cost him his life. What this proved to Post was that "people you count on *want* to be counted on. The Pig knew perfectly well that I was going to have to ask him to volunteer, and while I was figuring out how to say it, he saved me the trouble." To give Ruth the same opportunity to help him through this crisis, Post tells Chandler, would be "The highest compliment you could ever pay her. . . . That you need her, and need her so much that you had to tell her right away" (316). Like Mark McGranville, Lawrence Chandler must adjust his own assumptions about the limits of his wife's strength in order to be worthy of her compassion. The end of the story indicates that he will follow this course.

Although O'Hara did not turn to the suburban setting until relatively later in his career, his treatment of it reflects both concerns carried over from his earlier fiction and concerns particular to the suburban setting itself. Thematically, the tension common to these stories involves the disparity between appearance and truth—a theme integral to the suburban way of life, defined as it is in his stories by the sometimes overwhelming control of the *status quo* over his characters. His perceptive portrayal of the dynamics of marriage, particularly the problems of adultery, reflects a commitment to the belief that "ordinary" people harbor ideas and emotions that, if explored, are intrinsically interesting enough to merit a realistic treatment.

In terms of style and tone, his frequent reliance on dialogue, understatement, and reportage are consistent with his preference for indirect rather than explicit moral statements. In turn, his application of these techniques to the stories set in suburbia enhances their artistry. For, while much of his non-suburban fiction concentrates on portraying aristocratic, or, at the opposite end, lower-class characters, in these stories his goal is the evocation of lives that are, like his craft, filled with everyday detail, casual conversations, and apparently insignificant events.

This is not to underestimate his skill at portraying the world of Gibbsville or of pre–World War II Hollywood and New York; O'Hara displayed his intimate knowledge of these times and places as well until the end of his career. What we get in the suburban stories that is missing is much of his earlier work, however, is a sense of form reinforcing content: O'Hara's suburban stories frequently offer us a fragmented view of reality, a momentary inkling of truth, a glance at the inner life of a character—subjects that demand a more understated treatment.

These stories, then, shed additional light on the integrity of his fiction, a body of work which is due for the same careful re-evaluation that his biography has received over the past decade. They reveal that his writing was not as restricted to the traditionally recognized settings in his canon as his critics have assumed and show his ability to distill the essence of a setting that was developing contemporaneous to his writing about it. To paraphrase the title of Don Schance's interview with him, John O'Hara is alive and well in the *second* half of the twentieth century, too.[6]

Notes

1.   Sheldon Grebstein, *John O'Hara* (New Haven: Twayne, 1966), p. 33, divides O'Hara's fiction into two sections, Pennsylvania and New York-Hollywood. Charles C. Walcutt, *John O'Hara* (Minneapolis: Univ. of Minnesota Press, 1969), p. 6, finds three divisions: Eastern Pennsylvania, the movie industry in New York and Hollywood, and a Philadelphia-New York-Washington triangle of business, war, and society.

2.   John O'Hara, *Assembly* (New York: Random House, 1961), p. ix.

3.   Grebstein, pp. 134–35.

4.   Representative articles that reflect the popular image of postwar suburbia include the following: Harry Henderson, "The Mass-Produced Suburbs," *Harper's*, November and December 1953, pp. 25–32 and pp. 80–86; "Spur to Conformity," *Commonweal*, 64 (21 September 1956), 602; "Suburbia: The New America," *Newsweek*, 3 June 1957, pp. 83–90; Helen Puner, "Is It True What They Say About the Suburbs?" *Parents' Magazine*, July 1958, pp. 42–43, 96–97; "On the 5:19 to Ulcerville," *Newsweek*, 17 August 1959, p. 32; "The Changing Suburbs," *Architectural Forum*, 114 (January 1961), pp. 47–104; Peter Blake, "The Suburbs

Are a Mess," *Saturday Evening Post*, 5 October 1963, pp. 14–16; "Quit Picking on 'Suburbia,' " *Changing Times*, October 1963, pp. 34–36; Betty Friedan, "Women: The Fourth Dimension," *Ladies Home Journal*, June 1964, pp. 48–55; "Darien's *Dolce Vita*," *Time*, 2 November 1964, p. 60; and Donald G. Emery, "Memo from Scarsdale: A New Role for Suburban Schools," *Look*, 2 April 1968, p. 18.

5.   References to the stories of John O'Hara are to the following collections (publisher, unless otherwise noted, is Random House, New York): *The Cape Cod Lighter* (1962): "Appearances," "The Father," "Justice," "The Lesson," "Sunday Morning"; *The Hat on the Bed* (1964): "How Can I Tell You?" "Saturday Lunch," "The Twinkle in His Eye"; *The Horse Knows the Way* (New York: Popular Library, 1964): "The Clear Track," "The Jet Set," "The Madeline Wherry Case," "The Pig"; *The Time Element and Other Stories* (1972): "The Time Element," "Family Evening."

6.   Don Schance, "John O'Hara Is Alive and Well in the First Half of the 20th Century," *Esquire*, August 1969, pp. 84–86, 142–49.

Politics and the Social Order in the Work of John O'Hara

Lee Sigelman

Classic works of fiction almost always raise "penetrating questions about the foundations and effects of the political regime, i.e. human nature and its implications for society."[1] But popular fiction, too, can be an instrument of social and political understanding. As Gore Vidal has argued: "Writers of fiction, even more than systematic philosophers, tend to reveal unconscious presuppositions. One might even say that those writers who are the most popular are the ones who share the largest number of common assumptions with their audience, subliminally reflecting prejudices and aspirations so obvious that they are never stated and, never stated, never precisely understood or even recognized. John O'Hara is an excellent example of this kind of writer."[2] Taking a cue from Vidal, this paper focuses on the understanding of politics and the social order presented in the fiction of John O'Hara, a popular American novelist who has never been considered a political writer but who, as we shall see, formulated a highly sophisticated interpretation of the interplay between political and social forces.

O'Hara was one of America's best writers of short stories and, although his longer fiction may as a body of work fall short of his stories, he was undeniably a serious novelist and a skilled craftsman. More importantly, his major fiction presents a carefully composed, if not an altogether pleasant, portrait of American society. In a procession of novels and novellas that began with *Appointment in Samarra* (published in 1934) and ran through *A Rage to Live* (1949), *The Farmers Hotel* (1951), *Ten North Frederick* (1955), *A Family Party* (1956), *From the Terrace* (1958), *Ourselves to Know* (1960), *Sermons and Soda-Water* (1960) *Elizabeth Appleton* (1963), and *The Lockwood Concern* (1965), O'Hara put American society—or at least one corner of American society— under the microscope. In the foreword he wrote for *Sermons and Soda-Water* he explained his mission as a writer: "The United States in this Century is what I know, and it is my business to write about it to the best of my ability, with the sometimes special knowledge I have. The Twenties, the Thirties, and the

"Politics and the Social Order in the Work of John O'Hara," by Lee Sigelman reprinted with permission of the author and Cambridge University Press from *Journal of American Studies* 20 (1986): 233–57.

Forties are already history, but I cannot be content to leave their story in the hands of the historians and the editors of picture books. I want to record the way people talked and thought and felt, and to do it with complete honesty and variety."[3]

The residue of O'Hara's pursuit of this grand ambition is an uncommonly large and minutely detailed body of observations of American life—observations he drew to a considerable extent from his own life experiences. In his writing he focused on certain themes and certain character types, which together provided the organizing framework for the portrait of American society he began to compose in *Appointment in Samarra*. The primary theme he outlined in *Appointment in Samarra*, to which he returned ever after, was that society is a system designed to perform a function at which it is only sometimes successful: "covering up the disorder that lay beneath the surface of human intercourse."[4]

I

O'Hara was born in 1905 in Pottsville, a town of 25,000 in the coal-mining region of northeastern Pennsylvania. His father was a respected local physician, his family "lace-curtain Irish" in a three-tiered social stratification system. At the top was the Protestant Anglo-Saxon establishment; at the bottom were the Eastern and Southern Europeans (largely Slavs and Italians), most of whom held menial jobs and lived in poverty; sandwiched in between were the Irish and the Pennsylvania Dutch, both striving for upward mobility.

A young man growing up in Pottsville could not have been unaware of these social distinctions, and the young O'Hara, yearning for social acceptance, seems to have been quite a snob; many years later he put in the mouth of a character words that could just as easily have been applied to himself, even at an early age: "I consider myself an authority on the whole subject of snobbishness and I'm in favor of it."[5] He wanted more than anything else to attend Yale, which "was the objective correlative for all the things he admired, which may be summed up in the word *class*."[6] His enrollment was set for the fall of 1925, but shortly before then his father died, leaving the family in somewhat straitened circumstances. These circumstances, in combination with his highly developed snobbishness, conspired against him. As Bruccoli explains: "His brother Tom later attended Brown during the Depression, and Jimmy attended Lafayette. John could have attended Yale, but he obviously could not have attended in the style he aspired to. He was not an Alger hero. It wouldn't have been the real thing to be a bursary boy who waited on tables while the gentlemen browsed at J. Press and danced at the Fence Club. It had to be the right way or not at all."[7]

O'Hara's disappointment at not attending Yale remained with him all his life and, reinforced by the critics' savage attacks on his work, contributed to what can only be described as a chronic case of resentment combined with self-doubt. This whole episode inflicted so palpable a wound on him that it later served as the inspiration for a famous put-down by Ernest Hemingway, who, when asked what should be done with money left over from a fund collected during the Spanish Civil War, suggested that it be used to send O'Hara to Yale.[8] William Faulkner compounded the insult when he publicly called O'Hara "a Rutgers Scott Fitzgerald,"[9] as did Murray Kempton when he described O'Hara as "Penn State longing to be Yale."[10] The Yale episode is important not only because it says a great deal about O'Hara and his values (Yale, in the words of O'Hara's stepson, C. D. B. Bryan, had a "mythic significance" for O'Hara[11]), but also because it reinforced lessons he had learned from observing Pottsville society and ultimately helped make him the kind of writer he became.

O'Hara came of age during the 1920s, and his writing was forever marked by naturalism, the literary style of the day. The greatest influences on his writing were not the established naturalists of his youth, such as Crane, Norris and Dreiser, but were rather writers who themselves owed much to this first generation of American naturalists. During the 1920s Sherwood Anderson and Sinclair Lewis caused sensations by painting bleak portraits of American life in novels devoid of moralizing and full of descriptive detail. Contributing to the sensation, in Anderson's case at least, was a franker treatment of sex than had previously been seen in serious American fiction; because Anderson was the mentor of many of the best young writers of the 1920s, including Hemingway, Faulkner, Saroyan, Steinbeck, and Wolfe, his openness about sex carried well beyond his own work. To this franker treatment of sex, Hemingway, abetted by Fitzgerald, added the complementary element of resolution by violent death. Thus the emerging literary climate of the 1920s was one in which (a) a detached, if not wholly "objective," authorial perspective was used to compose (b) a scathing view of communities representing, in microcosm, the American experience, in which lived people who (c) were preoccupied with sex and (d) were ultimately destroyed in violent denoue-ments.[12]

II

O'Hara, who considered himself above all else a teller of stories, eschewed any attempt at stylistic pace-setting and disdained writers who did make such attempts. His locales were the places he knew best—New York, Hollywood, and especially "The Region," the area around his native Pottsville, which he rechristened "Gibbsville" in honor of his friend at The New Yorker, Wolcott

Gibbs. He set most of his major novels in The Region or close by, preserving it virtually intact. His characters, too, were often modeled upon people he knew or about whom he had read, though in this regard he displayed greater subtlety than in his borrowing of locales; his character transplants were so carefully done that even readers familiar with both the fictional character and the real-life model seldom made the connection.

This predilection for following the well-worn path rather than striking off in bold new directions can best be observed in O'Hara's formulaic approach to character and plot development. Once he had established a character who served his purposes, he literally could not let the character go. This reluctance was manifested in the cameo appearances central characters from one novel often made in another, but he recycled his main characters in another sense as well, endowing many of them with such similar characteristics that they became virtually indistinguishable. He not only permitted the very same characters, or at least the very same *types* of character, to walk through his novels and stories; he also permitted himself to tell and retell essentially the same story, adding a detail here and a nuance there. And yet this very sameness lent a rare degree of coherence and unity to his work, which taken as a whole comprises a comprehensive social history of The Region as seen from the naturalistic point of view and as colored by O'Hara's unique life experiences. This body of work is the product of a writer keenly attuned to the ubiquity of social distinctions and indelibly marked by the naturalist's pessimistic sense of the uncontrollable forces shaping human destinies. Although these themes permeated O'Hara's work, their first, and in many ways their best, expression came in *Appointment in Samarra*.

In *Appointment in Samarra*, which depicted the events leading to the suicide of young Julian English, a member of Gibbsville's smart set, O'Hara sketched out the themes to which he would repeatedly return. His starting-point was the observation that in spite of the egalitarian norms of American society, distinctions based on class were a basic fact of American life. Beginning with *Appointment in Samarra* and extending over the next thirty-five years, his writing was largely devoted to an extended documentation of the way the American class system worked.

But in *Appointment in Samarra* and its successors, O'Hara did much more than map the contours of the American class system. He was a keen observer of the outward manifestations of class, but in a sense his work was not *about* class at all. Rather, it was about the *implications* of class, for his enduring fascination with the concept of inevitability, reinforced by other elements of his naturalistic outlook, itself made it virtually inevitable that he would perceive class distinctions as a causal agent, a force determining action.

Thus, if we are to understand O'Hara's vision of society we must move beyond the mere existence of socially defined differences to a consideration of class hatred that is based on these differences. An atmosphere of anger and hatred runs through all O'Hara work, reflecting his focus on what James Tuttleton has called "the failure of the egalitarian dream": "Jealousy, envy, and hostility separate the classes, irritations are produced by social climbing, frustrations grow out of the arbitrary codes which imprison people in a social class—these are the origins of the hatred that O'Hara sees as the infected core of American social experience."[13]

Simmering just beneath the surface, this class hatred can boil over at any time, triggered by seemingly inconsequential and often unintended actions. How, in this context, can "normal" social intercourse be maintained? What is the centripetal force in a society composed of highly differentiated classes united only by their mutual loathing? What keeps class hatred from turning into class warfare?

These are questions that social and political theorists have been addressing for many centuries. They are also questions for which O'Hara, who was accused of many things but never of being a theorist, offered a rather sophisticated answer.

Interclass tensions in Gibbsville did not escalate into interclass warfare for two closely related reasons. The narrower reason stems from the class structure of Gibbsville, which, like that of the United States as a whole, was not dualistic. The effective counterweight to the Protestant Anglo-Saxon upper class was not the large Eastern and Southern European underclass, but the upwardly mobile middle-class Irish and Pennsylvania Dutch. The enduring class conflict, then, was not between polar opposites, which it might have been had the energies of the large, impoverished underclass not been wholly spent on the day-to-day realities of eking out a bare subsistence. The primary tensions that threatened to erupt were for the most part between those who occupied adjacent positions on the social ladder. While conflict is by no means unheard of between those who hold many values in common—most murders, as we are continually reminded, occur at home—tensions produce less social conflict when they occur between members of relatively like-minded classes than between members of classes that share few common bonds.

The broader answer, and the one that O'Hara emphasized, is that the most important parties to class conflict have a mutual stake in assuring that it does not turn into class warfare. The upper class is naturally concerned first and foremost with maintaining its privileged position. Moreover, because the middle-class Irish and Pennsylvania Dutch are upwardly mobile, they have no interest in obliterating class distinctions or in changing the bases upon which the social stratification system operates. The lace-curtain Irish may recognize that the best they can hope for is a fringe membership in Society, but they can still dream their dreams and try to insure that avenues of further social mobility remain open to their children. This makes them even more zealous about maintaining the status quo than are most members of the upper class. The underclass (the ethnics whom O'Hara portrayed as gross in their appetites and animalistic in their lack of self-control) does have something to gain from challenging the system, but lacks the energy, the imagination, and the skills to do so. Accordingly, there is a convergence of interests between the two most relevant social sectors, the upper and middle classes. Both wish to see the system maintained, and so both recognize and normally respect the rules— "unwritten but nonetheless inviolable"[14]—that govern social interaction.

O'Hara repeatedly emphasized this theme of convergence. Invariably, for example, he depicted his Pennsylvania Dutch characters in a nose-to-the-grindstone posture, seeking financial success and social assimilation. His Irish characters shared the same goals, though they may not always have emulated the Pennsylvania Dutch's example of stolid industriousness.[15] In any event, the willingness (indeed, the eagerness) of the middle class to work through the system rather than changing it in any fundamental way in effect preserves the system by affirming it. In the absence of that middle-class profession of faith in the system, class tensions could be transformed into class warfare. But faith can heal many wounds, even very hurtful ones. O'Hara made this point most forcefully in his novella *Imagine Kissing Pete*, which focused on Pete and Bobbie McCrea, a married couple fallen on hard times. In the novella's concluding scene, O'Hara repaid Pete and Bobbie for all their suffering by placing them at the 1960 Princeton commencement exercises, where their son, in the words of the story's narrator, ". . . led his class, was awarded the mathematics prize, the physics prize, the Eubank Prize for scholarship, and some other honors that I am sure are listed in the program, I could not read the program because I was crying most of the time."[16] The dream has been fulfilled, the faith rewarded, the system validated.

The system works as often as it does, according to O'Hara, owing to the shared interests and aspirations of its members. But there is much more to it than that, for shared interests and aspirations—a common stake—are necessary but by no means sufficient to insure the preservation of the status quo. What is needed to keep tensions within manageable bounds, to prevent class hatreds from getting out of hand, is a set of standards of appropriate behavior. In *Appointment in Samarra* O'Hara pointed up the need for such standards when he introduced his concept of "spurious democracy," which he elaborated as follows:

> [I]n order to get a ball game going the sons of the Gibbsville rich had to play with the sons of the non-rich. There were not even nine, let alone eighteen boys of Julian's age among the rich, and so the rich boys could not even have their own team. Consequently, from the time he was out of kindergarten until he was ready to go away to prep school, Julian's friends were not all from Lantenengo Street. . . . [W]hen they were going to play baseball or football, they would go down the hill to Christiana Street . . . and join the gang. The gang's members had for fathers a butcher, a motorman, a "practical" surveyor . . ., a freight

clerk, two bookkeepers for the coal company, a Baptist minister, a neighborhood saloonkeeper, a mechanic in a garage (which he called a garridge), and a perennial convict. . . .[17]

This may sound rather like organic solidarity, or even the American dream of melting-pot democracy. In what sense is such an arrangement "spurious"? As O'Hara made clear, the outwardly egalitarian interaction among the boys of Gibbsville's various social classes was contingent upon their adherence to a strict set of rules. Social inequalities could be set aside on the baseball diamond, but as soon as the game was over the agreed-upon sham of equality also ended. Julian and his friends went back up the hill to Lantenengo Street, while the members of the gang stayed on Christiana Street. The lesson, narrowly construed, is that unequals can profitably interact as equals, provided that they clearly understand the limits of their equality.

More often, social interactions are not between unequals who are playing at equality, but between unequals who fully comprehend their inequality. O'Hara provided countless examples of unequals interacting in ways that generated little tension between them. The key to these relationships was that the individuals involved had to watch carefully what they said and did, adhere scrupulously to their socially defined roles, and respect the sensitivities of others. By taking care to follow these rules, Julian found that he could enjoy a relationship with the members of the Christiana Street gang even after the ball game was over: "There were things not to talk about in the gang: you did not talk about jail, because of Walt's father; nor about drunken men, because there was a saloon-keeper's son; nor about the Catholics, because the motorman's son and one bookkeeper's son were Catholic. Julian also was not allowed to mention the name of any doctor."[18]

Society as O'Hara understood it "sets forth only one strong rule that a violator breaks at his great hazard; one must not publicly offend the dignity of others."[19] In *From the Terrace*, O'Hara presented a vivid case study of a thoroughly well-intentioned violation of one man's dignity by another. Tom Rothermel, risen from the working class, enters a social world where for the first time he observes, and is repelled by, the relationship between domestic servants and their masters. As a corrective, he attempts to treat a servant as his equal. In so doing he deliberately sets aside socially constructed definitions of place, violating the servant's own sense of propriety. Aristotle held that justice consists of treating unequals in proportion to their inequality, but Tom, no Aristotlean, fails to recognize that the servant does not object to—indeed, insists upon—being treated as a servant. For all his good intentions, Tom wins only the servant's contempt, which forces him to a new appreciation of adhering to an accepted code of conduct: "They were men together, . . . with one having more money and the other saying 'sir,' and the two keeping a precise distance that was no measure of one's respect for the other. The man with the money and the man saying 'sir' understood each other . . . and observed rules that kept the relationship successful."[20]

Playing by the established rules, as a corollary of not publicly offending the dignity of others, was a key to the maintenance of the social order as O'Hara understood it. In *A Rage to Live*, Sidney Tate lectures his wife Grace, whom he has just caught in an extramarital affair: "You see in this world, you learn a set of rules or you *don't* learn them. But assuming you learn them, you stick by them. They may be no damn good, but you're who you are and what you are because they're your rules and you stick by them, And of course when it's easy to stick by them, that's no test. It's when it's hard to obey the rules, that's when they mean something."[21]

If everyone were a Sidney Tate, there might be remarkably little social conflict. But O'Hara, never one to idealize, recognized that not everyone is a Sidney Tate and that any breach of the rules threatens the often-uneasy truce that binds the classes together. That very recognition provided the focus of his work, as he sought time and again to show what happened, not when the rules were adhered to, but rather when they were violated. "Through the intricate gradations of status," as Leo Braudy has written, O'Hara "searches for the false step, the slip, that will catapult someone outside the fold, with no hope of ever reentering."[22]

For Julian English, that moment arrives when he douses Harry Reilly, a crass Irish social climber, with a drink at the Lantenengo Country Club. For Charles Browning, a character in O'Hara's classic short story "Graven Image," it arrives at lunch with a fellow Harvardian who is now a high-ranking official in the Roosevelt administration. Browning, "with hat in hand," petitions his classmate for a government job, but for his efforts he is baited mercilessly because of his Republican sympathies and, it develops, because he had helped blackball his luncheon companion from a Harvard club. As the meal proceeds, the two reconcile and a government position is arranged. But then Browning slips:

" 'You know, I was a little afraid. That other stuff, the club stuff.' 'Yes,' said the Under Secretary. 'I don't know why fellows like you—you never would have made it in a thousand years, but'—then, without looking up, he knew everything had collapsed—'but I've said exactly the wrong thing, haven't I?' 'That's right, Browning,' said the Under Secretary. 'You've said exactly the wrong thing. I've got to be going.' He stood up and turned and went out, all dignity."[23]

In O'Hara's many stories and novels the same decisive moment arrives in an enormous variety of ways, but always, in O'Hara's scheme, it arrives— the moment of reckoning for one who has violated the rules. In one way or another the inevitable arrival of that moment and the forces that have brought it about became the paradigm to which O'Hara adhered in all of his writing.

III

Overtly political characters, ideas, and activity are distinguished primarily by their absence from O'Hara's work, reflecting, in part, the apoliticality of O'Hara the man. Like his characters, O'Hara did not often think political thoughts. He did pass through certain political phases, in a political trajectory paralleling that of his contemporary John Dos Passos. For a time he styled himself a radical, and during the 1930s and 1940s he greatly admired Franklin Roosevelt, but during the 1950s and 1960s his early leftist sympathies gave way to an ever more strident conservatism. Throughout his career he made no concerted attempt to translate his political views into either action or literature. He was, as one of his biographers has remarked, "always more interested in the personalities of the politicians than in political issues,"[24] probably because politician-watching furnished him with so many new quirks of character to use in his fiction. For O'Hara politics was a sometime thing which simply could not sustain his attention for any length of time.

In another sense, O'Hara's fiction was apolitical not by dint of personality but by conscious authorial design. In his novels of The Region he painted a richly textured portrait of American society, but he never squarely confronted the moral implications of his vision. He saw certain characteristics in the society about which he wrote at such great length, and he was so sure of what he saw that he piled up massive documentation of society's ways and endowed character after character with virtually identical traits. His vision—of people who reliably displayed thoroughly objectionable traits, and of a society that exacted a heavy toll on many of its promising members—could not have failed to unsettle him. But in spite of the common threads that ran through his work, he offered remarkably few generalizations and no prescriptions at all. He carried no brief for his characters, nor did he seek to condemn them. He was enormously concerned about descriptive accuracy,[25] which he refused to compromise, and he was deeply suspicious of the easy generalization. Writing time and again about certain *types* of people in a certain *type* of society, he detested the very thought that he was dealing in types rather than in individuals, that he was making statements rather than telling stories.

The overt apoliticality of O'Hara's novels can be traced to one final source as well: the solipsism of his main characters, who are strivers, dissatisfied with what they have and avid for more. Even (or perhaps especially) those characters who are engaged in what would normally pass for political activity betray no signs whatsoever that they might be able to think beyond purely personal considerations to any broader vision of *collective* welfare. They are preoccupied with *individual* striving for their own personal or familial benefit. Their political activity is thus motivated not by conviction but by their desire to feather their own nest. In O'Hara's play *Far From Heaven*, when a planning session for a returning political boss's "welcome home" celebration turns into a division of the spoils, Stitch O'Hearn, a late arrival, expresses outrage—but certainly not moral outrage:

STITCH: . . . Who got what so far? You got the program ads, Ray, I'll bet anything. Willie Devlin and Mona got the checkroom. Dick Sheridan's here, so I guess he got the orchestra contract. And I see Spider over there. You bringing a pair of dice, Spider? . . . What am I, a Jew or something? I want mine, just the same as everybody else.[26]

Unlike Steinbeck's farm laborers and Dos Passos' itinerants, O'Hara's characters have no vision that extends beyond their own day-to-day misery. They are certainly not out to reshape society. To the extent that they contemplate political activity at all, their motivations are entirely personal. Politics is about the spoils.

IV

Although he was not a political writer and was in some sense an apolitical writer, almost all of O'Hara's work focuses on what Zuckert considers the *foundations* of the political regime: the interplay between human nature and society.[27] Beyond this, three of his major works deal more explicitly with politics, focusing not only upon its foundations but more immediately upon distinctly (or, in one case, indistinctly) political phenomena.

The first of these political treatises, and by far the least distinctly political, is a novella. *The Farmers Hotel*, published in 1951, enjoyed great popular success, selling almost a million copies in paperback and winning some critical plaudits as well. On the surface, it describes the interactions among the members of a motley band of blizzard-bound guests at a hotel in The Region. The story climaxes when Joe Rogg, a coarse truck driver, murders two typically O'Haraesque members of the upper class who have offended him. Read literally, *The Farmers Hotel* is but a brief footnote to O'Hara's more extended treatments of the same subject-matter—*Appointment in Samarra* and *A Rage to Live* played out in Grand Hotel style. But O'Hara hoped that *The Farmers Hotel* would not be read literally, as this was his "experiment in symbolism."[28] The hotel apparently represents "the postwar world, specifically the United Nations, where people have gathered to escape the storm of war and to prepare for a harmonious present,"[29] and the murderous Joe Rogg stands for the Soviet Union. O'Hara only reluctantly owned up to any allegorical intentions,[30] and reviewers and the reading public alike missed his intended deeper meanings altogether. Despite the book's booming sales and favourable reviews, this was not a happy experience for O'Hara, who made no further gestures in the direction of political allegory.

If *The Farmers Hotel* was a popular success and an artistic failure, O'Hara's second political treatise, a never-performed play entitled *Far From Heaven*, can only be reckoned a total failure. Written in 1962, it is essentially a character sketch of John J. Sullivan, a Tammany district boss fresh from two years in Sing Sing. Sullivan has been a "guest of the state" as a consequence of pleading guilty to a charge of bribery in order to shield higher-ups in the Tammany machine. Returning from prison, Sullivan finds himself well cared for financially but unable to reclaim his post of district boss, for the machine is now eager to distance itself from him. Looking out for his own interests, Sullivan approaches a mobster, to whom he offers to peddle his inside knowledge of the machine. Word of this indiscretion inevitably leaks back to the machine, and the play ends with Sullivan being gunned down in retribution.

The Farmers Hotel says very little about politics. *Far From Heaven* says little enough, but it does say something. The third of O'Hara's political treatises, his novel *Ten North Frederick*, published in 1955, says a good deal. It won the National Book Award, and many consider it O'Hara's best novel[31] or at least his best after *Appointment in Samarra*.[32] Typically, O'Hara himself rejected the critics' verdict: he preferred the monumental *From the Terrace*.

Ten North Frederick is to Joe Chapin what *Appointment in Samarra* is to Julian English, or, for that matter, what *From the Terrace* is to Alfred Eaton, what *The Lockwood Concern* is to George Lockwood, and even what *Far From Heaven* is to John J. Sullivan: the chronicle of a proud man's downfall.

In *Ten North Frederick* O'Hara told the story of Joe Chapin, a prominent Gibbsville attorney who, though totally lacking in political experience or expertise, nurses a secret political ambition: he "had always wanted to be President of the United States, and thought he ought to be."[33] *Ten North Frederick*, like O'Hara's other "womb to tomb" portraits,[34] is a sprawling narrative, encompassing dozens of characters and locales observed over the course of many decades. A great deal of the book has nothing at all to do with politics; indeed, those who know *Ten North Frederick* only from the 1958 Hollywood movie may recall it as the story of a sudsy romance that contains only the barest hint of politics. But the core of the novel is distinctly political. It is the political application of the paradigm O'Hara outlined in *Appointment in Samarra* and elaborated in the rest of his work.

Ten North Frederick presents revealing portraits of the political outsider and the political insider. The outsider is Joe Chapin. The insider is Mike Slattery, the "realistic, crafty, treacherous" head of Gibbsville's dominant Republican machine.[35] Viewed on one level, *Ten North Frederick* is basically a chronicle of conflicting political styles and objectives and of the subjugation of naive idealism to the harsh realities of practical politics—the classic clash between the amateur and the professional, culminating, inevitably, in the triumph of the professional. "As soon as [Slattery] suspected that Joe Chapin was beginning to act like a man who wanted to be President he decided that Chapin was not presidential timber, and from that moment on Joe Chapin never had a chance," O'Hara informs his readers very early in the novel,[36] immediately alerting them to the inescapability of the downfall they are about to witness.

Slattery, as O'Hara depicts him, always acts in a manner calculated to maintain or even extend the dominance of the Republican political machine. He is subservient to no great cause and is no more of an ideologue than are the spoilsmen of John J. Sullivan's Tammany clubhouse. In fact, he actually prefers it when his party loses the presidential election, for as a professional he knows that losing an election can provide an opportunity to reshape the party for his own ends. His modus operandi has been established in classic nonfictional analyses of machine politics,[37] in large measure, he does favors for constituents and delivers votes to candidates. He is, then, a broker, a doer, a fixer. "Good old Mike. Instrumental," is the way one of the novel's characters summarizes the basis of Slattery's political power,[38] and there is considerable truth in that pithy characterization. In Slattery's own words, "We politicians have our uses,"[39] and these uses are only occasionally "political" in the narrow sense of the term. Politics as practised by Slattery has remarkably little to do with the great issues of the day.

Slattery's "uses" are vital to Gibbsville's lower and middle classes, who rely on him to find them jobs, get them out of trouble with the law, provide for their widows, and so on. But these uses are of more than passing interest to the Gibbsville establishment as well, and Joe Chapin himself has had occasion to avail himself of Slattery's services. When Chapin's daughter confesses that she has been carrying on with a local lout, Slattery arranges to have the miscreant run out of town; later, he arranges an annulment for the same wayward daughter, who has eloped with a different, but no less unsuitable, suitor.

In serving as a "fixer" for the members of the Gibbsville establishment, Slattery caters to their concern for the maintenance of good order. It surely will not do for a daughter of Joe Chapin to marry some Italian who plays in a band, and such indiscretions must be kept out of sight. What makes such episodes truly unbearable is the opportunity they give the locals to view one's dirty laundry, the insult of having one's private business become public knowledge, the shame of having one's name dragged through the mud. Concern about the disruption of good order is, as we have seen, the recurring O'Hara theme. He sometimes interrupts the narrative flow of a novel to muse about it at length, as when he discusses the marriage contract in *From the Terrace*:

[A]n adulterous man and woman who obstinately divorced their wife and husband and went on to a marriage of their own were held in low esteem. They had violated good order. . . . A man who allowed an illicit love to jeopardize his marriage and thereby to disturb good order forfeited what privileges he had and was likely to obtain. A similar punishment awaited the cuckolded husband who took his nasty discovery into the courts. He, too, had violated good order. . . . A man on his way up suffered his wife's infidelity rather than take public action that he knew would end his career. And the women knew it and made use of the knowledge. This unsuspected immoral effect of an apparently highly moral prohibition might have been truly laughable had the keepers of good order established their rules as a moral code. But in reality, . . . the purpose of good order and its enforcement was to keep the public in ignorance of the personal lives of these men and their families. No publicity was better than any publicity . . . A scandal attaching to a friend's name was unthinkable, and punishment awaited the disobedient.[40]

O'Hara is commenting in this passage about maintaining order in one particular type of relationship, but the applicability of his remarks extends well beyond the marital bond. Things are always going wrong in people's lives, he seems to be saying, and—life being what it is—that is simply to be expected. But such untoward situations must not be permitted to get out of hand. Appearances must be preserved, a façade maintained, or else the lives of the individuals immediately involved, and ultimately the uneasy truce that governs society, will be threatened; in Leo Braudy's words, "O'Hara's essential message is that social surfaces are a lie, but a lie that it is fatal to contradict."[41] The utmost discretion is required in order to keep such situations within manageable bounds, and Mike Slattery's usefulness to the Gibbsville establishment stems from his ability to do just that—to keep the lid from blowing off by keeping names not only off the police blotter but also out of the newspaper and removed from the gossip of the street.

The plot of *Ten North Frederick* focuses on the tension between Chapin and Slattery, which turns on the issue of who will control Chapin's political fate. Chapin fails to recognize that his political ambitions can be realized only if he approaches his political career in the prescribed fashion—by becoming a cog in the machine. O'Hara draws a sharp contrast between Chapin's determination to strike out on his own, and two Gibbsville politicians, Mayor Conrad L. Yates and Judge Lloyd Williams, who have both succeeded precisely because they are controlled by the machine and who have both freely accepted their subjection as a fact of political life. "A judge," Lloyd Williams sometimes calls himself, "thanks to the goodness of my fellow man and Mike Slattery."[42]

Slattery tries to "plant the bee in [Chapin's] bonnet about him getting into politics,"[43] and both he and Chapin are intrigued by the prospect. Both believe that he would make an attractive candidate. Neither gives even a moment's thought to what Chapin might hope to accomplish once elected, though Slattery's assumption is that Chapin, like Conrad Yates and Lloyd Williams, will do as the machine wishes.

Chapin resists Slattery's blandishments, but a seed has been planted, and on Chapin's fortieth birthday he and his wife have a very odd conversation: 'What would you like to do, or be?' 'I would like to be the President of the United States,' said Joe. 'You would?' 'I honestly would,' said Joe.[44] In pursuit of this lofty goal, Chapin immerses himself in local affairs, behind the scenes at first but more visibly as time passes. This concerns Slattery, for, as he puts it, "We don't want this fledgling to learn to fly without us."[45] Accordingly, he approaches Chapin again, this time prevailing upon him to accept a local judgeship—the unspoken promise being that even though this is a humble post, as long as Chapin remains a member in good standing he can expect to move up through the chairs. Again Chapin rebuffs him, announcing to his wife that he has no intention of playing Slattery's game: "No matter what Mike offers me, I'm going to refuse. All the way up to and including the governorship. He's not going to offer me the governorship, but if he did, I'd say no."[46] Instead, Chapin tries to arrange a federal appointment for himself, but the Senator with whom he tries to arrange the appointment is himself tied to the machine. Of course the appointment does not pan out, and word of Chapin's misstep is quickly passed back to Slattery. Shortly thereafter, Slattery and Chapin meet:

> "Joe, you know enough about mining to know what a pillar-robber is, don't you?"
> "Yes, of course," said Joe.
> "What is it?"
> "A man who pulls out timbers and the coal falls down for lack of support."
> "Correct. It's a dangerous job, highly paid."
> "All right, Mike. What's on your mind?" said Joe.
> "Do you have to go all the way to Washington, D. C., to be a pillar-robber?"
> "Who do you think you're talking to, Mike?"
> "I'm talking to a man with political ambitions. I'm talking to a man that goes behind my back to *further* his own political ambitions. I'm talking to a man that I could help, and that I offered to help. I'm talking to a man that goes out of his way to weaken the support of an organization that I built up. I'm talking to a man that pretends to be aloof from dirty politics, but that doesn't seem to need any lessons from me. Now what have you got to say?"
> "I say you can get the hell out of my office," said Joe.[47]

By deliberately bypassing the proper channels, by failing to observe the established niceties of politics in The Region, Chapin has signed his own death warrant. His indiscretion in trying to strike out on his own politically may outwardly seem a mere faux pas, but it is actually a grievous breach of the rules, an insult, and a threat—to Mike Slattery personally, to the political machine he heads, and, ultimately, to the social system the machine helps maintain. As if to underscore this point, O'Hara invented a very similar set of circumstances in *Far From Heaven* to help explain the hostility between John J. Sullivan and Ray Fallon, who is being groomed as his replacement:

JOHN: . . . You miserable son of a bitch. You double-crossing, two-bit bastard. I had you pegged five years ago. Five years ago you went to Bert

Ryan over my head, without consulting me, and you told Bert you
wanted to run for State Assemblyman.

RAY: All right, what if I did?

JOHN: What if you did? You son of a bitch, behind my back you snuck over to
Bert Ryan that hates my guts, and you knew he hated my guts, and
you told him you wanted to run for State Assemblyman. But you got a no
answer. Bert Ryan was afraid of me then. I was too big then. But I tell
you what happened, in case you think I don't know. Mr. Bert Ryan had a
meeting with Charley Reagan and Irving Goldberg and he told them,
he said John Sullivan is having trouble keeping his fellows in line. He said
Ray Fallon wants to run for assemblyman, with or without John
Sullivan's consent.

That was the first time Mr. Bert Ryan got anything to use against me.
You were the first one to put the knife in my back. It didn't go very deep,
but you convinced Mr. Bert Ryan that it could be done.

From that time on I had more and more trouble with Mr. Bert Ryan,
till finally it ended with me taking the rap and doing two years in
Sing Sing. You know who really put me in Sing Sing, Ray? You, you
miserable double crosser. How do you like that?[48]

Following his blunder, Chapin begins to make appearances around the
state. Slattery, certain that Chapin has learned his lesson, is content to let him
go about his business, and even encourages his interest in party affairs. Chapin,
it turns out, is laying the groundwork for a campaign for the lieutenant
governorship—the stepping-stone, he hopes, to the higher office for which he
yearns. In order to "convince Mike Slattery that he must convince the State
Committee that I'm the logical man for lieutenant governor,"[49] Chapin makes
an unsolicited gift of $20,000 to the machine. Slattery accepts this gift and
asks for another $100,000; Chapin agrees, but to Slattery's disgust threatens
to make no more contributions for the next twenty years if he is denied the
nomination for lieutenant governor. Slattery plays along, but this is all the
evidence he needs to conclude that Chapin has still not become a true party
man. Working quietly behind the scenes, Slattery orchestrates a series of
setbacks that culminate in a request from the party's state executive committee
that Chapin withdraw and in Chapin's compliance with that request. His
ambition dashed, his illusions shattered, Chapin lives out the rest of his life in
an alcoholic haze, using the bottle just as his townsman Julian English had
once used the automobile, to commit a lingering suicide.

V

If *Appointment in Samarra* is O'Hara's paradigmatic novel, then *Ten North
Frederick* should be viewed as "normal" O'Hara—detail work, a fleshing out

of the paradigm, or, more accurately, as an application, in a political context, of O'Hara's vision of society.

The numerous points of similarity between *Appointment in Samarra* and *Ten North Frederick* have passed largely unremarked during the three decades since the latter was published. Both novels are, of course, set in Gibbsville. Both focus on a member of the Gibbsville establishment. Both describe Gibbsville's social life in microscopic detail, *Ten North Frederick* far more voluminously than its briefer predecessor. The two novels even share some characters.

This much should be obvious. What has not been fully recognized is that in their essential characteristics the structures of the two novels are virtually identical. Each turns on a conflict between members of two different social classes in a highly class-conscious society, and the parties to the two conflicts, though not identical, are certainly similar enough: a member of Gibbsville's upper crust, thoroughly schooled in the social graces and accustomed to deference from his inferiors, pitted against a middle-class Irishman, crude by the standards of polite society but upwardly mobile, having risen from humble beginnings to middle-class respectability and yearning for more. Moreover, there are striking parallels in the conflicts that divide the two pairs of protagonists. Alone among analysts of O'Hara's work, Norman Podhoretz seems to have caught a glimmer of these parallels when he concludes that "[W]hat comes through as the cause of Joe Chapin's failure is precisely the same error that destroyed Julian English—a tactless move."[50] Podhoretz is perfectly correct, but he does not go nearly far enough. In the first place, he does not consider the *sources* from which the tactlessness of Julian English and Joe Chapin spring. Many different answers have been given to the question of why Julian English throws a drink in Harry Reilly's face, but in the end the best answer is simply that from Julian's perspective Reilly *deserves* to have a drink thrown in his face. Reilly, a crude Irishman, has overstepped himself socially and badly needs to be put back in his place. So Julian's action amounts to a reassertion, if an ultimately self-defeating one, not so much of his personal superiority over Reilly (though that is certainly part of it), but of the establishment's superiority over upstarts. Similarly, Joe Chapin, accustomed to having things his own way, naively assumes that a political career will work the same way: "Like picking an apple off a bowl of fruit. Or a paper off a newsstand. Drop a few pennies on the pile of newspapers, and walk away with the paper you want. That's really how simple I thought it would be, if I ever thought at all. At fifty-two I still went on thinking that because I wanted something, I could get it."[51]

Neither Julian English nor Joe Chapin intends to flout the rules or to destroy the social order—far from it. The action of both stem directly from the deference they and all concerned acknowledge to be their due. If Harry Reilly has overstepped himself, *someone* has to return him to his rightful place, and that someone might as well be Julian English. If Joe Chapin deems himself well-suited to be President, then those around him must do whatever they can to see that he becomes President. Julian English and Joe Chapin, then, are both asserting what they take to be their legitimate prerogatives, based on their social standing. Their interpretation of these prerogatives turns out in both cases to be fatally wrong, for by concentrating so single-mindedly on their own prerogatives both run afoul of an even more central component of the unwritten rules that govern society: the precept that one who publicly insults the dignity of another acts at his own peril, and at society's.

Nor does Podhoretz, despite his basic insight, seem to recognize that the parallels between Julian English's actions and Joe Chapin's extend far beyond their purely personal dimensions, to their *social implications*. In *Appointment in Samarra*, the paradigmatic work, an insult perpetrated by a member of one class upon a member of another class poses a threat to the social order and ultimately destroys the perpetrator. In *Ten North Frederick*, the application of the paradigm, the very same sequence is played out, modified only to fit a somewhat different set of circumstances. Julian English's humiliation of Harry Reilly, seen as a class action, threatens social disruption. By the same token, when Joe Chapin bypasses Mike Slattery, he offends Slattery personally, but more importantly he threatens the political machine and ultimately the social order to which that machine contributes. In both cases, then, interpersonal conflict is rooted in the social order, and in both cases the person who flouts the established rules and thereby poses a threat to the social order is crushed for his error.

As an application of the *Appointment in Samarra* paradigm, *Ten North Frederick* presents no unique lessons about society. It is, however, the sole occasion on which O'Hara devoted any extended attention to politics, and as such it, better than any other work, clarifies the political dimension of his understanding of society. Considered apart from O'Hara's broader vision of society, *Ten North Frederick* would have to be interpreted simply as a rather humdrum account of the conflict between a political machine and a political outsider. The focus of the novel, thus understood, would have to be seen as the triumph of the political machine over its challenger, and the novel's lesson would have to be simply that "you can't beat City Hall." Seen in such a light, *Ten North Frederick* as a political novel is indistinguishable from countless other novels of machine politics, and perhaps inferior to most. But *Ten North Frederick* cannot properly be understood apart from O'Hara's vision of the social order. Once that vision is taken into account, it becomes evident that the novel's denouement reflects the operation of a "machine" far more encompassing than Slattery's Republican organization. That more encompassing machine—the true focus of all of O'Hara's work—is society itself, which according to O'Hara's vision is based on scrupulous adherence to carefully-defined rules and roles. Politics, according to this vision, is best left to the politicians. The proper role of people like Joe Chapin is to do exactly what Mike Slattery asks: to bankroll the political machine and to provide a legitimate-looking front for it. The proper role for a Joe Chapin is most certainly not to try to arrogate political power unto himself, for if he tries to do so he will be overstepping his place as surely as Harry Reilly had overstepped his. The interests of a Joe Chapin, which consist most broadly of maintaining the social order, can best be served by ensuring the continuing hegemony of the political machine, not by challenging it. Seen in this light, Joe Chapin's attempt to sidestep normal, machine-dominated political channels threatens not only the Slattery political machine but also the machine-writ-large.

VI

It is not surprising that O'Hara's political insights have been so widely ignored, especially since in two cases out of three (*The Farmers Hotel* and *Far From Heaven*) these insights were so effectively camouflaged that they become virtually unrecognizable. That, of course, leaves *Ten North Frederick*, but even though it was a nationwide best-seller, won the National Book Award for fiction, and put politics in full public view, it has never made anyone's list of political novels, let alone great political novels. How can we account for this?

To some extent the widespread neglect of O'Hara as an author who has something serious and valuable to say about politics was—to use O'Hara's favorite word—inevitable, given the nature of his writing. In *Ten North Frederick* as in all his novels, he only hinted at the motivations of his characters. This steadfast refusal to psychologize was in the best tradition of naturalism, but his focus on external signs of character has been widely interpreted as symptomatic of shallowness in characterization[52] and has certainly contributed to superficial understandings of his characters. Further disguising the political content of *Ten North Frederick* was O'Hara's penchant for presenting descriptive materials of such encyclopedic scope and extraordinary density that certain nuances of plot and character were bound to pass unremarked. James Agee believed that a preoccupation with detailed description is often a passing phase in the novelist's development: "Most young writers and artists roll around in description like honeymooners on a bed . . . In the course of years they grow or discipline themselves out of it."[53] But O'Hara never did. In fact, he moved in precisely the opposite direction, as can easily be demonstrated by contrasting the spare prose of *Appointment in Samarra* against the relentless verbiage of *A Rage to Live, From the Terrace,* or *Ten North Frederick*.

So O'Hara, simply by being the kind of writer he was, made it difficult for his readers to grasp *Ten North Frederick*'s political insights. But it should not pass unremarked that *Ten North Frederick* has also been read with uncommon carelessness, even by many who are sympathetic to him and who are more than casually interested in the novel.[54] For example, O'Hara's biographer Finis Farr totally misstates the facts of a key episode, which he describes as follows:

"A famous scene in the story has Chapin interviewing a national political committee on his prospects of nomination for the presidency of the United States."[55] One need hardly have been hanging on O'Hara's every word to recognize that the office in question is not the presidency of the United States but the lieutenant governorship of Pennsylvania and that Chapin is appearing before a state committee, not a national one. Similarly, Sidney Alexander, in a review of *Ten North Frederick*, twists the plot virtually beyond recognition: "Spurred by his wife, Chapin assiduously builds up a personal following in the state, and finally secures the promise of a professional politician, Mike Slattery, to help him secure the nomination for lieutenant governor. But all of Slattery's influence and the thousands of dollars Chapin has thrown into the party chest cannot prevent the asphyxiation of his ambitions in a smoke-filled room. The politicians simply cannot risk an amateur against the hard-hitting Roosevelt-led Democrats."[56]

In this passage Alexander manages to get the office right, thereby improving on Farr's dismal performance, but he misunderstands virtually everything else—most notably the nature of Slattery's efforts on Chapin's behalf (which are, as O'Hara makes abundantly clear, merely half-hearted window-dressing) and the fact that in bypassing Chapin's candidacy the party bosses are motivated by a desire to maintain solidarity rather than any fear of electoral consequences. Even more egregious—for it betrays not a misreading of details but a failure to grasp the main point—is Edward Russell Carson's description of Slattery's defeat of Chapin as "the outcome merely of a personal quarrel,"[57] a reading so shallow and incomplete as to strip *Ten North Frederick* of any deeper meaning whatsoever.

There *is* deeper meaning in *Ten North Frederick*—deeper meaning about society and about politics. To be sure, most of the fiction that O'Hara composed over the course of his long career says nothing at all, in any direct fashion, about politics. Moreover, although he acknowledged that his work could be classified as "social history," he saw himself first and foremost as an artist, a craftsman, and a teller of stories, and only secondarily as a social historian. "When a novel's social history content begins to take over," he once said, "the author is in trouble . . . From Harriet Beecher Stowe to John Steinbeck the author who offers social history is most effective, perhaps even *only* effective, when his concern is for his characters rather than for his conditions. The difference between a novel about sharecroppers and a novel about Ezra Bumpkin, sharecropper, is the difference between a social-history report on the one hand and, on the other, Art."[58]

But all of this should make the bulk of O'Hara's work no less politically illuminating, for his microscopic portraits of social relationships, disciplined by his macroscopic vision of the social order, set the stage for political understanding. O'Hara has been called "the most complete, the most accurate, and the most readable" chronicler of twentieth century American life,[59] and it has been said that he possessed a "knowledge of how Americans live incomparably greater than that of any other fiction writer of his time."[60] By focusing so extensively and so convincingly on the distinctly *social* context in which all human action, including political action, unfolds, he sketched out a framework for sociopolitical analysis. He had clear notions about what holds society together and what tears it apart. He first outlined these notions in *Appointment in Samarra*, and over the course of the next thirty-five years he honed these notions in print—elaborating them, documenting them, and extending them to new contexts. To be sure, he never developed any theory of the *roots* of socially determining forces. He largely ignored the issues of how class distinctions emerge in the first place and, more importantly, why it is so necessary to maintain them. For all his emphasis on social order he never really addressed, let alone answered, the question "Order for what?" And it was never entirely certain where his true sympathies lay—with the proud individual crushed by overwhelming social forces, or with the "orderly" society and the maintenance of class prerogatives. So O'Hara's work was limited in the questions to which it was addressed and the answers it offered. His focus was on the consequences, not the causes, of the social forces he so painstakingly chronicled. His real contribution to social and political analysis lies in his compelling portraits of the clash between individual and society.

Only very rarely, as in *Ten North Frederick*, did O'Hara articulate these notions in a political context. When he did focus directly upon the play of political power, he did it, in true theoretical fashion, by trying to spell out the political corollaries of his broader view of social structure and social conflict. He was not interested in politics *as such*, for in his view there was nothing generic about politics. Rather, he viewed politics as an epiphenomenon, a secondary manifestation of the operation of the broader social order in which he was so keenly interested and which, in his view, "superseded all other considerations."[61] As surely as Marx was an economic determinist, O'Hara was a social determinist. If O'Hara's insights were taken as seriously as those found in classic works of fiction, it would be more widely recognized that his work contains elements of a well-articulated, socially based theory of politics.

Notes

1.   Catherine Zuckert, "On Reading Classic American Novelists as Political Thinkers," *Journal of Politics* 43 (August 1981), 685.

2.   Gore Vidal, *Homage to Daniel Shays: Collected Essays 1952–1972* (New York: Random House, 1972), p. 165.

3.   John O'Hara, *Sermons and Soda-Water* (New York: Random House, 1960), p. 8.

4.   Frank MacShane, "Introduction: The Power of the Ear," *Collected Stories of John O'Hara*, ed. Frank MacShane (New York: Random House, 1985), pp. vii–viii.

5.   John O'Hara, *Elizabeth Appleton* (New York: Random House, 1963), pp. 152–53.

6.   Matthew J. Bruccoli, *The O'Hara Concern: A Biography of John O'Hara* (New York: Random House, 1975), pp. 21–22.

7. Ibid., p. 42.

8. Ibid., p. 164.

9. Frank MacShane, *The Life of John O'Hara* (New York: E. P. Dutton, 1980), p. 152.

10. Charles Mann, "John O'Hara: Pennsylvania Novelist," *John O'Hara Journal*, 2, (Summer 1980), 1.

11. C. D. B. Bryan, "My John O'Hara," *Esquire* (July 1985), p. 102.

12. This paragraph draws freely on Geoffrey Perrett's excellent chapter on literary trends in the United States during the 1920's in *America in the Twenties: A History* (New York: Simon and Schuster, 1982).

13. James W. Tuttleton, *The Novel of Manners in America* (Chapel Hill, N.C.: University of North Carolina Press, 1972), p. 195.

14. Scott Donaldson, "Appointment With the Dentist: O'Hara's Naturalistic Novel," *Modern Fiction Studies*, 14 (Winter 1968–69), 437 [reprinted in this volume].

15. O'Hara's treatment of his Irish characters caused considerable consternation among many Irish-American readers. William Shannon, *The American Irish* (New York: Macmillan, 1963), p. 249, accused O'Hara of harbouring an "inverted hostility" toward the Irish. Joseph Browne, "John O'Hara and Tom McHale: How Green Is Their Valley," eds. Daniel J. Casey and Robert E. Rhodes, *Irish-American Fiction: Essays in Criticism* (New York: AMS Press, 1979), p. 130, went even further, accusing O'Hara of being "repelled by anyone who is Irish."

16. *Sermons and Soda-Water*, p. 143.

17. John O'Hara, *Appointment in Samarra* (New York: Harcourt, Brace and Company, 1934), pp. 183–84.

18. Ibid., p. 185.

19. Sheldon N. Grebstein, *John O'Hara* (New York: Twayne Publishers, Inc., 1966), p. 39.

20. John O'Hara, *From the Terrace* (New York: Random House, 1958), p. 688.

21. John O'Hara, *A Rage to Live* (New York: Random House, 1949), p. 245.

22. Leo Braudy, "Realists, Naturalists, and Novelists of Manners," ed. Daniel Hoffman, *Harvard Guide to Contemporary American Writing* (Cambridge, Mass.: Belknap Press, 1979), p. 125.

23. John O'Hara, "Graven Image," *The New Yorker* (13 March, 1943), 18.

24. MacShane, *The Life of John O'Hara*, p. 216.

25. This fixation on descriptive detail sometimes carried O'Hara to extreme lengths. For example, he attached a foreword to *Ten North Frederick* so that he could publicly confess to his readers that even though in the novel they were about to read Joe Chapin's grandfather was said to have served as lieutenant governor of Pennsylvania, this would have been impossible, for the office was not created until 1873. For O'Hara getting the details right was a hallmark of good writing.

26. John O'Hara, *Two by O'Hara* (New York: Harcourt Brace Jovanovich, 1979), p. 111.

27. Zuckert, p. 685.

28. Orville Prescott, *In My Opinion: An Inquiry Into the Contemporary Novel* (Indianapolis: Bobbs-Merrill Company, Inc., 1952), p. 74.

29. MacShane, *The Life of John O'Hara*, p. 154.

30. He did feel compelled to alert his publisher, Bennett Cerf, of the novella's symbolic thrust:

I also want to reveal to you that this is an allegory. . . . However, I am not calling it an allegory; I am presenting it as a short novel, and if the more alert critics and other readers spot it as an allegory (which I am sure they will), fine. It stands as a short novel, without the allegorical connotation. If you, as publisher, feel you would like to pass the word that it also is an allegory, you can use your own judgment about that, but I am not going to make any public statement to the effect until after the second meaning has been detected, and even then I am not going to do any interpreting.

From *Selected Letters of John O'Hara*, ed. Matthew Bruccoli (New York: Random House, 1978, p. 235). Several weeks later, he seems to have had second thoughts about even admitting publicly that the novella was an allegory: "People I have talked with," he wrote, "are now about 50-50 on the wisdom of letting it known [sic] that the book has a secondary meaning"; *Selected Letters*, p. 236.

31. Louis Auchincloss, "Marquand and O'Hara: The Novel of Manners," *The Nation* (19 November, 1960), 383–88; Rex Roberts, "On *Ten North Frederick*," *John O'Hara Journal*, 2 (Summer 1980), 69–87.

32. Robert Weaver, "Twilight Area of Fiction: The Novels of John O'Hara," *Queen's Quarterly*, 64 (Summer 1959), 302–25.

33. John O'Hara, *Ten North Frederick* (New York: Random House, 1955), p. 10.

34. Sidney Alexander, "Another Visit to O'Haraville," *The Reporter* (26 January, 1956), 44.

35. O'Hara, *Ten North Frederick*, p. 11.

36. Ibid.

37. See, for example, Robert K. Merton, *Social Theory and Social Structure* (New York: Free Press, 1967).

38. *Ten North Frederick*, p. 25.

39. Ibid., p. 25.

40. *From the Terrace*, pp. 420–21.

41. Braudy, p. 127.

42. *Ten North Frederick*, p. 75.

43. Ibid., p. 205.

44. Ibid., p. 260.

45. Ibid., p. 263.

46. Ibid., p. 264.

47. Ibid., pp. 269–270.

48. *Two by O'Hara*, pp. 144–45.

49. *Ten North Frederick*, p. 338.

50. Norman Podhoretz, "Gibbsville and New Leeds: The America of John O'Hara and Mary McCarthy," *Commentary* (March 1956), 271.

51. *Ten North Frederick*, p. 357.

52. In one variant of this criticism, O'Hara's characters were "not adequately motivated," "they just act"; Charles W. Bassett, "John O'Hara," ed. James J. Martine, *American Novelists, 1910–1945, Part 2: F. Scott Fitzgerald–O. E. Rolvaag*, vol. 9 of *Dictionary of Literary Biography* (Detroit: Bruccoli Clark, 1981), 278. In a somewhat different expression of the same basic criticism, he was taken to task for engaging in a form of characterization that consisted simply of following to its logical conclusion the assumption that "mankind was vile by nature, and without surprises"; Brendan Gill, "The Dark Advantage," *New Yorker* (15 September, 1975), 55.

53. James Agee and Walker Evans, *Let Us Now Praise Famous Men* (Boston: Houghton Mifflin 1960), p. 215.

54. This problem was not restricted to *Ten North Frederick*. Perhaps because he insisted on remaining "outside" of his characters, O'Hara left much to the reader's imagination and thereby virtually invited superficial interpretations of his work. That invitation was often accepted, as can be seen in Clifton Fadiman's dismissal of *Appointment in Samarra* as totally

meaningless—*Party of One: The Selected Writings of Clifton Fadiman* (Cleveland: World Publishing, 1955), p. 447: "The suicide of Julian English . . . is a tragedy in a vacuum, the tic of a young man who has had a couple of hard days and too much hard liquor." Albert Van Nostrand in *The Denatured Novel* (Indianapolis: Charter Books, 1960), p. 213, accepted the same invitation: "O'Hara keeps telling the same story that E. A. Robinson superbly told, of 'Richard Cory' who put a bullet through his head for no known reason."

55. Finis Farr, *O'Hara: A Biography* (Boston: Little, Brown, 1973), p. 225.

56. Alexander, p. 44.

57. Edward Russell Carson, *The Fiction of John O'Hara* (Pittsburgh: University of Pittsburgh Press, 1961), p. 22.

58. *"An Artist Is His Own Fault": John O'Hara on Writers and Writing,* ed. Matthew J. Bruccoli (Carbondale, Ill.: Southern Illinois University Press, 1977), p. 29.

59. Clarence A. Glasrud, "John O'Hara," *20th Century American Literature* (New York: St Martin's Press, 1980), p. 435.

60. Gill, p. 55.

61. Podhoretz, p. 269.

All in the Family: John O'Hara's Story of a Doctor's Life

GEORGE MONTEIRO

Those contemporary reviewers who liked John O'Hara's "A Family Party" (1956) described it as "warm-hearted" and "mellow."[1] Most of the subsequent criticism has sounded a similar note. The story has been called "a sentimental portrait of a doctor who devoted himself to the well-being of a town,"[2] and the author's "tribute to his father and to Dr. O'Hara's profession,"[3] one in which the "author's motivations"—"kindness and 'respect' "[4]—are perfectly clear. O'Hara himself insisted that it was a "simple, honest story."[5] Only Robert Emmet Long has acknowledged the subtlety of the story. It is "one of O'Hara's cruelly ironic monologues," he concludes, in which the narrator "unwillingly" reveals that "the honored guest's life has been lonely and anguished."[6]

Long's comments on "A Family Party," though brief, are the most useful to date. It is true that while the author intends to pay loving homage to his anguished father-physician, he does such a good job of undermining the narrator whose testimonial monologue constitutes the story we have that his speaker, who embodies and expresses the values of the town, becomes, in this respect, as important to the narrative as is the guest of honor. What he chooses to say and how he says it tell us volumes about the ethos of the town of Lyons, Pennsylvania. It is clear that the author's attitude toward the speaker (and by extension toward the entire town) is at best sardonic, that the speaker's (and the town's) attitude toward the doctor who is being honored is both sentimental and profoundly mendacious, and that the author's attitude toward the doctor is compassionate and considerate.

"A Family Party" opens with a short section, printed in italics to set it apart from the rest of the tale, that tells of the circumstances surrounding the principal narrative that follows and explaining that that narrative is a stenographic report of an address given by the main speaker at a dinner honoring a small-town physician on the occasion of his retirement from the profession after forty years of practice. This "report" on the stenographic report

Reprinted with permission from *Studies in Short Fiction* 24 (Summer 1987): 305–308. © 1987 by Newberry College.

that constitutes the "story" told in "A Family Party" identifies the speaker and the honoree, gives the date of the dinner and its location, lists the organizations sponsoring the affair, names the clergymen who have official duties, and nods in the direction of the high school orchestra performing under its female leader. In short, this note presents the information more or less that a newspaper reader would have every right to expect in a headnote preceding the printing of the speech itself. Its prose is plain in style, neutral in tone, and consciously workmanlike. As such, it contrasts distinctly with the style, tone, and authorial intention of the address by "Mr. Albert W. Shoemaker, president of the Shoemaker Printing Company and former editor and publisher of the Lyons *Republican*, at a dinner in honor of Dr. Samuel G. Merritt."[7]

"Bert" Shoemaker's tone is breezy and marked by studied conviviality. His diction is informal, the syntax of his sentences folksy. The speech is "marred" as prose by repetitions and awkward self-interruptions, not to mention the coy references to things he will not talk about (because to do so would be indiscreet, by the standards of others, or by the speaker's own). Here is the first paragraph (following the obligatory words of address to the dignitaries and guests), which is typical enough in tone and style to stand for those aspects of the speech as a whole:

> Back in February of this year, when a few of us old-timers accidentally discovered that we had in our midst a man who had held the same job for close on to forty years, that seemed such a remarkable accomplishment in these days that a few of us decided we ought to do something about it. This town of ours used to be an important railroad center, before they put in the buses and before the business of mining coal was all shot to—well, a certain place that I understand they have all the coal they need, if the reverend clergy will pardon me.

To be singled out are such folksy and colloquial examples of speech as "us old-timers," "close on to forty years" and "this town of ours." We can almost hear the knowing wink when he makes his little joke about the place he will not name but which rhymes with the "well" that usurps its position.

The purpose of the speech is to honor the town's retiring physician. Dr. Merritt is too-obviously well-named for he has manifested, according to all the evidence, the qualities that the townspeople are now called upon to admire and reward: selflessness, sacrifice, professional competence, and civic-mindedness. The speaker asserts as much and in every instance tells an illustrative anecdote: the doctor's handling of injuries at a train wreck, his easy way with those patients in his debt, and his fund-raising for the creation of a hospital that at the last moment he decides altruistically to allow others to build in (and credit to) a nearby town. To round out his account of the doctor's character, moreover, the speaker lets it be known (as he must) that he is privy to some of the doctor's secrets of character and motivation (the doctor and his family, he reveals, put up $30,000 of their own money to prime the fund-raising pump for the town's proposed hospital). The doctor has his foibles, though. He chews tobacco, if only a few people know it, and he plays poker, so badly though that his card-playing poses no danger to his standing as a Methodist.

All this "Bert" Shoemaker handles with confidence and obvious aplomb. He is clearly a man comfortable among fellow townspeople at this "family party." Effortlessly in this unwritten speech—he has only a few jottings on crib-cards ("Family" and "Hobbies," for example) that he sometimes anticipates—he reaches the last phase of his performance. It is the most difficult thing he has to do, it turns out, for it involves bringing up the large unspoken matter in the town, so far unmentioned: the madness and continued confinement of the doctor's wife. The speaker tackles this dreaded subject by telling a lightly sentimental story of adolescent courtship, deferred marriage, two pregnancies and the death of the babies, and depression that deepened into permanent madness. At first the speaker appears to be dwelling unduly on the matter. But, as it turns out, the story is fully appropriate to the occasion, for the prize the townspeople have for their doctor is a check for $20,000 on a silver platter engraved: *"Presented to Samuel G. Merritt, M. D. at a Family Party in Honor of His First Forty Years of Service To His Community."* The money is intended for the maternity ward of the Johnsville Hospital, to be known— in honor of the doctor's wife—as the "Alice C. Merritt Ward."

This evening's "family party" culminates in this showing of communal appreciation. Even the reference to the "first" forty years is intended only as a well-meaning joke. But this aura of well-being, orchestrated skillfully by the town's spokesman, may not be entirely warranted. There are indications to the contrary. Early in his speech "Bert" Shoemaker refers to the ancient practice among railroaders for bestowing a gold watch upon an employee at his retirement. The check for charity and the engraved silver platter are the townspeople's equivalent of the railroader's watch. And they are, in their own way, as inadequate to compensate for a life of service as the watch is to compensate the worker for his labor on the railroad's behalf. And yet, the speaker's tone is nothing if not smug and self-satisfied. The question, all but asked, is how *can* this town adequately thank this man whose rewards have been to be taken (patients who could pay for his services do not do so), hated (when during the strike he will not return the townspeople's contributions to the hospital fund), and even robbed (his shotgun is stolen from his car while he ministers to the victims of the train disaster). Yet, the speaker's "mister-smooth-it-all-away" tone would persuade us that the equation has been given and at the last everything is all right. But it is not, and the point should be put clearly. "A Family Party" is not the heart-warming story about a doctor's dedication to his patients and their expression of gratitude for his forty years of service that *Collier's* paid for and published. Rather it is the story of the town of Lyons, which, in turn, is the story of the American small town that invariably "uses" its benefactors, scraping up its thankfulness at the last in one showy gesture. An evening of gratitude, it is expected, will even things out. They have chosen their spokesman well ("Bert, you're it," they tell him) not only because he is the doctor's best friend but because, as O'Hara makes deftly clear, he is the self-satisfied, self-congratulatory, self-deceiving voice of the suggestively named town of Lyons. What should be recognized is the subtlety of O'Hara's execution of his decision to tell his "small-town story" as a poker-faced parody, drawing upon the familiar form of the honoring speech at a retirement dinner. Entirely in the hands of a "heart-warming," not entirely reliable narrator, "A Family Party" offers his readers a special instance of O'Hara's narrative virtuosity and, perhaps, his feelings as a doctor's son.

Notes

1. Robert Emmet Long, *John O'Hara* (New York: Ungar, 1983), p. 181.
2. Frank MacShane, *The Life of John O'Hara* (New York: E. P. Dutton, 1980), p. 167.
3. Matthew J. Bruccoli, *The O'Hara Concern: A Biography of John O'Hara* (New York: Random House, 1975), p. 232.
4. Finis Farr, *O'Hara: A Biography* (Boston and Toronto: Little, Brown, 1973), p. 226.
5. Quoted in MacShane, p. 167.
6. Long, pp. 181–82.
7. This and subsequent quotations refer to John O'Hara, *A Family Party* (New York: Bantam Books, 1957).

Gibbsville: John O'Hara's Small-Town Armageddon

CHARLES W. BASSETT

Reviewing John O'Hara's last "big" novel, *The Lockwood Concern*, in 1965, Webster Schott called O'Hara "America's most distinguished out-of-date novelist. . . . Like a man on a couch searching for an explanation, he keeps repeating the same story with wondrous invention: how to go to hell in style. . . ."[1] Schott went on to predict that posterity would account O'Hara a great writer, a prospect that appears very unlikely nearly three decades later. Nevertheless, in the 1950s and 1960s O'Hara was probably the most popular *serious* writer in America, and he owed his popularity in part to that very repetition, focus, and verisimilitude. As the contemporary Italian novelist Alberto Moravia once told a reviewer: "Good writers are monotonous, like good composers. Their truth is self-repeating. They keep trying to write the same book. That is to say, they keep trying to perfect their understanding of the one problem they were born to understand."[2] Clearly, the problem that John O'Hara was born to understand is the pathetic waste engendered by the class and status anxieties of a materialistic American society, particularly the dangerous illusions that snobbery generates in those who seek identity and security in social form, the symbolic value of *things*, and the power of established wealth. These themes dominated O'Hara's huge canon: 13 novels, or 18 if separately published novellas are included; 402 short stories, most of which are gathered in 13 collections; and eight plays, most notably *Pal Joey*. A native of the small anthracite town of Pottsville, Pennsylvania, O'Hara recreated his hometown (he called it Gibbsville) and its environs in nine novels and 63 stories.

Conversely, O'Hara's range made him something more than the Pied Piper of Pottsville, PA. He also used New York City, Hollywood, Cleveland, and various suburbs, summer colonies, and retirement villages as settings; in fact, for a time, O'Hara rivaled two other Johns, Cheever and Updike, as the best known chronicler of the lives of upper-middle-class Americans. Cheever's intellect endeared him to those critics who considered his settings too conven-

This essay was written specifically for this volume and is published here for the first time. An earlier version was presented at a Mid-American American Studies Association meeting in May 1987.

tional; and Updike, even more sexually explicit than O'Hara, routinely endowed his heroes with theological languors that offset their bourgeois anxieties. On the other hand, O'Hara's characters were considered excessively stereotypical (read "shallow") suburbanites—*too* consumerist, *too* envious, *too* obsessed with the insecurity of their places in a venal and competitive culture.

In fact, however, O'Hara might better be called a hybrid: one part novelist of manners (in the James-Howells-Wharton tradition); another part thoroughgoing naturalist after Dreiser, Norris, and London. Probably his major literary inspiration was that other hybrid, Sinclair Lewis. As he wrote in the foreword to the Modern Library edition of *Appointment in Samarra*: "In the matter of influences . . . chiefly [Scott] Fitzgerald and Lewis. . . . I can see countless instances of the effect of my reading Fitzgerald and Lewis."[3] O'Hara's first nationally published piece was a 500-word imitation of Lewis in F. P. A.'s "The Conning Tower" column in the New York *World*—"A Speech by George F. Gabbity. . . ."[4] This Lewis-O'Hara connection has been clear to all of O'Hara's biographers and critics. Frank MacShane in fact considers O'Hara the more skillful author: "Where Sinclair Lewis makes sarcastic judgments about his characters, O'Hara lets them reveal themselves through their own words."[5] Wolcott Gibbs had similar feelings: "All of O'Hara's pieces give evidence of a remarkably accurate ear and also a clear perception of the difference between satire and burlesque: unlike the very similar characters in 'Main Street' and 'Babbitt,' whose conversation was frankly heightened to absurdity since they were little more than animated symbols of Mr. Lewis' general contempt for American thought."[6]

Whatever the respective merits of the two novelists, O'Hara's fictional Gibbsville owes something to Lewis' Gopher Prairie and Zenith. As Robert Emmet Long puts it: "It is extraordinary how seriously both Lewis and O'Hara take the American small town, down to the minutest manifestations of its life, how accurately they place their characters within local hierarchies. They are mimics of distinctively American types, and give unusual importance to their speech."[7] Yet those who recognize the techniques of the literary naturalist would hardly characterize Lewis and O'Hara's attention to the American small town and its distinctive idiosyncrasies as "extraordinary"; the naturalists find such verisimilitude of setting and speech absolutely crucial to a clear understanding of their characters.

Still, naturalism's quotidian and even obsessive mimesis has fallen out of critical fashion in this age of metafiction, relegating both O'Hara and Lewis to the literary ash heap. In her fine book on literary naturalism, June Howard explains this disparagement:

"I suspect that many critics find naturalist novels somehow scandalous. They fail to be well-made novels; they insist tactlessly upon a relation between literature and reality; they traffic brazenly with the formulas of popular culture and journalism; and they are obsessed with class and commodities in a most embarrassing fashion."[8]

Though naturalism may seem passé to post-modern literary critics, this important genre and its practitioners remain a mother lode for cultural historians, whose perceptions of changes in American values are often triggered by George Babbitt's or Julian English's obsessions with "class and commodities." Moreover, O'Hara wrote of his avowed precursor: "Lewis was born to write *Babbitt*, and no one else could have written it."[9] For O'Hara, Lewis was a key to his era.

At the same time, despite his admiration for Sinclair Lewis as novelist and social historian, John O'Hara had to forge his own style and vision out of a wholly different experience of the world. These two writers, both doctor's sons, felt excluded from their rightful place in their towns—Lewis because of looks and personality, O'Hara because of his Roman Catholicism and Irish ethnicity. But Lewis got to Yale, unhappy as that experience might have been for him; O'Hara never did, and he never forgot the failure. For O'Hara satire was not enough to assuage the wounds; he could write like Lewis (and did for the *New Yorker* from 1928 to 1932, in satiric monologues at the Orange County Afternoon Delphian Society and the Hagedorn & Brownmiller Paint and Varnish Co.), but generally O'Hara's imagination produced bleaker portraits of the bourgeoisie. Lewis' kind of *Smart Set-American Mercury-New Yorker* sarcasm seemed to O'Hara to be quintessentially of "the Twenties," not an accurate portrayal of the America of the 1930s.

Little wonder, then, that the novel that made O'Hara's reputation as the prophet of the Hangover Generation was *Appointment in Samarra* (1934). The book won O'Hara some respectful criticism from the more liberal reviewers (the Communist *New Masses* said "O'Hara reports like Sinclair Lewis and has more guts than Hemingway," but it was demonstrably a more misanthropic and deterministic novel than were any of Lewis' great novels of the 1920s.[10] And *Appointment*'s frankness about sexual matters in Gibbsville earned a pan from genteel H. S. Canby in one review headlined "Mr. O'Hara and the Vulgar School." Weighing in with a similar assessment was one Harry Sinclair Lewis, who claimed that O'Hara's book was "infantile . . . the erotic visions of a hobbledehoy behind the barn."[11]

In 1994, the carnal candor of *Appointment in Samarra* would bring no blush to the cheek of a sophomore at Sauk Center High. But the novel was strong stuff in 1934, and O'Hara's protagonist—Julian English—does not flinch from sex like Carol Kennicott or equivocate like George Babbitt. Julian's pride—indeed his very identity—stems from his success with women in bed, and the final, fatal blow to his self-esteem in *Appointment in Samarra* is his failed seduction of a gauche Gibbsville newspaperwoman. O'Hara's fiction highlights the dangers of an improvised erotic life in a conservative social milieu, and Julian English's heedless libidinousness plays a major role in his disintegration.

Nevertheless, sexual outspokenness is hardly the only quality separating O'Hara's Gibbsville from Lewis' Gopher Prairie. For all of his putatively nasty satire and his contempt for the style and values of American provincials, Lewis' fiction of the 1920s was actually optimistic. Will Kennicott might be vulgar and Vergil Gunch vaguely menacing, but the future seemed bright enough even to the Babbitts. Depression Gibbsville, on the other hand, is a thoroughly frightened little city. O'Hara's novel chronicles just three days in the life of Julian English: 24, 25, and 26 December 1930. John O'Hara himself had perceived the lesson that his protagonist would learn with great difficulty—"1930 was the worst year of my life."[12]

Gibbsville, the once-thriving center of the southern anthracite fields, had never recovered from the "disastrous strike of 1925. . . . Anthracite markets disappeared. Domestic sales were hurt permanently; the oil burner was installed in thousands of homes."[13] But economic disaster went beyond the coal region. As Richard Pells puts it: "For most Americans the 1920s was a period not so much of prosperity as of sheer survival, with little money left over after the bills were paid to enjoy the party others seemed to be throwing."[14] The people of Gibbsville, PA, however, kept hoping that President Hoover—a mining engineer, the most trustworthy of professionals in the anthracite fields—would work a miracle and that the Black Friday of the great crash would continue to be known as "a strong technical reaction."[15]

Julian English is O'Hara's Jazz Age anachronism in this Depression decade; he's an insecure and reckless child / man whose personal attractiveness, superficial charm, and inherited social status have given him an unwarranted and self-deceiving sense of freedom from personal responsibility and economic retribution. Ironically, in 1930, Julian is also proprietor of the Gibbsville Cadillac Motor Car Company, selling fewer and fewer luxury cars and deeply in debt to Harry Reilly, Gibbsville's parvenu Irish entrepreneur. In a fit of jealous, drunken petulance at the Lantenengo Country Club, Julian throws a drink in Reilly's face, triggering the detonation of events that leads to his death.

The reasons for Julian's suicide are the central question in *Appointment in Samarra*. More psychologically sensitive than Lewis, O'Hara can dramatize the sources of English's failure of will: his physician father's coldness has denied Julian a stable identity; his mother is an ineffectual shadow; his wife controls him by indulging his immaturity and using her sexual favors to keep him "proper." Yet Julian has never been a rebel; rather, he is completely establishmentarian, an anthracite region aristocrat, until his heedless gesture threatens the stability of Gibbsville's stratified class structure. Then the masks are off, the latent violence unloosed, the fragile order tottering. Class is tenuous and slippery at the best of times in Gibbsville; it is hypersensitive to injury at the beginning of the Great Depression. O'Hara's American small town is a "spurious democracy," marked by classic hatred among its entrenched social classes.[16]

The *intensity* of this class-based animosity and its connection to the dangers of lubricious sexual promiscuity and the imminence of violent retaliation differentiates O'Hara's town from the earlier, more manageable conflicts in Lewis' fictional Gopher Prairie and Zenith. More graphically than Lewis, O'Hara focuses on the venal, small-minded, and bloody antagonisms of Gibbsville's citizens—inescapably defined by money, family, occupation, region, religion, education, and ethnicity.

The chief catalyst for conflict in Gibbsville is liquor. By Christmas 1930, no one saw anything amusing in Prohibition; O'Hara's generation couldn't smirk anymore at Babbitt's clumsy and falsely cheery ministrations of home-made gin to Chum Frink and the "boys." Almost *everyone* in Gibbsville drinks or sells booze or transports it. Big Ed Charney rules Lantenengo County as its boss bootlegger, making him nearly equal to Julian's patrician friend, Whit Hofman, whose coal-land millions have even managed to survive the crash of the 1930s. *Appointment in Samarra*'s hoods are no bathtub amateurs; they are amoral gangsters who bribe and shoot and whore their way to power. Gibbsville *needs* whiskey—to forget, to smooth over, to goad, to dull, to lubricate.

At the same time, drink exacerbates inter- and intra-class animus in the little city of 25,000 people, where Julian English scurries fecklessly like a laboratory animal in a rum-soaked maze. Weakly, Julian drinks and drinks, relishing the chimerical sense of license that alcohol lends to his irresponsibility. But throwing the drink is a step too far. Exclusion and scapegoating ensue for Julian as the conservative Pennsylvania Dutch middle class join Reilly's fellow Irish in spurning this drink-throwing "baby." And the mobsters stir ominously at Julian's drunken public tryst with bootlegger Charney's mistress. Caroline, English's wife, leaves him for his gross infidelity. "Julian . . . felt the tremendous excitement, the great thrilling lump in the chest and abdomen that comes before an unknown, well deserved punishment. He knew he was in for it."[17]

Punishment is consequently inevitable because O'Hara knows that Gibbsville enjoys nothing more than a self-righteously indignant slash at an elitist miscreant. And Julian's plight seems leagues more serious than similar exclusions in *Main Street* and *Babbitt*. In Gibbsville, every act—however trivial—has social consequences, and in a culture increasingly fragmented by the lack of shared values, the merely irresponsible suffer as grievously as the truly monstrous. Life in O'Hara's town is more dangerous than life in Lewis'. Gopher Prairie and Zenith may be hypocritical and smug, philistine and provincial, but forgiveness is not impossible there. And confidence, hope, and ambition are not mortal sins. By contrast, Gibbsville is cancerous, a society far gone in self-destruction.

Appointment in Samarra climaxes with Julian English's suicide; he, more pathetically than Carol Kennicott and George Babbitt, has found that he cannot flee the torments of his town: "you did not really get away from what he was going back to, and whatever it was, he had to face it."[18] However, Depression despair has turned this small town into a combat zone. " 'The war's over,' " Julian tells an antagonist at the Gibbsville Club. The reply—" 'Yeah, that's what you think' "[19]—underscores the latent violence informing all relations in Gibbsville. Caught, Julian punishes himself one last time; the self-destructive weapon he uses is the carbon monoxide from his own Cadillac in his own garage. The war finally *is* over for Julian, whose wife thinks of him as "some young officer in an overseas cap and Sam Browne belt." Julian was like someone "who had died in the war," for, she concludes, "it was *time* for him to die."[20]

These "times" are central to O'Hara's view of the world. The Depression is eternal in *Appointment*'s Gibbsville—economic, social, and cultural depression. The world cannot be made right. And O'Hara's new pessimism is echoed as well by other connoisseurs of small-town America: Anthony Hilfer's *The Revolt from the Village*, a study of cultural iconoclasts like Lewis and Anderson and Mencken and Wolfe, ends its analysis with 1930 when *different* revolts began to boil.[21] Finally, in *Small Town America*, Richard Lingeman uses O'Hara's novel to argue that the class war had spread permanently from the city to the country.[22]

O'Hara's Gibbsville is still another symbol of the loss of possibility in American life. Mobility has characterized the American Dream from the beginning, men and women fleeing to the moving frontier for freedom and identity. Alternately, rural Americans thronged to the city in search of the same elusive goals. By 1934, city, town, and country had become indistinguishable; we had no place to go, except perhaps into the garage where the Cadillac's carbon monoxide promised permanent escape. John O'Hara might be in eclipse in 1994, but historians of the culture of the American small town would do well to examine his vision again. He could be on to something.

Notes

1.   Webster Schott, "How to Go to Hell in Style," *New York Times Book Review*, 28 November 1965, 4.

2.   Quoted in Melvin Maddocks, Review of *Command, And I Will Obey You* by Alberto Moravia, *Atlantic Monthly* 224 (August 1969): 90.

3.   "Foreword," in *Appointment in Samarra* (New York: Modern Library, 1953), n.p. O'Hara offered further comments on Lewis in a letter dated 17 February 1959 to Mark Schorer: "Lewis was a great American novelist and long before the Nobel people got around to giving him the prize, I said I thought he deserved it. . . . He observed well, he retained, he had a good sardonic sense of humor, and he also had a sense of history. . ." *Selected Letters of John O'Hara*, ed. Matthew J. Bruccoli (New York: Random House, 1978), 288–89.

4.   Reprinted in Matthew J. Bruccoli, *The O'Hara Concern: A Biography of John O'Hara* (New York: Random House, 1975), 46–47.

5.   Frank MacShane, *The Life of John O'Hara* (New York: E. P. Dutton, 1980), 35.

6.   Wolcott Gibbs, "Preface" to *Pipe Night* by John O'Hara (New York: Duell, Sloan & Pearce, 1945), ix. Gibbs was O'Hara's colleague on the *New Yorker* in the 1920s and 1930s, a boon drinking companion, and the eponymic of the Gibbsville of O'Hara's fiction.

7.   Robert Emmet Long, *John O'Hara* (New York: Frederick Ungar Publishing Co., 1983), 167.

8.   June Howard, *Form and History in American Literary Naturalism* (Chapel Hill: University of North Carolina Press, 1985), xi.

9.   *Selected Letters of John O'Hara*, 288.

10.   Quoted in Finis Farr, *O'Hara: A Biography* (Boston & Toronto: Little, Brown & Co., 1973), 173.

11.   Canby reviewed *Appointment in Samarra* in *Saturday Review of Literature* 11 (18 August 1934): 53, 55. Lewis sideswiped O'Hara in a review of Canby's *The Age of Confidence* in *Saturday Review of Literature* 11 (6 October 1934): 41.

12.   The quote is from a November 1931 letter to his boyhood friend Robert Simonds. *Selected Letters of John O'Hara*, 55.

13.   *Appointment in Samarra* (New York: Harcourt, Brace and Co., 1934), 63–64. O'Hara is uncharacteristically inaccurate about the length of the 1925 strike; it lasted 170 days. See Donald L. Miller and Richard E. Sharpless, *The Kingdom of Coal: Work, Enterprise, and Ethnic Communities in the Mine Fields* (Philadelphia: University of Pennsylvania Press, 1985), 292. Moreover, the unique rigidity of social stratification in O'Hara's native Pottsville—the source of the conflict in *Appointment in Samarra*—has been challenged. Historian Edward J. Davies II found neighboring Wilkes-Barre to be far more class-conscious and hierarchical than Pottsville during O'Hara's youth. See *The Anthracite Aristocracy: Leadership and Social Change in the Hard Coal Regions of Northeastern Pennsylvania, 1800–1930* (DeKalb: Northern Illinois University Press, 1985).

14.   Richard Pells, *Radical Visions and American Dreams: Culture and Social Thought in the Depression Years* (New York: Harper & Row, 1973), 12.

15.   *Appointment in Samarra*, 65.

16.   *Appointment in Samarra*, 183. James W. Tuttleton was the first to accent the "spurious democracy" theme. See *The Novel of Manners in America* (Chapel Hill: University of North Carolina Press, 1972), 193–94.

17.   *Appointment in Samarra*, 182.

18.   *Appointment in Samarra*, 242.

19.   *Appointment in Samarra*, 236.

20.   *Appointment in Samarra*, 293–94.

21.   Anthony Channell Hilfer, *The Revolt from the Village 1915–1930* (Chapel Hill: University of North Carolina Press, 1969).

22.   Richard Lingeman, *Small Town America: A Narrative History 1620–The Present* (Boston & New York: G. P. Putnam's Sons, 1980), 414.

The "story behind the story": John O'Hara's Handling of Point of View

Thomas P. Coakley

Critics generally have taken the position that John O'Hara weaves a rich but thin tapestry—realistic details without thematic context—no "religious or philosophical dimension" as one critic puts it.[1] To embrace such a view is to ignore what Matthew Bruccoli calls "the theme of isolation" which pervades O'Hara's work.[2] Many of John O'Hara's protagonists are destroyed by their rejection of or by other people.

Julian English, Joe Chapin, Alfred Eaton, Robert Millhouser, George Lockwood, and countless other O'Hara characters share a tendency to withdraw from the world. They isolate themselves—or allow themselves to be isolated—emotionally and even physically at times, as in the case of George Lockwood. The need to make meaningful contact with the rest of mankind is the central moral issue in O'Hara's fiction. O'Hara characters fail, not because they are "bad" or "unlucky" or "immoral," but because they sever their ties with the world.

Ironically, O'Hara's considerable technical skill has caused many critics to miss his preoccupation with this theme. His subtleties are sometimes so subtle that they are overlooked. For example, he has been widely credited—sometimes grudgingly—with having a sensitive ear for dialogue. However, as O'Hara himself observes, those who say that he has a "phonographic ear" are not reading carefully: "It is one thing to admit or claim that I write credible conversations, naturalistic speech. But it is something else to say I have a phonographic ear. My dialog is good because I never allow a character to say anything he would not say, that is not a product of his social and educational background and of the occasion on which he is speaking, relaxed, under stress, drunk, sober, tired, or whatever the occasion may be."[3] In actual conversation, O'Hara notes, people seldom finish their sentences; a writer must maintain constant "control" of dialogue whereas speakers ordinarily need not do so.[4] It is thus a careless critic who will attribute O'Hara's "naturalistic" dialogue to a "phonographic" ear.

Unfortunately, too many critics have read his work carelessly. As Sheldon Grebstein observes,

This essay was written specifically for this volume and is published here for the first time.

240

Critics have too often read him as one reads an entertainer, not as one reads an author whose very survival during more than a generation of shifting literary taste, whose productivity, whose hold upon a large and loyal audience, whose depiction of certain crucial segments of our life and times, and whose power to win distinguished adherents to his cause, all demand that he be given consideration as a serious artist, possibly as a serious artist of major stature. Not having read him closely, the very subtlety of his effects and the very saliency of his insights have escaped them. Not having read him closely, they have missed much of the best that is in him.[5]

One subtle effect that critics tend to miss is his exploration of a character's consciousness. O'Hara manipulates point of view so skillfully that the reader is frequently misled into believing that he is still dealing with surfaces when, in fact, he has already descended into the interior consciousness of a character. "As a result," writes Grebstein, "the reader—without realizing just how and when—moves from the vantage place of third person to first person, from outside to inside."[6] Grebstein argues that O'Hara's technical mastery "conjoins the finished and conclusive effect derived from the objective mode with the immediate and concrete effect of the subjective."[7]

O'Hara's handling of point of view allows the reader to understand and experience a character's movement toward isolation. The reader is always positioned in a way that will allow him to perceive the functioning of a character's consciousness—regardless of whether the point of view is dramatic monologue (*A Family Party*), interior monologue ("Alone"), a blending of omniscient narrator with interior monologue (*Appointment in Samarra*), or a combination of all of these (*Ourselves to Know*). For example, in *Appointment in Samarra* the omniscient narrator leads the reader through the consciousnesses of Julian and the other characters, creating an ironic tension between Julian's sense that he is being relentlessly driven toward isolation and destruction and the generally held view of Julian as a well-liked and enviable young man.

O'Hara frequently uses variations on a technique that might be called "dramatic interior monologue." With this device, O'Hara takes the reader inside the mind of a character in a story. O'Hara uses the diction the character would be expected to use but refers to the character in the third person. The effect is that of a narrator repeating the specific thoughts of the character. The use of the character's diction, coupled with a kind of associative process by which one thought leads to another, simulates a stream of consciousness effect; however, the third-person references to the character serve as a reminder that the narrator is processing the character's thoughts and allows O'Hara to retain the clarity of more conventional forms of narration, without making the narrator obtrusive. As a result, the subjectivity of the character is ordered by the objectivity of the narrator, and the reader receives a privileged look at the character's thoughts without getting lost in a chaotic flow of unrelated thoughts and images.

Grebstein calls this technique "shifting perspective" and "interior monologue" at different points in his discussion of O'Hara's work.[8] He sees it as a useful disguise for the omniscient narrator and a means for furthering the "felt life" of a story.[9] "*Dramatic* interior monologue" is the term used here because the added modifier reflects the tendency of O'Hara's characters to reveal to the reader aspects of their personalities of which they themselves are not aware. In conventional dramatic monologue, the speaker unknowingly reveals motives and attitudes that would normally be kept hidden in his or her secret thoughts; in a dramatic interior monologue, the character's consciousness reveals motives and attitudes normally hidden in the subconscious. This is a rather awkward but important distinction: O'Hara employs the dramatic interior monologue to allow the reader to know more about a character than the character knows about himself or herself; in other words, he adds a dimension to the interior view that simply reveals a character's secrets. Critics who complain that O'Hara fails to go beneath the surface appear to have missed this extra dimension.

O'Hara began experimenting with the dramatic interior monologue quite early in his career. "Ella and the Chinee" is an unremarkable story, but it does offer a useful illustration of O'Hara's early use of the technique: "He was an old geezer, and if he'd of been a Mick or a Wop or a Kike, she wouldn't of worried about him. But she'd never had any experience with Chinees. She had read somewhere that every single one of them took dope, and they were all constantly under the effects of it, but not the same way Ella's Uncle Larry used to get. They never showed any kind of emotion because of the dope."[10] This simple passage is no deeper than Ella herself, but it is revealing. The structure of phrases such as "he'd of been" and "wouldn't of worried" suggests a lower-class background, as do the derogatory ethnic epithets. The spelling "Chinees" indicates that when the character hears the word "Chinese," she thinks of it as the plural form of "Chinee": one native of China is a "Chinee," two or more are "Chinees." This touch, combined with the thesis which Ella draws from something she "had read somewhere" implies that she is a less than attentive reader. Her train of thought ("Chinees"—"dope"—"Uncle Larry"—"emotion") is associative, but O'Hara would probably be quick to point out—as he did in reaction to comments about his "phonographic ear"— that her thought pattern never escapes the writer's control. Ella's conscious thoughts are read by the reader who, as a result of reading them, knows that Ella is shallow and unattractively naive. Presumably these are characteristics of which Ella is not aware.

By the time he wrote *Appointment in Samarra*, O'Hara was able to use the dramatic interior monologue effectively in exploring the minds of characters more complex than Ella. In that novel and in much of his later work, he employs the dramatic interior monologue in a way that often blurs the movement from outside to inside (from the narrator's comments to character's thoughts) or the movement from one character's thoughts to those of another character. The last chapter of *Appointment in Samarra* opens with a comment by the narrator and then flows from what appears to be a newspaper report into the minds of people who have known Julian. One section of that chapter opens in the mind of Julian's father, then jumps—after a one-line break in the text—to Caroline's mind, and concludes with a dialogue between Caroline and her mother. The passage, besides serving to illustrate the narrative progression, also contains an effective word-portrait of a mind in a state of shock:

> Dr. English was not afraid of what he knew people were saying—people with long memories. He knew they were recalling the death of Julian's grandfather. But inevitably they would see how the suicide strain had skipped one generation to come out in the next. So long as they saw that it was all right. You had to expect things.

> It was a lively, jesting grief, sprightly and pricking and laughing, to make you shudder and shiver up to the point of giving way completely. Then it would become a long black tunnel; a tunnel you had to go through, had to go through, had to go through, had to go through, had to go through. No whistle. But had to go through, had to go through, had to go through. Whistle? Had to go through, had to go through, had to go through, had to go through. No whistle? Had to go through, had to go through, had to go through.
> "Caroline dear, please take this. Sleep will do you good," her mother said.
> "Mother darling, I'm perfectly all right. I don't want anything to make me sleep. I'll sleep tonight."
> . . . .
> "Oh, dear, what am I going to do with you?" said Mrs. Walker.[11]

Dr. English's egoism and rationalization, Caroline's relentlessly chugging grief, and Mrs. Walker's mindless patter blend together here to provide a panorama of grief; the reader is simultaneously inside the minds of individual mourners and outside, critically surveying the aftermath of Julian's tragedy. He can judge Dr. English's concern for appearances, empathize with Caroline's confused and desperate resolve to penetrate and pass the blackness, and pity Mrs. Walker's ineffectiveness.

The dramatic interior monologue is particularly effective in dramatizing the theme of man's isolation. In novels such as *Appointment in Samarra*, *Ten North Frederick*, and *The Lockwood Concern*, O'Hara uses this technique to provide the reader with several views of the events of each novel. He allows the reader to enter the closed universes of isolated characters and to share the feelings of "aloneness" that confront them; at the same time, this entry into the minds of several other characters provides the reader with a multifaceted vision in which one character's perceptions are clarified by the perceptions of another.

In *Appointment in Samarra*, O'Hara's use of the dramatic interior monologue makes it possible for the reader to share Julian's view of himself as hopelessly isolated, and, at the same time, understand that other characters neither recognize nor wish to further Julian's isolation. His tragic end is unnecessary in the sense that nothing he or anyone else has done demands it, but it is also inevitable because Julian cannot open himself to others; he cannot expose his feelings and thereby earn a clarifying or supportive response from others. If Julian had developed a relationship of mutual trust with his wife, he would have at least one person to whom he could turn for understanding and support; however, as his dramatic interior monologues show, he views Caroline as an enveloping, protective force—like the "coonskins" in his car[12]—in which he can lose rather than express his "self." When he believes that he has lost her protection, he is doomed. O'Hara's use of the dramatic interior monologue reveals the complexity of Julian's character, which belies the image others have of him as a charming but self-indulgent and reckless snob.

The fact that O'Hara provides no dramatic interior monologues for Joe Chapin in *Ten North Frederick* is equally revealing. Joe spends most of his life in the artificial, protective worlds created by his mother and his wife. As long as he remains within the confines of those worlds, he does not feel the "aloneness" that confronts all fully realized human beings. He is not fully human until he encounters Kate Drummond. Only then can he say, "I have a soul now," "I feel as though my full life had just begun. . . ."[13]

The reader knows nothing of Joe "that could not have been seen or heard by the people whose lives were touched by Joe Chapin's life."[14] Dwelling in the artificial worlds created by Charlotte, Edith, and finally alcohol, Joe Chapin has no "self" to reveal in dramatic interior monologues; the self which comes to life briefly during his affair with Kate makes itself known in dialogue that has considerably more emotional intensity and insight than the reader is accustomed to find in the conversations of Joe Chapin. Joe's vision of his future reflects this increased intensity: " 'Tonight I'll be in Gibbsville, going from the station to my house. And I'll know every face I see, and the houses I've passed a thousand times. I know which sidewalks are brick and which ones are concrete. Everything the same as when I left yesterday morning. But I won't be the same. Practically nobody in the town will know I've been away, and won't know I've come back to what? To nothing. To everything that's away from you, Kate. To nothing. To death. To the end of life. To death. To life away from you.' "[15] Joe's life, the real life of his "self," *is* "nothing"; aside from his brief affair with Kate, he has no self to reveal in dramatic interior monologues. The elaborate social ritual of his funeral which opens the novel stands in ironic contrast to the "nothing" that is his life.

O'Hara does employ the dramatic interior monologue in dealing with other characters in the novel. The thoughts of Charlotte, Edith, and Mike Slattery reveal how carefully and completely Joe's life has been manipulated by those around him. O'Hara also uses the dramatic interior monologue to show that Edith's manipulation of Joe is motivated by the same fear of isolation that underlies Joe's willingness to submit himself to her control. Edith's desire to "own a human being" proceeds from the same insecurity that forces her to seek "greatness";[16] she must enlarge herself by absorbing Joe in order to escape the feeling that she is powerless and alone in a vast universe. To the funeral-goers, Edith is rich, sensible, and possessed of inner strength; O'Hara's use of the dramatic interior monologue allows the reader to understand that Edith fears life as much as Joe fears it.

O'Hara makes extensive use of the dramatic interior monologue in *The Lockwood Concern*. Abraham Lockwood's dramatic interior monologues provide insights into the family background and the original nature of the Concern; they also reveal the extent to which Abraham manipulates his son. The dramatic interior monologues of Adelaide and Agnes Lockwood reveal their attitudes toward the Lockwood men; those of characters such as Harvey Fenstermacher reflect the attitudes of the outside world.

Most of *The Lockwood Concern*, however, is seen through the eyes of George Lockwood; the narrator spends almost all of Books Two and Three—and part of Book One—either with George or in his mind. O'Hara makes the reader spend a great deal of time with George because there is no better way to arouse a reader's sympathy for a less than admirable character; as Wayne Booth puts it, "*If* an author wants intense sympathy for characters who do not have strong virtues to recommend them, *then* the psychic vividness of prolonged and deep inside views will help him."[17] In other words, the more time the reader spends walking in George's shoes—or at least, keeping close track of his footsteps—the more likely it is that he will be able to understand and sympathize with him. George has some serious character defects, but O'Hara cannot risk making him a complete monster; *The Lockwood Concern* is essentially George's story, and, if the reader sees him as completely unattractive, O'Hara may lose the reader's interest. If the reader is to see George's death at the foot of his secret stairway as something more than the deserved fate of an insensitive brute, he must understand the fears and hopes that make George act as he does. Like Edith Chapin, George is one of the less appealing victims of isolation; however, Edith has a likeable victim, Joe Chapin, to help her hold the reader's interest. George must carry the load himself. He is both victim and victimizer: manipulated by his father, he seeks to manipulate those around him. O'Hara's extensive use of the dramatic interior monologue for telling George's story allows the reader to understand both sides of his personality. O'Hara's success in maintaining the reader's interest in George Lockwood may not be as complete as his success in dealing with Julian English and Joe and Edith Chapin; however, in George's case, the task is more challenging.

A major problem with another novel, *A Rage To Live*, may be traced in part to the fact that O'Hara denied himself the option of presenting an interior view of his protagonist, Grace Caldwell Tate. She is one of the few major characters in the book who have no dramatic interior monologues. He explained his intentions in a letter to Frank Norris:

I have employed a device in this novel which I doubt if any critic is going to catch on to. I have given you a complete picture of Grace, the superficial things such as a spottily good vocabulary with a naturalistic use of grammar; her clothes, her drinks, etc. But I also have let you know how she thinks and feels AND YET AT NO TIME DO I, THE NOVELIST, ENTER HER MIND [O'Hara's caps]. At no time am I the omniscient, ubiquitous novelist. The God. You read that book and you *think* [O'Hara's emphasis] you have been inside her thinking moments, but the fact is there is nothing told about Grace that could not have been actually seen or overheard by another human being. That, my friend, is a triumph of writing. I am very proud of it, because in my own estimation it makes me really a pro.[18]

In other words, O'Hara tried to do with Grace what he was later to do with greater success in dealing with Joe Chapin. Joe, however, is a conventionally attractive character whose ability to hold a reader's sympathy is magnified by the reader's awareness that he is being manipulated and victimized by others. Grace is less apparently a victim, and less conventionally attractive. Until his involvement with Kate, near the end of the novel, Joe lives by an aristocratic code, and his role as victim makes the reader sympathize with his violation of that code. Grace is not victimized by Sidney, and *her* adultery is less likely to be acceptable to the reader. The fact that O'Hara felt compelled to defend Grace against charges of lewdness is an indication of his artistic failure in her case.[19]

Grace fails to earn the reader's sympathy. Despite O'Hara's intentions and his belief that he had succeeded, the reader does not really get to know and understand her. George Lockwood is a far less attractive character, but O'Hara's use of the dramatic interior monologue allows the reader to understand him; on the other hand, even the most broad-minded reader may not understand Grace's sexual rages. Thus, after the death of Sidney—a likeable character whose attractiveness is enhanced by the reader's ability to see his mind at work—the reader's interest in the novel lags. This has prompted a number of even sympathetic critics to argue that the novel should end with Sidney's death.[20] It seems likely that O'Hara's desire to render a portrait of both the woman and her city might have been better served by providing Grace with the dramatic interior monologues that would reveal her more completely.[21]

While *A Rage To Live* might have been improved if O'Hara had allowed his reader to see the workings of Grace Tate's mind, *From The Terrace* might have benefited from less extensive use of the dramatic interior monologue. This latter book is so seriously flawed that one risks oversimplifying its problems in stressing any single failure;[22] however, *From The Terrace* provides a useful illustration of the dangers inherent in excessive use of the dramatic interior monologue.

In a novel like *Appointment in Samarra*, the dramatic interior monologues of secondary characters serve the useful function of clarifying events which might be distorted if the reader saw them only through the eyes of the protagonist. In *From The Terrace*, the novel's size tends to diffuse the effects of the dramatic interior monologue; there are so many characters and so many dramatic interior monologues that they tend to annul each other. For example, less than 100 pages after Mary Eaton admits that she does not believe in love,[23] a dramatic interior monologue reveals her great love for her children;[24] 84 pages later, another dramatic interior monologue discloses that the death of her oldest son has given her "confirmation of her disbelief in love."[25]

These apparent inconsistencies may be resolved by noting the changes that take place in Mary's life during the period. *From The Terrace* takes place over such a broad expanse of time that the lives and views of many characters— Tom Rothermel, Jim Roper, Mary Eaton, even Alfred Eaton—can be expected to change, and they do. As a result, information gleaned from dramatic interior monologues seems transitory and insignificant. As the dramatic interior monologue becomes a less reliable source of information for the reader, it loses its clarifying function. Alfred's dramatic interior monologues are useful because they contribute to the reader's interest in and sympathy for the protagonist but the inside views of other characters do little more than contribute to the confusion caused by O'Hara's overly ambitious goals for the book.

O'Hara used the dramatic interior monologue with varying degrees of emphasis in many other novels as well. In *Butterfield 8, The Big Laugh, Elizabeth Appleton, The Instrument, Lovey Childs*, and *The Ewings*, O'Hara used the device as he had used it in *The Lockwood Concern*: to gain a maximum of reader sympathy for characters who, viewed only from the outside, would seem too depraved to merit the reader's or the novelist's interest. Gloria Wandrous is a promiscuous young woman lost in a maze of one-night-stands, lesbian affairs, and alcoholic stupors. Hubert Ward is a "shitheel" whose inherent evil proves alluring for movie audiences. Elizabeth Appleton is a junior league version of Grace Tate; she acquires a lover, uses him for five years to satisfy her sexual needs and her craving for excitement, and then dumps him unceremoniously. Yank Lucas is a playwright who uses women to fire his creativity and then destroys them. Lovey Childs is a richer and shallower version of Gloria Wandrous. Bill Ewing is a cold, driving young business executive who makes up in looks, luck, and business sense what he lacks in sensitivity.

One senses that O'Hara's motivation for presenting portraits of such characters derives from his "theological theory" that "good" and "evil" as conventionally conceived are irrelevant terms for dealing with the complexity of human lives.[26] To present a character who may readily be designated "good" or "evil" is to omit something, and for O'Hara, that is dishonest: "It is not now, it never has been the serious author's job to make his characters nice. The author who does make his characters nice is a hack and a liar. He is a hack in the sense that he is writing nice people [*sic*] for those moments when we only feel like reading about nice people. If he is reporting, as a novelist, on characters he has fully understood, but reports incompletely for the sake of niceness or for fear of that awful-people criticism, he is professionally a liar."[27] The biggest challenge facing the novelist, according to O'Hara, is to tell the *whole* truth: "The novelist's privilege, and in my opinion his duty, is to tell all he has to, even when it means dispensing with the pretty reticences that his characters may affect or that he himself may have."[28] To tell the complete story of a "shitheel" is a challenge; to tell that story and retain the reader's interest is a major accomplishment.[29] O'Hara uses the dramatic interior monologue to raise the reader's understanding of a Hubert Ward or an Elizabeth Appleton to a level of sympathetic tolerance. Perhaps O'Hara's designation of these works as "morality" novels is based on his hope that his readers will be able to extend such tolerance beyond their pages.[30]

In *Ourselves To Know*, O'Hara used a modified form of the dramatic interior monologue in combination with other narrative devices. The novel takes its title from the last line of Pope's *Essay on Man*. O'Hara used the complete line as an epigraph for the novel: "And all our Knowledge is, ourselves to know." Twice before, O'Hara had turned to Pope's work for titles: *A Rage To Live*, as many critics have pointed out, came from Pope's "Epistle II: To a Lady."[31] (O'Hara also used the phrase in describing Charlotte Chapin's death: ". . . she died of nothing but a rage to live.")[32] He had also planned at one point to use a phrase from Pope's "Ode on Solitude"—"and not a stone"— as title for the novel published as *Ten North Frederick*.[33]

Ourselves To Know, even without the allusion to Pope, would be an appropriate title for a work that on one level is an exploration of the relationship between an artist and his creation. Gerald Higgins, the character who narrates most of the novel, is what Wayne Booth calls a "self-conscious narrator," one of that class of narrators who are "aware of themselves as writers."[34] Using one of O'Hara's rare metaphors, Gerald assures the reader, ". . . that the story behind the story is relevant. I have often wondered, as I watched newsreels of structural workers on skyscrapers and mountain climbers on precipices, what the anonymous cameraman was thinking and doing."[35] On another occasion, Gerald tells his reader, ". . . obviously I have intruded myself as a character in this chronicle. . . ."[36] As narrator, writer, and character, Gerald provides O'Hara with an opportunity to explore the consciousness of a narrator—a figure who "processes" the consciousness of characters in stories. In other words, Gerald processes the thoughts of Robert Millhouser, the protagonist of *Ourselves To Know*, just as the anonymous narrator of *Appointment in Samarra* processes the thoughts of Julian English and other characters in that novel; because the narrator in *Ourselves To Know* assumes a name and an active role, he becomes available for the reader's scrutiny. In effect, this novel represents an opportunity for the reader to *watch* the narrator as he explores the mind of his subject. *Ourselves To Know* dramatizes "the story behind the story." If one assumes that in other novels the anonymous narrator is O'Hara himself, then it is reasonable to see Gerald Higgins as O'Hara's alter-ego in this novel.

The biographical similarities between Higgins and O'Hara provide support for such a view.[37]

Ourselves To Know reveals both the artistic principles and the dangers that O'Hara saw as inherent in the act of creation. As a part of his "fictional method,"[38] Gerald recreates a conversation between Robert Millhouser and Chester Calthorp in which Calthorp explains the "restrictions" every artist confronts and stresses the intense and minute control the artist must exercise over his medium. Among these restrictions are the width and length of the painter's canvas. In terms of the novelist's craft, these dimensions might translate into point of view; as the painter chooses his canvas and then must restrict himself to the space it provides—"a certain number of square inches in which he has to put everything he wants to say"—so the novelist, having chosen a point of view, must restrict himself to observations available from that vantage point. Calthorp's observations regarding the painter's perfect control of "every bead of paint" reflect O'Hara's belief that the writer must exercise the same perfect control over every word that he uses: "'. . . every fractional, minute stroke must count for something, every bead of paint in every stroke must count. He must have absolute, perfect and uninterrupted control. Infinite control. Infinite because it gets down to amounts of paint that are too tiny to be measured, and that is achieved only through a combination of muscular and nerval co-ordination that originates in the brain and the soul, and instantaneously passes down the arm to the tips of the fingers.' "[39] A third restriction, according to Calthorp, is the artist's "cruel, secret knowledge of the limitations of his talent"; an artist's greatness consists of reaching and recognizing those limitations.

In applying these artistic principles, certain dangers become apparent. Having chosen a particular point of view, the writer must do everything in his power to fully exploit that view. When that point of view involves the dramatic interior monologue—as it often does in O'Hara's work—the writer/ narrator must open his own consciousness to the consciousness of the character he is creating: "we're all limited in what we know of others by what they know of us."[40] If he succeeds in giving his character life, he risks exposing himself so fully to that character that he finds himself trapped in his own creation:

> An author's creations and God's partook of the same animate unreality once God's creatures were no longer in this life and provided that the author had given life to his. And so it was with so many of the people in Robert Millhouser's story, who were not in this world during my lifetime. Zilph Millhouser, Dr. Willetts, Moses Hatfield's father, the blind soldier after Gettysburg were no less real to me than Fitzgerald's Rosalind or Tarkington's Marjorie, and Robert Millhouser was already more truly alive in his past than he was now or ever since "for where no hope is left, is left no fear." . . .
>
> I must say these things at this point in Robert Millhouser's story because it must be apparent to the reader that I, Gerald Higgins, had begun at this point

to realize that I had so filled my life with the life of another man that much of the time I was Robert Millhouser.[41]

Gerald's "fictional method" involves "plowing through hundreds of pages of irrelevant material [provided by Millhouser] to unearth a single essential fact."[42] His "plowing" is analogous to the narrators' activity in the other O'Hara novels discussed. Implicitly extensions of O'Hara himself, they plow the minds of characters like Julian English, Edith Chapin, and George Lockwood; "process" the masses of material they have gathered; and form it into dramatic interior monologues. In entering the minds of these characters, the narrators are attempting to bridge the gap between the reader's (and the novelist's) consciousness and the consciousness of the character. As the narrator's success in bridging that gap increases, so does the danger that the character will absorb the narrator's personality: "It was as though his notes were stimulating *my* memory. Sometimes I could hardly wait to see what I would do next, and I believe that during those days I would have answered to his name. . . . This was no relationship of biographer to subject. It was becoming (and I knew it) an absorption of biographer by subject. . . . But I could not halt the loss of my own personality unless I gave up the whole project, and for that I did not have the courage."[43]

Early in his relationship with Higgins, Millhouser asks, "What do I know of my fellow man, my fellow townsmen—and what do they know of me, Gerald?"[44] (Note the similarity to the question Jim Malloy asks at the end of *Sermons And Soda-Water*: "What, really, can any of us know about any of us. . .?")[45] Millhouser must open himself to Gerald in order to escape his own isolation in at least a limited way. The more he allows Gerald to know of him, the more he will know Gerald: ". . . what they know of us has a great effect on . . . how much we can know of them."[46] Gerald runs the risk of getting too close to his subject, of being absorbed. As the artist tries to penetrate the consciousness of a character he has created, he faces the dangerous possibility that that character may overcome him. The loneliness and isolation of Robert Millhouser may become the loneliness and isolation of Gerald Higgins. On the last page of the novel, Millhouser warns Gerald not to look too closely at the story of Millhouser's life: "He made a cold chuckling sound. 'Look out, Gerald. You may find what you're looking for. Yourself.' "[47]

The "story behind the story is relevant" because the stories of Robert Millhouser and Gerald Higgins have merged again in the last lines of the novel, where Higgins thinks of Millhouser in order to take his mind off his own unfaithful wife.[48] O'Hara leaves it to the reader to determine whether Higgins will finally be able to separate his own fate from that of Robert Millhouser.

Ourselves To Know has a complex narrative structure. The novel consists of 25 sections, ranging in length from 56 pages down to less than one page. Gerald Higgins speaks directly to the reader in six of these sections. In another section he introduces a dialogue that takes place between himself and Millhouser. In two other sections, Higgins reproduces portions of the material Millhouser has provided, allowing Millhouser to tell his story in the first person. The bulk of the novel—16 sections—consists of Higgins' "fictional" re-creation of Millhouser, the accounts of other characters, and Higgins' intuition; this portion of the story is told in the third person, with dramatic interior monologues by Millhouser and Hedda, a considerable amount of dialogue, flashbacks, and italicized asides from Higgins to the reader. In terms of form, these 16 sections constitute one massive dramatic interior monologue, in that they consist largely of material derived from the consciousness of Robert Millhouser and processed by the narrator, Gerald Higgins.

Indeed, many characters function as processors in this novel. Hedda's thoughts, one must assume, have been re-created and processed by Robert, whose mind in turn has been processed by Gerald Higgins. There are actually two Geralds involved. The narration of the 24-year-old Gerald has been "rewritten and edited" by the 44-year-old Gerald.[49] And of course O'Hara stands behind all of these other processors.

As might be expected, such complexity caused many critics to throw up their hands in confused dismay. "O'Hara," says Matthew Bruccoli, "was bitterly hurt by the critical response to *Ourselves To Know*, which he regarded as one of his peak achievements."[50] On one level, the novel was O'Hara's parable about his artistic process; Gerald Higgins telling the story of Robert Millhouser *is* John O'Hara studying and re-creating the minds of his protagonists. In a letter written to his daughter several months before the novel was published, O'Hara made his enthusiasm apparent: "Every surgeon, every composer, every author adds to the knowledge and techniques of his own profession. Next February, when my new novel comes out, there will be reviews which will comment on how different this book is from all my earlier ones. (Mr. Cerf already likes it better than anything I've ever done.) There will, of course, be the usual panning, but practically nothing that was an innovation in writing, music, or art was accepted right away. Even Debussy, whom we take for granted now, was considered daring and unmusical."[51] The novel's failure to earn widespread critical acclaim was especially painful to O'Hara because the critics seemed as intent on discounting his methods and ignoring his "innovations" as they were in finding fault with Millhouser and his story.[52]

Of course, O'Hara did not limit himself to building all of his novels around variations of the dramatic interior monologue. He had used Jim Malloy as a first-person narrator in *Hope of Heaven*, and again in the same capacity in *Sermons And Soda-Water*, the book which followed *Ourselves To Know*. Malloy, though, is always something of an outsider; it is as though O'Hara's close identification with the character limits Malloy to the role of an uninvolved observer rather than a participant. This is especially noticeable in *Hope of Heaven*, where Malloy takes an almost clinical view of his abortive love affair with Peggy Henderson. The defect is less disturbing in *Sermons And Soda-*

Water, where Malloy's relationships with Charlotte Sears, the McCreas, Polly Williamson, and Charley Ellis are like that of Nick Carraway to Jay Gatsby, the Buchanans, and Jordan Baker—involved just enough to keep things interesting.

O'Hara used modified forms of the first-person narrator for his *Pal Joey* letters and in *A Family Party*. In both, the form is actually that of the conventional dramatic monologue, and the real subject is the narrator himself, writing or speaking. In *The Farmers Hotel*, a play revised to the form of a short novel,[53] he combined what Booth calls an "implied author" ("who stands behind the scenes, whether as stage manager, as puppeteer, or as an indifferent God, silently paring his fingernails")[54] with a great deal of dialogue and an occasional interior monologue. In this case, the interior monologue is *not* "dramatic." Rather than being used to indicate a character's subconscious, it serves to point out something that would be visible to the audience of a play: "In the light of the lobby Ira noticed for the first time that the man and woman were wearing riding boots and breeches under their polo coats."[55]

In writing his novels, O'Hara drew upon many different techniques, but the dramatic interior monologue was the technique that allowed him to probe and reveal his characters most thoroughly. O'Hara employed the dramatic interior monologue in 12 of his 16 separately published novels and novellas. He used the technique to elicit reader interest in characters who, judged only by their actions and seen only from the outside, would have been considered unworthy of such interest. He also found the technique invaluable in treating what appears to be his central theme: human isolation. Because the feeling of isolation is one which, almost by definition, remains hidden within the sufferer, O'Hara used the dramatic interior monologue to allow the reader to enter the consciousness of the victim; rather than telling the reader what is going on in the victim's consciousness—as an omniscient narrator would do—O'Hara carefully reproduced the victim's diction and expression, thus re-creating that consciousness. He gives the reader, not a chaotic "stream of consciousness," but a *processed* stream, a controlled participation in the victim's pain. O'Hara's intense desire to create fully realized characters, without sacrificing artistic control and without endangering the reader's "willing suspension of disbelief" finally "culminated in the complex structure of *Ourselves To Know*," according to Bruccoli.[56] That work, despite its defects and complexity, deserves close study by any critic who wishes to understand and measure O'Hara's achievements. In the works of John O'Hara, "the story behind the story" is indeed "relevant," and that story has often been ignored by his critics.

Notes

1. Sheldon Norman Grebstein, *John O'Hara* (New York: Twayne Publishers, 1966), 144.

2. Matthew J. Bruccoli, "Foreword," *Two by O'Hara: The Man Who Could Not Lose, An Original Screen Story & Far from Heaven, A Melodrama* by John O'Hara (New York: Harcourt Brace Jovanovich, 1979), x–xi.

3. "The Rider College Lectures: Dialog, Detail, and Type" in *"An Artist Is His Own Fault": John O'Hara on Writers and Writing*, ed. Matthew J. Bruccoli (Carbondale, Ill.: Southern Illinois University Press, 1977), 9.

4. "Rider College Lectures," 8–10.

5. Grebstein, *John O'Hara*, 22.

6. Grebstein, *John O'Hara*, 127.

7. Grebstein, *John O'Hara*, 127.

8. Grebstein, *John O'Hara*, 42–43, 127–28.

9. Grebstein, *John O'Hara*, 41–42.

10. John O'Hara, *The Doctor's Son and Other Stories* (New York: Harcourt, Brace and Co., 1935), 83.

11. *Appointment in Samarra* (New York: Harcourt, Brace and Co., 1934), 288–89.

12. *Appointment in Samarra*, 182.

13. *Ten North Frederick*, (New York: Random House, 1955), 386, 384.

14. *Ten North Frederick*, 408.

15. *Ten North Frederick*, 384–85.

16. *Ten North Frederick*, 164.

17. Wayne C. Booth, *The Rhetoric of Fiction* (Chicago: University of Chicago Press, 1961), 377–78.

18. *Selected Letters of John O'Hara*, ed. Matthew J. Bruccoli (New York: Random House, 1978), 227–28. Actually the reader does get at least one glimpse at the inside of Grace's mind. See John O'Hara, *A Rage to Live* (New York: Random House, 1949), 580.

19. "Remarks on the Novel" in *"An Artist Is His Own Fault"*, 101.

20. Grebstein, *John O'Hara*, 52–53.

21. *Selected Letters of John O'Hara*, 226–27.

22. See Grebstein's discussion of *From the Terrace* in *John O'Hara*, 63–69.

23. *From the Terrace* (New York: Random House, 1958), 552–53.

24. *From the Terrace*, 644–45.

25. *From the Terrace*, 728.

26. See his letter of 4 January 1966 to William Maxwell in *Selected Letters of John O'Hara*, 480–81.

27. "Remarks on the Novel," 92.

28. "Remarks on the Novel," 101–2.

29. One indication that O'Hara succeeded in retaining his readers' interest is his commercial success. Presumably the majority of the people who bought his books also read them. See Matthew J. Bruccoli, *The O'Hara Concern: A Biography of John O'Hara* (New York: Random House, 1975), 126, 247n, 285, 292, 307, 320, 327, 340.

30. *Selected Letters of John O'Hara*, 480.

31. Alexander Pope, "Epistle II: To a Lady" in *Poetry and Prose of Alexander Pope*, ed. Aubrey Williams (Boston: Houghton Mifflin Co., 1969).

32. *Ten North Frederick*, 187.

33. Bruccoli, *O'Hara Concern*, 228n.

34. Booth, *Rhetoric of Fiction*, 155.

35. John O'Hara, *Ourselves to Know* (New York: Random House, 1960), 89.

36. *Ourselves to Know*, 203.

37. Bruccoli, *O'Hara Concern*, 13–14.

38. *Ourselves to Know*, 141.

39. With the exception indicated in note 38, all other quotations in this paragraph are from *Ourselves to Know*, 101–2.

40. *Ourselves to Know*, 48.
41. *Ourselves to Know*, 179.
42. *Ourselves to Know*, 141.
43. *Ourselves to Know*, 179–80.
44. *Ourselves to Know*, 47.
45. *Sermons and Soda-Water* (New York: Random House, 1960), vol. 3, "We're Friends Again," 110.
46. *Ourselves to Know*, 48.
47. *Ourselves to Know*, 408.
48. *Ourselves to Know*, 408.
49. *Ourselves to Know*, 266.
50. Bruccoli, *O'Hara Concern*, 260.
51. *Selected Letters of John O'Hara*, 307.
52. See O'Hara's letter of 27 February 1960 to Charles Poore, reviewer for the *New York Times*, in *Selected Letters of John O'Hara*, 323–24.
53. Bruccoli, *O'Hara Concern*, 206.
54. Booth, *Rhetoric of Fiction*, 151.
55. *The Farmers Hotel* (New York: Random House, 1951), 19.
56. Bruccoli, *O'Hara Concern*, 259n.

Index

♦